Eileen Rositzka
Cinematic Corpographies

Cinepoetics

—
Edited by
Hermann Kappelhoff and Michael Wedel

Volume 3

Eileen Rositzka
Cinematic Corpographies

Re-Mapping the War Film Through the Body

DE GRUYTER

This book has originally been written and submitted in partial fulfilment for the degree of PhD at the University of St Andrews.

ISBN 978-3-11-070912-4
e-ISBN (PDF) 978-3-11-058080-8
e-ISBN (EPUB) 978-3-11-057971-0
ISSN 2569-4294

Library of Congress Control Number: 2018941437

Bibliographic information published by the Deutsche Nationalbibliothek
The Deutsche Nationalbibliothek lists this publication in the Deutsche Nationalbibliografie; detailed bibliographic data are available on the Internet at http://dnb.dnb.de.

© 2020 Walter de Gruyter GmbH, Berlin/Boston
This volume is text- and page-identical with the hardback published in 2018.
Cover image: Collage of a film still from *Paths of Glory* (Stanley Kubrick, USA 1957) and a map of the Western Front in 1917
Typesetting: Integra Software Services Pvt. Ltd.
Printing and binding: CPI books GmbH, Leck

www.degruyter.com

Acknowledgments

Thanks to my supervisor, Robert Burgoyne, for his invaluable feedback and support in finding my way, and to staff and fellow PhD students at the Department of Film Studies, University of St Andrews, for making my PhD the time of my life.

I would also like to thank Hermann Kappelhoff, who has been influencing my research ever since I started walking the path of academia, and whose parable of "Napoleon on a hill" inspired this study.

Last but not least I thank my parents for their loving guidance, and especially my mother, who taught me to never stop exploring.

Contents

1 Introduction —— 1
1.1 Cartographic Cinema, Embodiment, and the Navigating Spectator —— 5
1.2 The War Film as a Corpographic Genre —— 12
1.3 Pathos, Affect, and Expressive Movement —— 18

2 Measuring the Trenches: Corpographies of the First World War —— 25
2.1 The Great War in Literature and Film —— 26
2.2 Geographies of Fear: ALL QUIET ON THE WESTERN FRONT —— 30
2.3 Images of the Paths: Stanley Kubrick's PATHS OF GLORY —— 45

3 From Above and From Within: Aerial Views and Corpographic Transformations in the WWII Combat Film —— 57
3.1 Documenting War: The United States, Britain, and the Burma Campaign —— 59
3.2 OBJECTIVE, BURMA! / Subjective Burma: The Illusion of Overview —— 63
3.3 Corpography and Conversion: FURY's Hell on Wheels —— 80

4 Dismembering War: Touch and Fragmentation in Anthony Mann's MEN IN WAR —— 97
4.1 The Forgotten Subgenre: The Korean War Film of the 1950s —— 100
4.2 Forgetting to Remember: In and Out of Touch in MEN IN WAR —— 106
4.3 Vectors, Bodies, and Blind Spots —— 117

5 Uncharting Territories: The Vietnam War's Shattering of the Senses —— 126
5.1 Shattered Senses —— 128
5.2 THE BOYS IN COMPANY C: Sonic Envelopes and Aural Traces —— 133
5.3 Off-screen Monstrosity —— 138
5.4 RESCUE DAWN: Into the Abyss —— 142

6 ZERO DARK THIRTY: Corpographies of the War on Terror —— 151
6.1 Echoes of Terror: Black Screens and Black Sites of 9/11 —— 153
6.2 Behind the Surface —— 158

6.3	Tracking Shots —— **163**	
6.4	Night Visions / Night Calls: The Canaries —— **168**	

7   **Conclusion —— 173**

Bibliography —— 182

Filmography —— 193

Subject index —— 195

Name index —— 198

Film index —— 201

1 Introduction

There is much more to be said about losing oneself in worldly space than can be referenced – or remedied – by recourse to the abstract objectivity of a map.
                                                                    Vivian Sobchack[1]

Nowhere becomes the notion of a measurable landscape more evident and decisive than on the battlefields of war. The strategic planning and effective progress of battle action heavily relies on the soldier's ability to evaluate and make use of the given territory, which encompasses cognitive processes of abstraction and anticipation, as well as attuning the body to different geographical conditions. The sense of vision therefore plays a major role in seeing and comprehending combat events, since "metaphors of sight constantly surface in our claims to know something: the emphasis on observation, on evidence (from the Latin videre meaning 'to see), and the common use of 'I see' when we mean 'I understand.'"[2] Nevertheless, it seems paradoxical to talk about war and "the soldier's body" without actually acknowledging the impact of battle on *all its senses* – without accounting for the thundering sounds of explosions, the smell of smoke, or considering how it feels to wade through mud and water, especially when the actual objective, or the enemy, is more or less *invisible*.

Likewise, when it comes to analyzing how spaces of military conflict are perceived and mediated through cultural practices, this omission turns out to be even more paradoxical when we leave the primary framework of war and turn our attention to what has long been an established philosophical position: Within a larger phenomenological context, visual perception is embedded into a considerably more complex interplay of cognitive activity and sensuous processes. That is, regarding the body's relationship with its environment, vision lies at the heart of what could be conceived as a somatic experience of space and landscape: It predestines a cartography, a sense of orientation, that not only works in terms of mathematical coordinates, but first and foremost by navigating the body through a given space in order to implant its own presence into its surroundings. This navigation is thus not about seeing or understanding geographical conditions independent of our physical existence, but more about creating a certain space while interacting with it – a perspective which connects our senses to both geography and history:

---

[1] Vivian Sobchack, *Carnal Thoughts: Embodiment and Moving Image Culture*, Berkeley 2004, 15.
[2] Derek Gregory and Noel Castree, "Editors' Introduction: Human Geography," in *Human Geography*, Vol. 2, ed. Derek Gregory, Noel Castree, London 2012, xxv–lxxix, here: xli.

https://doi.org/10.1515/9783110580808-001

> Geography is no longer ruthlessly partitioned from History; time and space are no longer absolutes but defined in relation to people, events and objects, and these are not located 'in' time and space but enter into the co-production of time-space; and 'physicality' now carries a much livelier, more sensuous charge.[3]

Now this conception, in turn, can be used to mark a paradigm shift in the theoretical discourse of war representation, as events of war always designate distinct focal points and ruptures within historical experience. Indeed, the interdependencies between concrete bodies and concrete battle circumstances have come to be discussed more extensively. No longer is military conflict reduced to the primary of vision (as it has been from the very first accounts of optical warfare to the many Virilian analyses of modern "screen wars", or even to the discussions of war and video games), but is considered affecting all senses, as a condition shaping and being shaped by human bodies.

It is exactly this historically grounded production of somatic experience I seek to apply onto forms of audiovisual representations of war, and – more precisely – onto war cinema. In this study, I explore the ways the sensory experience of combat is staged as a corporeal apprehension of space in the Hollywood war film. Placing an emphasis on films that foreground tactile and sonic experience in battle as a key dimension of symbolic meaning in the depiction of war, I move beyond the emphasis on optics and weaponized vision that has largely dominated contemporary writing on war and cinema in order to highlight the wider sensory field that is powerfully evoked in this genre. As a cinematic field, however, it can only be explored if it presupposes a sense of direction and movement – a dynamic navigational process undergone by the explorer (i.e. the character, and, ultimately, the spectator); a process in which sensuous perceptions become graspable as aesthetic figurations.

In my conception of war cinema as staging a somatic experience of space, I am applying a term recently developed by Derek Gregory within the theoretical framework of Critical Geography, or, more precisely, Human Geography. What he calls "corpography" establishes a direct connection between notions of cartography and nature to the physical perception of war, conveyed through first-hand accounts of battle experience (notes, letters of soldiers, poems, and other forms of written memory). Although Gregory accounts for the important role the sense of vision plays in seeing and comprehending combat events, he addresses the dysfunctionality of military maps for the individual soldier in a battle zone, who has to rely on his tactile and acoustic perceptions instead to gain a sense of orientation. War, in this sense, implies a constant re-mapping of landscape through the soldier's body.

---

[3] Gregory and Castree, "Editors' Introduction," xlix.

From the First World War to WWII and the Vietnam War, Gregory traces the corpography of war as a more visceral and sensuous form of what Raymond Williams would have called a "structure of feeling."[4] The writings he draws on for the purposes of his study share a common ground in being products of an "intersubjective and trans-formative process" – a process "rooted in human bodies as bio-physical forms becoming intimately entangled with other bodies and other bio-physical forms."[5] Defined by Gregory as a "co-production of nature and military violence,"[6] corpography (and the way it is represented throughout media history) not only reveals repetitions from one theater of war to another but also reversals, echoes, silences, parallels and departures in the perception of war and continues to structure the somatic and cultural implications of modern warfare.[7]

Consequently, these contingencies and shifts also influence, and are performed by, cinematic representations of war. To my mind, Gregory's assumptions – although they don't directly aim at challenging theoretical accounts of film and media studies – articulate the missing link between already established theories of cartographic film narration, and ideas of (neo)phenomenological film experience, as they also imply the involvement of the spectator's body in sensuously grasping what is staged as a mediated experience of war. More than that, the notion of corpography can help to reframe the concept of film genre in terms of expressive movement patterns (as done by Hermann Kappelhoff[8]) and embodied history / genre memory (as exemplified by Robert Burgoyne[9]), avoiding reverting to the usual taxonomies of generic texts. For the question here is not so much whether a specific war is represented accurately or authentically (one would have to refer to an ideal audiovisual image in this regard) – instead, it must be investigated how the body of the spectator, that is, their concrete sensuous

---

[4] Williams understands structures of feeling as specific relationships between texts and conventions, ways of thinking and experiencing that emerge from certain inner dynamics of form. Cf. Raymond Williams, *Marxism and Literature*, Oxford 1977, 128–135.
[5] Derek Gregory, "The Natures of War," *Antipode* 48 (1), 2016, 3–56, here: 38.
[6] Gregory, "The Natures of War," 4.
[7] Gregory, "The Natures of War," 40.
[8] Hermann Kappelhoff, *Front Lines of Community: Hollywood Between War and Democracy*, Berlin 2018.
[9] For instance, this specific concept of embodied history is outlined in Robert Burgoyne, "Generational Memory and Affect in Letters from Iwo Jima," in *A Companion to the Historical Film*, ed. Robert A. Rosenstone, Constantin Parvulescu, Malden, MA 2013, 349–364. For further reading on genre memory and the representation of war, cf. Robert Burgoyne and Eileen Rositzka, "Goya on his Shoulder: Tim Hetherington, Genre Memory, and the Body at Risk," *Frames Cinema Journal* 7 (2015), http://framescinemajournal.com/article/goya-on-his-shoulder-tim-hetherington-genre-memory-and-the-body-at risk/.

world, establishes spatiotemporal correlations with the (historical) events of war depicted on screen. Therefore, this approach does not entail an interpretation of the filmmaker's intention, nor does it generalize and reduce the experience of individual spectators to one possible way of reacting to the films in question. The object of this study, then, is not an empirical or historical spectator; rather, it presumes the film viewer's active participation in the interaction with the expressive qualities of audiovisual images, and, in this case, images of war that are shaped by specific genre poetics. Naturally, since film can never be an absolute reproduction of battle experience, it is much more a reflection on sensuous perception itself, an interface relating the audience physically to an idea or a memory of war, rather than to the reality of combat. Thus, like every work of art, a film provides its viewers with a number of sensory coordinates that invite them to move along, and be moved by, the parcours that is cinematic experience.

While cinematic codes of war have long been oriented almost exclusively to the visual, i.e. cartography and the overview, Gregory's study of somatic imagery and spatial apprehension in war-related history, literature, and poetry testifies to a paradigm shift in the theoretical discourse of war representation. No longer is military conflict reduced to the primacy of vision (as it has been from the very first accounts of optical warfare to the many Virilian analyses of modern "screen wars," or even to the discussions of digital images, and the relation between war and video games), but is considered affecting all senses, as a condition shaping and being shaped by human bodies – which implies an understanding of space not as a medium *over* which war is conducted, but as a medium *through* which war is conducted, making bodies "both vectors and victims of military violence."[10]

I therefore demonstrate in my study that the war film can essentially be qualified as a genre that, throughout the history of cinema, has been elaborating on the corpographic and symbolic role of the body in military conflict, and has continuously shaped the ways spectators sensuously engage with war and its cinematic dimensions of affect. As a first step, and in order to situate Gregory's concept within the realm of cinema and media studies, I will provide a literature review of recent academic works that have explored the relationship between cartography and film (especially those by Tom Conley and Giuliana Bruno), and of texts approaching audiovisual representations of war in terms of genre poetics and affect (with a special emphasis on Hermann Kappelhoff and Robert Burgoyne).

My case studies will reveal the transformations the Hollywood war film has undergone in terms of somatic staging patterns and genre poetics, analysing

---

[10] Gregory, "The Natures of War," 3.

audiovisual representations of combat in relation to the varying historical, territorial, and technological conditions of war that provoked palpable changes in the cultural perception of military conflict. Ultimately, I argue that descriptive investigations of narratives and plot constellations fall short in taking into account what I would consider a constitutive factor of cinematic experience, and of war cinema in specific: the body as both an aesthetic concept and sensuous link between film and spectator. In my phenomenological approach to the war film genre, I will therefore identify stylistic devices, aesthetic compositions, and expressive movements that, in establishing a specific relation between filmic space-time and the spectator, make up the cinematic corpography of war.

Each chapter of this book focuses on a different war, covering WWI, WWII, Korea, Vietnam, and the so-called "War on Terror" after 9/11, isolating the Hollywood war film in its respective cultural-historical context and tracing both representational consistencies and shifts in each case study. My analysis thus intends to show that cinematic depictions of war as a somatic experience change over time, while still maintaining the genre imprint of the past.

1.1 Cartographic Cinema, Embodiment, and the Navigating Spectator

In conducting a study on what I have come to term *cinematic corpography*, I do not assume that the concept of navigating filmic space through the senses is self-evident. The idea itself is a conglomeration of not only different scholarly disciplines (geography, philosophy, and film / media studies) but also of different perspectives on spatial perception and subject positions within their respective theoretical frameworks. Thus, in order to be able to set and use corpography as an analytical tool for describing certain staging patterns of the Hollywood war film, that is, to provide an alternate approach to the genre as such, an explanation of the word itself must go beyond Gregory's specified definition. It must certainly clarify in what ways cinema can enable us to orientate ourselves within filmic space in the first place, and, last but not least, given that the term's etymology represents an amalgam of corporeality and aspects of cartography, it has to be made clear what conceptions of spectators, bodies, and navigational processes actually inform corpography as a characterization of film staging and film viewing.

What cannot be overlooked as a development in film studies is "the growing premium attached to the locational properties of the moving image, and the concomitant processes of spatial and temporal navigation – historiographical, ontological, geographical, archaeological, architectural – that these make possible."¹¹ Here, Les Roberts identifies five thematic areas of cinematic cartography: maps and mapping in films; mapping of film production and consumption; movie mapping and cinematographic tourism; cognitive and emotional mapping; and film as spatial critique. While most of these clusters can hardly contribute to an understanding of cinematic corpography, the theme of mapping in films as well as the more spectator-oriented matter of cognitive and / or emotional mapping localize several important points of interest for the purpose of corpographic analysis. For studying a historically grounded genre like the Hollywood war film, it is furthermore necessary to include some of the basic implications of a so-called "cinematic geography,"¹² based on the assumption that "social and cultural meanings are intertwined with space, place, scale and narrative."¹³ In this perspective, continuities and changes in the genre's aesthetics of spatial perception would allow us to make inferences about respective media-historical shifts within the cultural reception and audiovisual representation of war.

Hence, the first question to consider would be about the relation between cinema and cartography, about what it is that qualifies films as mapped or mapping constructs? As geographers Kitchin and Dodge write,

> [m]aps are of-the-moment, brought into being through practices (embodied, social, technical), always re-made every time they are engaged with; mapping is a process of constant re-territorialization. As such, maps are transitory and fleeting, being contingent, relational and contextdependent. Maps are practices – they are always mappings.¹⁴

This reterritorialization is of central importance both for Gregory's idea of a corpography of war and for its cinematic renditions within the war film genre. Maps and corpographies are representations of spatial orientation just as they are recalibrated through the senses of those who read, use, and experience them (in this case the film spectator). It is therefore important to note that, as a model for analysing filmic space, corpography cannot only be reduced to being the result of yet another spatial turn in the humanities; moreover, its basic assumptions derive from a change of perspective within the original science of studying space

---

11 Les Roberts (ed.), *Mapping Cultures: Place, Practice, Performance*, London / New York 2012, 68.
12 For a more detailed description of cinematic geography, cf. Chris Lukinbeal, "The Map that Precedes the Territory: An Introduction to Essays in Cinematic Geography," *Geo-Journal* 59 (4), 2004, 247–251.
13 Lukinbeal, "The Map that Precedes the Territory," 248.
14 Rob Kitchin and Martin Dodge, "Rethinking Maps," *Progress in Human Geography* 31 (3), 2007, 331–344, here: 331.

itself – a phenomenological turn within the field of critical geography and philosophy. In this conception, a film (like a map) creates a territory, rather than just depicting it. However, this creative process is not restricted to representational codes, or to the spectator's cognitive capacities alone – its premises lie in what Sibylle Krämer describes as mapping: the "logical and mathematical laws of cartographic projection" as well as in the "technical, semiotic, aesthetic, political, and ideological conditions of mapmaking."[15] Thus, what turns maps into performative practices also renders the act of film viewing a cultural and phenomenological mapping process, a poetic practice of transforming a text into an experiential space.[16]

So far, many theoretical approaches to cinematic mapping have either focused on the formal elements of film itself (like the filmic syntax and narrative, or the symbolic function of landscape in film in shaping individual and national identities[17]), or on the cognitive / sensuous activity of the spectator – although both factors can hardly be separated from one another as they engage in a symbiotic process of generating a distinct aesthetic experience.

In a neoformalist sense, the relation between various formal elements of film narrate a topography which is then cognitively and emotionally apprehended by the audience; within the context of apparatus theory, cinema's spatiality extends to the space between film/screen and projector, and thus describes the spectator as a transcendent subject caught in, or woven into, the reality effect of cinema as an ideological construct of visual perception. On the other hand, as the distinction between reality and illusion must presume an absolute and objective ideal of the non-diegetic world, it tends to mask out different levels of sensuous subjectivity shared and exchanged between film and spectator. Very early on, Robert Kolker and J. Douglas Ousley, in sketching out a "phenomenology of cinematic time and space," had already voted against measuring the film experience by cinema's illusionary potential and instead suggested talking of film as "surrogate spaces."[18] But although this idea indeed considers the perceptive relation between film and spectator, it falls short in describing film viewing as an act of adopting and creating sensuous experiences. Moreover, it omits the multisensory as well as

---

15 Sibylle Krämer, "Karten erzeugen doch Welten, oder?" *Soziale Systeme* 178 (1 & 2), 2012, 153–167, here: 155.
16 This would be a variation of Michel de Certeau's distinction between place and space: "In short, space is a practiced place." For further reading, cf. Michel de Certeau, *The Practice of Everyday Life*, Berkeley 1988, 117.
17 Cf. Martin Lefebvre (ed.), *Landscape and Film*, London / New York 2006.
18 R.P. Kolker and J. Douglas Ousley, "A Phenomenology of Cinematic Time and Space," *British Journal of Aesthetics* 13 (4), 1973, 388–396, here: 396.

the somatic appeal of cinematic images to an audience that not only conceives of the filmic world as a *substitute* for reality but as *part* of their reality. Nevertheless, despite Kolker and Ousley's hesitation to further develop their approach in theoretical terms, their basic claim to put the intellectual primacy of "film language" into perspective is still relevant for contemporary film phenomenology (as most prominently advocated by Vivian Sobchack), according to which cinematic experience is created through the spectator's sensing body. In this context, film itself cannot merely be regarded as a pregiven semiotic system; it is only realized as an aesthetic experience through the spectator's bodily perception.

Taking this into account, the navigation of filmic space thus implies a certain text or form as much as it calls for the spectator's mental and sensuous mobility in order to be immersed into the diegetic universe. This would mean that, from a phenomenological point of view, even if we conceive of maps and mapping processes as sign- and text-based forms of communication, our embodiment of such communication is a premise for the dynamics of meaning making,[19] just as Mark Johnson, in his capacity as linguist, reminds us: "[A]ny adequate account of meaning and rationality must give a central place to embodied and imaginative structures of understanding by which we grasp our world."[20] Although it has to be emphasized that, if we recall Merleau-Ponty's original and essential notion of embodiment, bodily perception creates its own significance which has "no equivalent in the universe of the understanding."[21] It is an expressive space which is itself the source for any emerging meaning.[22] Thus, embodiment does not imply a mimetic adaptation of a certain experience, but it describes a modification of this experience through our own subjectivity.[23] For what concerns the functionality

---

[19] Thomas Morsch, *Medienästhetik des Films: Verkörperte Wahrnehmung und ästhetische Erfahrung im Kino*, Munich 2011, 96.

[20] Mark Johnson, *The Body in the Mind: The Bodily Basis of Meaning, Imagination, and Reason*, Chicago 1987, xiii.

[21] Maurice Merleau-Ponty, *Phenomenology of Perception*, trans. Colin Smith, London 2002 [1962], 46–47.

[22] The French original reads: "Notre corps n'est pas seulement un espace expressif parmi tous les autres. Il est à l'origine de tous les autres, le mouvement même d'expression, ce qui projette au-dehors les significations en leur donnant un lieu." Maurice Merleau-Ponty, *Phénoménologie de la perception*, Paris 1945, 183.

[23] As straightforward as this application of Merleau-Ponty to linguistics and film studies seems (being part of a general somatic turn in the humanities), this phenomenological concept of embodiment as meaning making marks a fundamental shift from psychoanalytical theory, which propels an antagonistic relation between semiotic processes and the body. When psychoanalytical theorists speak of somatic experience as "pre-symbolic," they do not regard it as generator of significance but always as a residuum, the raw material for symbolic transactions (from somatic

of cinema, and according to Sobchack, moving images would therefore make themselves "sensuously and sensibly manifest as the expression of experience by experience"[24]:

> Objectively projected, visibly and audibly expressed before us, the film's activity of seeing, hearing, and moving signifies in a pervasive, primary, and embodied language that precedes and provides the grounds for the secondary significations of a more discrete, systematic, less "wild" communication. Cinema thus transposes, without completely transforming, those modes of being alive and consciously embodied in the world that count for each of us as direct experience: as experience "centered" in that particular, situated, and solely occupied existence sensed first as "Here, where the world touches" and then as "Here, where the world is sensible; here, where I am."[25]

As a matter of fact, in re-conceptualizing the poetic processes of film viewing in terms of sensuous engagement, Sobchack at the same time implicitly formulates the premises for a theory of cinematic mapping. Not until fifteen years later, film scholar Tom Conley took the initiative to publish a comparative study on "cartographic cinema," where he first of all looks into existing paradigms of films and / as maps. Conley conceives of cinema as form of "locational imaging," which concerns the filmic text as well as the location of the spectator, allowing them to think about their relation to the diegesis and their being in the (real) world. This of course touches upon questions of history, society, and ideology. Once a map is seen in a film, it is not only a diegetic object, but a text revealing the production mechanisms of cinema, superimposing codes on the film which are not part of its language. We are dealing with aspects of enunciation and "bilocation," as Conley puts it. The map in a film tells us that we are and are not where it says it is taking place,[26] which, in the words of Sybille Krämer, is a fusion of first-person ("I am here) and third-person perspective ("I am there").[27] Conley continues:

> The map can bring forward issues that cause it to become a point of departure for an interpretive itinerary. When a cartographic shape – be it a projection, a globe, an icon of the world, an atlas, a diagram, a bird's-eye view of a landscape, a city-view – is taken as a point of departure, it becomes a model, a patron, or even a road map from which transverse

---

stimuli to mental representation (cf. Morsch, *Medienästhetik des Films*, 40)). Hence, in this view, the body would be a negation of subjectivity instead of being conceived of as an extension of subjectivity.
24 Vivian Sobchack, *The Address of the Eye: A Phenomenology of Film Experience*, Princeton, NJ 1992, 3.
25 Sobchack, *The Address of the Eye*, 4.
26 Tom Conley, *Cartographic Cinema*, Minneapolis 2007, 3–4.
27 Cf. Krämer, "Karten erzeugen doch Welten, oder?," 158. This duality of perspectives, in turn, corresponds to Sobchack's remarks on embodied experience ("Here, where I am").

readings can be plotted. It lifts the viewer from the grip of the moving image and thus allows our gaze to mobilize its faculties.²⁸

Here, Conley's argument is close to Christian Metz's theory of enunciation, and even closer to what Metz terms "mobile topography," a "changing geography" that is underscored in an impersonal meta-discourse, that is, "when speech or gesture are discerned in the context of camera angles, intertitles, voice-in and voice-off, film-in-the-film, and other techniques."²⁹ As textual references, maps *in* films also reveal films' nature *as* maps, as topographies or geographies that, however constructed, form unique spaces that are not congruent with the pro-filmic world. Instead, they are subject to their own laws of spatiality and continuity. Conley refers to André Bazin when he describes how the cinematic image's simultaneously visible, tactile, and material qualities initiate a dialogue between the characters and objects moving within it, and how they constitute a world rather than being a mere representation of it: the filmic image "is a map to the degree it is at once a geography, a totality, and a form liable to contain topographies or places in the image that can be called localities with specific characters and historical traits."³⁰ Consequently, it takes an active, sensuously perceiving spectator to unlock this totality, which then unfolds dynamically over the course of the film. Temporality is thus a key factor of a distinctly cinematic cartography, that is, the topography of moving images. It is only through time, rhythm and duration that we can speak of a cartography that is developed and explored as an aesthetic experience.

In addressing and interacting with the spectator, cinematic maps not only invite their audience to extract a certain meaning from a filmic text, but they also initiate processes of meaning making, of meaning that is first produced and modified through the sensing body of the spectator. As Conley reminds us paraphrasing Marie-Claire Ropars-Wuilleumier, the so-called "mapping impulse"³¹ of cartographic cinema "can be associated with the relations of writing to space. The force of the former engenders perception (or even the creation) of the latter and [...] the latter tends to fissure the meaning of the former."³² This is another

---

28 Conley, *Cartographic Cinema*, 208.
29 Christian Metz, *L'Enonciation Impersonnelle, ou le Site du Film*, Paris 1991, 210.
30 Conley, *Cartographic Cinema*, 20.
31 In accordance with Conley, Teresa Castro also speaks of cinema's "mapping impulse" – yet she identifies it as part and effect of a visual regime that dictates our ways of perceiving places and spaces in general. Cf. Teresa Castro, "Cinema's Mapping Impulse: Questioning Visual Culture," *The Cartographic Journal* 46, 2009, 9–15.
32 Conley, *Cartographic Cinema*, 212. Conley paraphrases a passage from Marie-Claire Ropars-Wuilleumier, *Ecrire l'espace*, Paris 2003.

important historiographic point, as it links the "then" of a film's production with "now" of its reception through an audience. Hermeneutically speaking, acts of meaning making and interpretation naturally conflate images of the past with the present, but not to conserve them as artefacts of bygone moments; rather, as Giuliana Bruno writes, by means of mapping, we compare the present with the past in order to "assess if it is really offering something new."[33] It is this type of judgment which leads back to Conley's concept of bilocation: if a map in a film tells us that we are and that we are not where it says it is taking place, it also tells us that we are and are not *when* the film tells us it is taken place. But in order to ultimately evaluate the differences between images of then and now, we always have to immerse ourselves into the filmic world as a "now." In other words, we are always re-living cinematic images of the past as a present, as an embodied, subjective experience. And if this is true for any kind of film, it most evidently applies to the war film as a genre that calls for our emotional investment in the conflicts of the past to situate ourselves in the present. In order to do so, however, it is essential to part from mapping theories that solely focus on cinematic cartographies designed to orientate the spectator within the plot of a film. Here, Conley avoids describing specific genre patterns or stylistic developments in detail, although he underlines the importance of maps in the war film, the road movie, the Western, the adventure film, education films, etc. Remarkably, he describes cartography often as allegory of a certain message a film tries to convey, or as narrative strategy.

While pointing out spatial clues as coordinates for a film's narrative is only one way to situate an audience within a diegetic time and space, it certainly fails to explore the filmic image as an affectively grounded, embodied experience. An important step towards what Roberts calls "emotional mapping" has been made by Giuliana Bruno. In her pioneering book, *Atlas of Emotion*, she sheds light on how this (emotional) investment on the part of the spectator is intricately connected with affective responses to spatial structures. Offering a pre- and parallel history of cinema as a means of private, imaginative and subjective travel, Bruno shifts the (proto)cinematic subject "from spectator-voyeur to spectatrix-voyageuse,"[34] taking a decidedly feminist point of view. She interweaves a vast array of European cultural practices from the sixteenth to the twentieth centuries that provide a particular genealogy of cinematic spectatorship as mobile, embodied and typically feminine. These include cartography, travel and travel writing, architecture, museums, fashion, gardens, cemeteries and many other habitable

---

[33] Giuliana Bruno, *Atlas of Emotion: Journeys in Art, Architecture, and Film*, New York 2002, 418.
[34] Bruno, *Atlas of Emotion*, 157.

spaces, as well as contemporary visual art and cinema itself. In drawing these links, Bruno reinvents the critical genealogy of both cinema and its antecedents. Perhaps the most fascinating and beautifully developed of these intermodal linkages is cinema-cartography. Bruno argues that cartography is not necessarily a medium for mastering space, but that it can extend subjectivity and emotion into space. By this she not only refers to cinematic spaces as such but to the ways the affective geometries and geographies of films can influence our understanding of extra-diegetic landscapes and architectures.

This, in turn, is key to a thorough understanding of the corpography of war and its symbolic dimension: the aesthetic experience of combat as explored in film opens up new modalities of sensing war, *and* of reflecting on the cultural image of military conflict. Seen through the eyes of different aesthetic forms (poetry, fiction, film, music), wars are constructed as alternate spaces that establish sensuous connections to individual spectators as much as they relate this subjective experience to a way of perceiving the world. Ultimately, the ways film is able to incorporate aesthetic qualities and modalities of other media allow for a multisensory, corpographic, experience of war that contradict the technocratic conception of contemporary military conflict as "hygienic" and "bodiless": even the codes of surveillance and control implemented in the digital images of modern warfare are undone by how war films stage the somatic environment of the battle space. As a corpographic genre, the war film enables what Kappelhoff calls a "poiesis of viewing films,"[35] to create and explore cinematic spaces with all their cultural, historical, and technological connotations through the act of viewing, sensing, and meaning making.

1.2 The War Film as a Corpographic Genre

Over the years, the corpus of scholarly work on the relationship between war and the media has grown significantly, being discussed widely within the fields of history, sociology, cultural psychology, and, of course, cinema and media studies. A pressing research question in this regard has always been as to whether (or to what extent) images of war could be regarded as propaganda, investigating what moral or political values they would communicate to their recipients.

---

[35] This concept is outlined in Kappelhoff's *Front Lines of Community: Hollywood Between War and Democracy* (Berlin 2018) and informs the work of the *Cinepoetics – Center for Advanced Film Studies* based at Freie Universität Berlin.

Many texts, in perpetuating the discourse of pro-, anti-, and paramilitarist functions of war films and documentaries,[36] enquire the authenticity and historical accuracy of media images to eventually reconstruct their underlying ideology;[37] others merely summon different audiovisual representations of military conflicts to weave them into the genealogy of a historical discourse of war, and into the framework of what is often referred to as "military-entertainment complex," including films, TV series, and videogames.[38]

From the production and circulation of news images (as examined in Hoskins and O'Loughlin's *War and Media*, or Susan L. Carruthers' *The Media at War*) to critical studies of films about specific wars,[39] the foci of various publications testify to the attempt to categorize images of war as instruments of affect mobilization – without actually going into detail about the aesthetic strategies of this mobilization. Above all, these comparatively empirical findings are used to illustrate that, within certain sociocultural and industrial contexts, war representations serve the purpose of (national) identity-building.[40] Yet the communicative function of said representations cannot be grasped by means of content-based analysis alone,[41] as neither psychological constitutions of identity nor the emotional involvement of an audience into the world of film can be reduced to narrative functions and effects. Nevertheless, most comprehensive studies of the war film, too, have defined it as a cycle of films with similar narrative and iconographic structures. Before scholars such as James Chapman, Guy Westwell, and

---

36 Cf. for instance Alisa Lebow, "The Unwar Film," in *A Companion to Contemporary Documentary Film*, ed. Alexandra Juhasz, Alisa Lebow, Hoboken, NJ 2015, 454–474.
37 One example would be Jo Fox, *Film Propaganda in Britain and Nazi-Germany: World War II Cinema*, New York 2007.
38 Two publications are especially worth mentioning in this regard: James Der Derian, *Virtuous War: Mapping the Military-Industrial-Media-Entertainment Network*, 2nd edition, London 2009; Tim Lenoir and Henry Lowood, "Theaters of War: The Military-Entertainment Complex" (2002), http://www.stanford.edu/class/sts145/Library/Lenoir-Lowood_TheatersOfWar.pdf (accessed December 10, 2016).
39 There are numerous monographs and edited collections on the Vietnam War in film and television, for instance: Michael Anderegg (ed.), *Inventing Vietnam: The War in Film and Television*, Philadelphia, PA 1991, and: Linda Dittmar and Gene Michaud (eds.), *From Hanoi to Hollywood: The Vietnam War in American Film*, New Brunswick / London 1990; on the Iraq War, cf. for instance Martin Barker, *A 'Toxic Genre': The Iraq War Films*, Chicago 2011.
40 Examples include Guy Westwell, *War Cinema: Hollywood on the Front Line*, New York / London 2006, and Elisabeth Bronfen, *Specters of War: Hollywood's Engagement with Military Conflict*, New Brunswick, NJ 2012.
41 James Chapman and J. David Slocum each have provided war-related publications with a focus on content analysis: James Chapman, *War and Film*, London 2008; J. David Slocum (ed.), *Hollywood and War: The Film Reader*, New York / London 2006.

Robert Eberwein[42] published their respective takes on the historical developments of this particular genre (each with a strong focus on the Hollywood war film), Jeanine Basinger has even gone so far as to propose a detailed anatomy of the WWII combat film, a compendium of films sharing comparable plot and character schemes, which paved the way for several other typological approaches to war and cinema.[43]

However, a genre like the war film is by no means a generic prototype of any sort. First, its themes and plot schemata can be connected to the larger framework of the historical film[44]; second, it is a hybrid of different modes of dramatic expressivity and affective address: the triumphant excess of battle explosions, the agony of the wounded and exhausted soldier, scenes of playful comradeship on the one hand, and of mourning and grief on the other – all these are elements of a variable dramaturgic arrangement of modalities that, in altered combinations, can be found within the context of other genres: equivalents would be the sentimental sadness of the melodrama, the horror genre's thrilling fear, or laughing as a constitutive mode of comedy. As Christine Gledhill notes: "[A]ction and sentiment, pathos and spectacle, presumed today to appeal to differently gendered audiences, are drawn into a composite aesthetic and dramatic modality, capable of different emphases and generic offshoots."[45]

Within the field of genre studies, more recent theoretical works like Gledhill's have moved on to conceive of genres as dynamic systems of different aesthetic modalities that find themselves in a process of constant refiguration. Thus, to comprehend the war film in its complexity (even when the canon is limited to Hollywood productions), it must be analysed within a larger framework of generic exchange mechanisms and cultural practices.

Such an approach can be found both in Robert Burgoyne's elaborations on genre memory, and Hermann Kappelhoff's study on genre and sense of commonality. Furthering Gledhill's argument, and taking the war film as a prime example, they consider genres as open ensembles of narrative and dramaturgical patterns, which, in their concrete poetic concepts, activate their viewers' sense of self in order to relate it to a certain sense of commonality. It is on this level that historical constellations have to be reconstructed and examined to eventually analyse genre cinema as part of a specific sociocultural framework. Burgoyne classifies

---

42 Robert Eberwein, *The Hollywood War Film*, Chichester / Malden, MA 2010.
43 Jeanine Basinger, *The World War II Combat Film: Anatomy of a Genre*, New York 2003.
44 Robert Burgoyne, *The Historical Film*, Malden, MA 2008.
45 Christine Gledhill, "Rethinking Genre," in *Reinventing Film Studies*, ed. Christine Gledhill, Linda Williams, London 2000, 221–243, here: 230.

the war film as one of five subtypes of the Hollywood historical film (along with the epic, the biographical film, the topical film, and the metahistorical film), the primary project of which is to make the world of the past knowable and visible in its "otherness."[46] In re-enacting the past, war films as historical films create a highly immersive experience for the spectator, which, for Burgoyne, lies in the genre's impression of "witnessing again."[47] More than simply "re-living" the past, the spectator can perform and rethink it, which, at the same time, provokes a dialogue with the present. Furthermore, Burgoyne goes on to say that "the striking impression of verisimilitude in combat films serves a particular type of rhetorical argument; the weight of the experience, the amplified impression of reality, implies that the event is worth revisiting, that it has national significance."[48] In a later essay on Clint Eastwood's LETTERS FROM IWO JIMA, he extends this notion to the concept of "generational memory,"[49] the spectator's distinctly emotional connection to the past, which he otherwise describes as "somatic empathy."[50]

As I will later explain in more detail, Kappelhoff, too, defines the war film genre as an aesthetic construct that can visualize the links between affective experience and collective memory – precisely through the ways it mobilizes emotions and orchestrates various expressive modalities of film.[51] Thus, corpography can be used to inquire the ways filmic bodies are portrayed navigating through historically grounded spaces, and also to map out what media-technological conditions and sociocultural contexts cooperate in shaping the idea of our bodies in history, that is, of bodily perception as a premise for the experience of *being-in-the-world*[52]. As Burgoyne notes for the war film, the body (of the soldier) conveys "in visceral form a vision of history produced from intensive sensual impressions"[53] and serves as a "medium of experience."[54]

---

46 Burgoyne, *The Historical Film*, 2.
47 Burgoyne, *The Historical Film*, 8.
48 Burgoyne, *The Historical Film*, 56.
49 This term was originally coined by Johannes von Moltke and refers to German wartime memory. Cf. Johannes von Moltke, "Sympathy for the Devil: Cinema, History, and the Politics of Emotion," *New German Critique* 102 (3), 2007, 17–43.
50 Robert Burgoyne, "Generational Memory and Affect in Letters from Iwo Jima," in *A Companion to the Historical Film*, ed. Robert A. Rosenstone, Constantin Parvulescu, Malden, MA 2013, 349–364, here: 359.
51 Cf. Hermann Kappelhoff, *Front Lines of Community: Hollywood Between War and Democracy*, Berlin 2018.
52 A term Merleau-Ponty discusses regarding human subject's perceptive relation to the world. Cf. Maurice Merleau-Ponty, *Phenomenology of Perception*.
53 Robert Burgoyne, "Embodiment in the War Film: Paradise Now and The Hurt Locker," *Journal of War & Culture Studies* 5 (1), 2012, 7–19, here: 8.
54 Burgoyne, "Embodiment in the War Film," 15.

Taking this into account, it is surprising that the role of the body has been largely neglected in the analysis of war and the media. There is, in fact, a growing number of publications on the war film's representation of gender and identity[55], but in these contexts, the body is much more rendered an image, a representation of political discourses itself, rather than a perceiver and producer of sensory experience. Even in the wake of Virilio's perennial *War and Cinema*, audiovisual representations of military conflicts have mainly been discussed against the background of a "crisis of vision", although Virilio himself, despite foregrounding the optical sensorium as an agent in defining the cultural imaginary of war, has opted for describing the relationship between war and cinema as a "logistics of perception" that would naturally include bodily senses beyond vision. Yet, perhaps less surprisingly regarding their themes and the time they were published, most of Virilio's books have been associated with the First Gulf War as a thoroughly televised conflict. Within this context they have spawned discussion about military technology and "hygienic", or "virtuous", warfare[56] – a conception of combat expounding the problems of the distance between soldier and target, and, last but not least, between (audiovisual) images of war and their recipients. As the war itself became the subject of a media-philosophical turn towards the digital age, the sensing body seemed to disappear from theoretical accounts of battle as a mediated experience. Following the events of 9/11, leading theorists were even less concerned with bodies of / at war, but instead reflected on the monstrous (in)visibility of terrorism and its effect on the ontology of media images per se.[57] However, as Gregory points out, while these conflicts have indeed transformed the optical-cartographic imaginary in requiring new investments in digital cartography and satellite imagery, they are "still shaped and even confounded by the multiple, material environments through which they are fought and which they, in their turn, re-shape."[58]

What becomes apparent in revisiting existing academic work on the war film genre is that only recently scholars have started to approach it in terms of its poetics of affect, or, more specifically, with regard to its somatic appeal to the spectator, although war itself, as a state of pure violence, is unthinkable (and

---

[55] One of the most recent collections has been edited by Karen Ritzenhoff and Jakub Kazecki, *Heroism and Gender in War Films*, New York 2014; preceded by Karen Randell and Sean Redmond (eds.), *The War Body on Screen*, London / New York 2012 [2008].
[56] Cf. Der Derian, *Virtuous War*.
[57] For further discussion, cf. Jean Baudrillard, *The Spirit of Terrorism and Requiem for the Twin Towers*, trans. Chris Turner, London / New York 2003; also: Slavoj Žižek, *Welcome to the Desert of the Real! Five Essays on 11 September and Related Dates*, London 2002.
[58] Gregory, "The Natures of War," 40.

unrepresentable) without considering its impact and dependence on the human body. Returning to Linda Williams' influential essay on genres and modes of excess, "Film Bodies," German film scholar Michael Wedel was one of the first authors to classify the post-classical war film as a reflexive "body genre" that, in the words of Williams, would "both portray and affect the sensational body."[59] And it would do so in displaying the spectacle of a sensuous, emotional body, the sensation of overwhelming pathos, and the ecstasy of a body being "beside itself" – states that, in the case of the war film, are all projected onto, and negotiated through, the male.

With regard to their effectivity, body genres can be described as staging the elementary opposition of bodies that do not solely operate on the basis of identification processes; rather, these bodies entangle their viewers in a perceptive process of involuntary physiological mimicry: the filmic sensations and emotions are somatically transferred to the spectator.[60] More than creating historical verisimilitude, war films aim at aesthetically confronting characters and viewers alike with the lethal violence performed by modern military technology in order to test the limits and transgressions of somatic experience.[61]

In his essay, which would later inform a book co-authored with Thomas Elsaesser, Wedel sets out to trace significant modifications of the war film's body concept, and to demonstrate their effects on corresponding changes in style, dramaturgy, motives, and iconographies, beginning in the late 1970s. For him, the last phase of New Hollywood cinema marks a decisive historical moment in which the war film develops a critical perspective on its own form and the media-technological, aesthetic, and socio-political partaking in the reality and perception of its subject. Thus, the post-classical war film could be regarded as a mode of thinking about and with the body, conveyed through somatic and empathic effects.[62] However, from my point of view (and in retrospect), the war film has been a body genre from the very beginning, only gradually varying in the extent to which the body is addressed as a sensing, vulnerable subject. And just as combat films have to be understood in their oscillations – not polarizations – between individual and community,[63] they also have to be categorized in their interrelations between bodily and geographical space.

---

59 Linda Williams, "Film Bodies. Gender, Genre, and Excess," *Film Quarterly* 44 (4), 1991, 2–13, here: 4.
60 Michael Wedel, "Körper, Tod und Technik – Der postklassische Hollywood-Kriegsfilm als reflexives Body Genre," in *Körperästhetiken: Filmische Inszenierungen von Körperlichkeit*, ed. Dagmar Hoffmann, Bielefeld 2010, 77–99, here: 84.
61 Wedel, "Körper, Tod und Technik," 83.
62 Wedel, "Körper, Tod und Technik," 83.
63 Wedel, "Körper, Tod und Technik," 89.

To carve this out more precisely in terms of affect, I refer to Kappelhoff's recent categorization of the war film's expressive modes of staging, which, amongst other insights to the mobilization of affect through cinema, sheds light on the genre's complex of somatic warfare – something Gregory would subsume under "The Natures of War."

1.3 Pathos, Affect, and Expressive Movement

Following a qualitative analysis of numerous Hollywood combat films from the 1940s to present day, Kappelhoff's team of researchers identified eight types of standard scenes that – in contrast to Basinger's narrative typology – are ostensibly characterized by their respective affective dimensionality. They defined them as "pathos scenes", audiovisual compositions of moving images in war films seeking to modulate affective responses as a perceptive experience of the spectator.

Expanding on Aby Warburg's "pathos formulas" (a concept also taken up by Elisabeth Bronfen in her book *Specters of War*[64]), these pathos scenes do not solely comprise iconographic figurations and narrative constellations but take them as a semantic frame within which the film image becomes graspable as an affective expressivity. That is, pathos scenes are based upon the expressive qualities of cinematic staging (sound, framing and montage, lighting and colour composition, gestures, etc.) and their dynamic link to audiovisual movement figurations. Kappelhoff's analytical method is thus built on the concept of "expressive movement," an idea of inter-affectivity developed in cultural psychology, linguistics, anthropology, and film theory, but in this case defining the act of film viewing as an embodied subjective experience of the world that is grounded in felt sensations.[65] That is, each level of cinematic staging takes part in abstracting bodily movement from everyday experience and subjecting it to the affective dynamics of film.

Thus describing specific plot constellations of the war film on the one hand, and clearly defined domains of affect on the other, the pathos scenes do not represent subjective experiences of certain film characters, but they relate different

---

[64] Elisabeth Bronfen, *Specters of War: Hollywood's Engagement with Military Conflict*, New Brunswick, NJ 2012.
[65] Hermann Kappelhoff and Cornelia Müller, "Embodied Meaning Construction: Multimodal Metaphor and Expressive Movement in Speech, Gesture, and Feature Film," *Metaphor and the Social World* 1 (2), 2011, 121–153, here: 137.

types of affect-images to one another; only the spectators realize these images as a process of modulated sensations, as a *feeling* – a feeling that is not necessarily represented as an emotion of a film character but instead generated by means of an affective resonance between interacting bodies. A film's arrangement of pathos scenes therefore makes up the temporal structure of cinematic perception and constitutes – in correlation with the spectator's cognitive and sensuous apprehension of representations and actions – its poetics of affect.[66]

Out of Kappelhoff's eight pathos scenes[67], three are of special significance for a corpographic approach to the war film: first, *Battle and Nature*; second, *Battle and Technology*; and, third, *Suffering / Victim / Sacrifice*. Each category entails a close relationship between bodies and spaces, transforming the cinematic space of battle into a sensuous terrain to navigate and reflect on changing physical conditions of the self. I will briefly outline the formal constellations and affective dimensions of said scenes: stemming from the cinematic concept of the horror film, that is, employing "the eerie uncertainty about that which one sees or hears, the fear of being abandoned, of losing one's bodily self and one's identity in chaos,"[68] the category *Battle and Nature* applies to scenes in which the experience of nature as physical threat replaces the battle against the enemy. Here, nature can either provide cover for the enemy, or inscribe signs of exhaustion and death in the body of the individual soldier, blurring the lines between physical entities, and eventually creating spaces of tension within the cinematic composition. As it is written on the project's website:

> On the one hand, the individual soldiers who are moving forward and must maintain a clear view appear to be in an alliance against nature that both orders and destroys nature. On the other hand, nature is portrayed as an agent of chaos, in relation to both the perception and orientation of each individual as well as to the efforts of the corps to maintain the order it needs to remain in action.[69]

---

66 For the theoretical background of expressive movement, cf. Hermann Kappelhoff, *Matrix der Gefühle*, Berlin 2004; the empirical method of analysing media is outlined in: Hermann Kappelhoff and Jan-Hendrik Bakels, "Das Zuschauergefühl. Möglichkeiten qualitativer Medienanalyse," *Zeitschrift für Medienwissenschaft* 5 (2), 2011, 78–95.
67 These are: (1) Transition Between Two Social Systems; (2) Formation of a Group Body (Corps); (3) Battle and Nature; (4) Battle and Technology; (5) Homeland, Woman, Home; (6) Suffering / Victim / Sacrifice; (7) Injustice and Humiliation / Moral Self-Assertion; (8) A Sense of Community as the Shared Filmic Remembrance of Shared Suffering. Cf. http://www.empirische-medienaesthetik.fu-berlin.de/en/emaex-system/affektdatenmatrix/kategorien/index.html (accessed December 5, 2016).
68 Empirische Medienästhetik, "Battle and nature," 2011.
69 Empirische Medienästhetik, "Battle and nature," 2011.

Battle and Technology can be used to describe scenes which foreground an experience of omnipotence (typically induced by the presence and display of powerful weapons technology, and most evident in battle scenes as cinematic fantasies of destruction). First, this implies a merging of human bodies and machines that together form one seemingly almighty entity. At the same time, what goes hand in hand with this physical transformation is the dissolution of the individual body in order to be adapted to the group body, the military corps (which is in itself technologically structured).

While this complex characterizes the metamorphosis of bodies and sensations on screen, a second complex affiliated with this type of pathos scene accentuates the strong ties between weapons technology and cinematic technology – a relationship Virilio has also described as a mode of spectatorial perception. Kappelhoff's definition reads as follows:

> At the fore is a specific form of viewer pleasure that stems mostly from their perspective, which allows them to experience and enter the perceptual and affective/emotional space of a filmic battle without getting as much as a scratch. Everyday perception is expanded by the technological capabilities of cinema.[70]

Contrastingly, the pathos scene *Suffering / Victim / Sacrifice* focuses on the experience of bodily pain portraying the vulnerable, agonizing, or even dying, soldier. When killed in battle, the dead soldier is either staged as a victim, becoming aware of his vulnerability in the moment of unexpected death, or as having made a heroic sacrifice for a greater cause, the army, the nation. In this sense, the "inside view of an indissoluble, irreconcilable experience of suffering characterizes the central pathos of American war films."[71] This is also what Burgoyne points out in his work on war and cinema. Like Wedel, he argues that the war film has to be conceived of as a body genre, as he nominates the soldier's "body at risk" as one of its central tropes, both being a vehicle for the somatic experience of film viewing and the corporeal engagement with history:

> Situated in a kind of shadow zone between organic life and national symbol, between sacrificial object and agent of sovereign violence, the body of the soldier conveys in visceral form a vision of history produced from intensive sensual impressions. From the early sound films depicting World War I to the portrayals of self-sacrifice and loss in *Letters from Iwo Jima* (Eastwood 2006) and *Saving Private Ryan* (Spielberg 1998), the body in the war film expresses in a singular way our immersion in history, framing the past in a way that foregrounds corporeal experience.[72]

---

[70] Empirische Medienästhetik, "Suffering / victim / sacrifice," 2011.
[71] Empirische Medienästhetik, "Suffering / victim / sacrifice," 2011.
[72] Burgoyne, "Embodiment in the War Film," 8.

According to Burgoyne, the war film plays a crucial role in the formation of generational cultures of memory in that it organizes affect around certain conflicts and figures and shapes the ways in which the past is apprehended from one generation to another.[73] What is more, these shifts in (re)constructing the past through cinema become evident in the palpable intensification of somatic imagery, which changes the war film's mode of address and produces "a new visual and acoustic landscape of war."[74] Therefore, the natures of war, both as geographical settings and as recurrent topoi of media warfare, form the ground on which the specific somatic experience of combat can emerge as a spectatorial experience. These landscapes, from the muddy trenches of World War I to the ruins of World War II Europe, the jungle of Vietnam, or the deserts of North Africa and the Middle East, are the very sites of negotiation for the mediated image of war – an image, which is always shaped by and developing with history and media. Seen in this way, it is possible to distinguish continuous patterns from certain historical and aesthetical turning points in the war film genre by means of *corpographic* transformations.

My categorical assumption is that corpography reveals the overarching friction between orientation and disorientation in space. Moreover, it affirms the notion of the war film as a body genre in that it highlights its pronounced expression of a "crisis of the senses," a crisis articulated through the constant reterritorialization of the body on several levels of cinematic staging. Corpography hereby encompasses various modes, each one focusing on a specific sensory apprehension of space and time.

First, it concerns all stylistic devices that provide characters and spectators alike with visual coordinates that they use to orientate themselves within the cinematic space and / or the narration. This includes the display of geographical maps as objects, camerawork and editing to establish a specific filmic space, as well as signs and texts designating the historical time and space of the events depicted. Second, the location of the body can be measured by acoustic coordinates signifying closeness or distance, prominently linked to the affective dimension of fear due to visual disorientation. Third, cinematic space can be staged as being apprehended through touch, i.e. when a soldier is shown navigating the muddy trenches of the Western Front, or fighting his way through dense jungle vegetation.

Fourth, the spatial confusion that especially characterizes the war films of the post-Vietnam period is also created and conveyed through eruptive cutting

---

[73] Burgoyne, "Generational Memory and Affect," 350.
[74] Burgoyne, "Generational Memory and Affect," 350.

and the juxtaposition of multiple image types (analogue, digital, film footage, news images or mobile phone videos). The specific temporalities and modes of perception brought about by these intertextual strategies articulate how the technological conditions of modern warfare not only change how soldiers navigate through actual battle zones, but they also challenge the ways we situate our sensing bodies within the contemporary media landscape of war.

In Chapter Two, I demonstrate how war films about the First World War set and shape the expressive codes of the war film genre. First, in a case study on ALL QUIET ON THE WESTERN FRONT (Lewis Milestone, 1930), I emphasize the explicitly haptic qualities of the film in comparison and intimate connection to literature and poetry of the Great War. Drawing on a literature study by Santanu Das (*Touch and Intimacy in First World War Literature*), I point out the close relationship between literary and cinematic images of sensuous war experience, foregrounding dimensions of sight, sound, and touch. A second case study on Stanley Kubrick's PATHS OF GLORY (1957) illuminates the essential importance of these sensory modes of expression for the war film genre and its mediation of spatial perception. PATHS OF GLORY challenges the iconography and expressive patterns of earlier films about the Great War (in a period of combat films about the Second World War), in that its treatment (and eventual deconstruction) of an optic sensorium not only exposes the war film's persistent aesthetic structures established in the 1930s but produces a palpable sense of time and history that turns into a visceral experience.

Chapter Three puts an emphasis on the decidedly cartographic aspects of corpography as exemplified with OBJECTIVE, BURMA! (Raoul Walsh, 1945). This film is paradigmatic for the expressive modes of staging of the American WWII combat movie (being at its height during the 1940s). Its excessive use of maps, models and optical devices to visualize the opaque jungle of Burma articulate both the attempt of and inability to make this landscape transparent – a condition that will become especially important in films about the Vietnam War. With regard to the film's setting and cartographical narration, OBJECTIVE, BURMA! can be seen as a preceding contrast to Post-Vietnam films (which I will examine closely in the respective chapter). My second case study for this chapter focuses on David Ayer's FURY (2014), a film about tank warfare in WWII Germany. Here I explore the self-sacrificing corporeal adjustment of the soldier to the mechanical body of the tank and the ways it affects the experience of the battle zone as a space of transgression. The claustrophobic space of the tank is strictly opposed to the aerial perspective deployed in OBJECTIVE, BURMA!, but relates to the film's corpographic setting of the jungle: as I will foreground and analyse, conflicts and contrasts between human body and technology, as well as between body and nature, make up two essential tropes of the war film genre.

In a different rendition, and due to a representational predicament in the Cold War period, said conflicts seem intensified through cinematic techniques of repetition and fragmentation, which will be the focus of the fourth chapter. Within the context of US-American history, the Korean War (1950–53) is also known as the "Forgotten War." Temporally framed by the preceding Second World War and the subsequent Vietnam War, it has also been neglected by the film industry from the very beginning, serving as generic template for arbitrary combat stories or family melodramas. Yet, as a subgenre, the Korean War film is more than a mere continuation of the WWII combat film against the background of a different battle theater. As I demonstrate in this chapter, the Korean War film homes in on the governing socio-political uncertainties of the 1950s by establishing a more intimate perspective on warfare as such, and by treating combat as a deeply unsettling, personal matter. This is exemplified by Anthony Mann's MEN IN WAR (1957): the film's pronounced corporeality, its portrayal of spatial, physical and mental confinements, translates the representational confinements of the Cold War into aesthetic figurations of touch, intimacy and claustrophobia. The cinematic fragmentation of spaces and bodies testifies to what I call a process of "*dis*membering" as opposed to the poetics and politics of remembrance deployed in classical combat films.

The Vietnam War marks a distinctive turning point in the audiovisual representation of war. As the first televised and controversially discussed war, it could hardly be situated and classified – also because of the massive amount of fragmentary information about its events. It is this overflow of sensuous perception and disorientation that is primarily negotiated in post-Vietnam war films. In incorporating media images, sounds and technology into their form, these films deal with an expressive richness of detail that for the most part reflects on their own ontology and create profound synesthetic effects (for instance through the fusion of sound and colour). In case studies of THE BOYS IN COMPANY C (Sidney Furie, 1978) and RESCUE DAWN (Werner Herzog, 2006) I explore two conceptual poles of staging the physical experience of war: in Furie's film, visual control is suspended by aural traces which, in turn, are not the solution to the problem of disorientation, but rather articulate this problem in the first place. The attention drawn to the film's acoustics serves to disclose the disparities between sound and image, the sensory detachment of the soldiers to their immediate environment. RESCUE DAWN, in turn, describes the fall, imprisonment, and escape of its protagonist (an American pilot) as an extremely visceral ordeal, developing a distinct counter-image to the aerial view as a representational trope of the war film.

Finally, I will turn to a case study on the mediation of contemporary conflicts. Amongst others, Kevin McSorley and Patricia Pisters have pointed out recently that the incorporation of media technology into the practice of soldiering has gotten to another level with the post-9/11 wars in Afghanistan and Iraq. Media interfaces are at the very heart of the soldier's and spectator's experience in modern warfare, especially for what concerns configurations of drone warfare. Thus, navigation through space has become more and more virtual, challenging the notion of the "body at risk." I argue that these changes in perception and corporeal engagement create uncanny, unstable perceptions of space that nurture the phantasm of a constant threat. Thus, the so-called "War on Terror" becomes a sensuous conflict involving disembodied aerial or satellite views, chaotic urban spaces, and, on a compositional level, irritating disjunctions of sight and sound. Here, and within the context of contemporary war thrillers, my analysis will focus on ZERO DARK THIRTY (Kathryn Bigelow, 2012).

2 Measuring the Trenches: Corpographies of the First World War

According to Paul Virilio, "the history of battle is primarily the history of radically changing fields of perception."[1] Thus, he argues, the Great War became the first mediated military conflict insofar as physical confrontation had been replaced by long-range artillery warfare, which, in turn called for ever more accurate sighting. Photography and film, in this regard, provided the technical opportunity to get a clear overview of the front. The first military films were therefore supposed to "reconstitute the fracture lines of the trenches, to fix the infinite fragmentation of a mined landscape alive with endless potentialities."[2] From then onwards, Virilio, in his study on "war and the logistics of perception," emphasizes the importance and power of sight within the framework of armed conflict, and how it converges with cinematic technology. In order to point out the reverse of this visual mastery, he further develops this paradigm in later works such as *The Vision Machine* and *Desert Screen*, where he talks about the elimination of human subjectivity through forms of telecommanded and televised war. With regard to the Gulf War, and similar to Jean Baudrillard,[3] Virilio foregrounds the notion of a thoroughly automated war machine aligned to media technology and perception.

Many contemporary critical discussions of war cinema take Virilio's observations as a starting point, reading recent war films as exercises in technological display, and finding in earlier war films powerful antecedents. For many theorists and critics of films of war, the thematic issue that returns, again and again, as the central problematic around which the genre turns is a crisis in vision, where issues of concealment, visuality, optical control, knowledge and mastery are set forth in terms of a problematics of vision, expressed in the cinematic language of the panorama, the map, the aerial overview, and targeting coordinates.

Although Patricia Pisters, for example, notes that contemporary media images of war are anything but dehumanized, that they in fact bear strong subjective and affective intensity,[4] the connection between these intensities is rarely

---

[1] Paul Virilio, *War and Cinema: The Logistics of Perception*, London 1989, 7.
[2] Virilio, *War and Cinema*, 71.
[3] In *The Gulf War Did Not Take Place*, Baudrillard argues that the Gulf War of 1991 was in fact a hyperreal simulacrum, a pure media event. See Jean Baudrillard, *The Gulf War Did Not Take Place*, Bloomington 1995.
[4] Patricia Pisters, "Logistics of Perception 2.0: Multiple Screen Aesthetics in Iraq War Films," *Film-Philosophy* 14 (1), 2010, 233–252, here: 241.

demonstrated. More precisely, the body of the soldier, through which war and its images are mediated, is, in many readings, a mere appurtenance of vision, the target of an optically superior emplacement or the instrumentalized projection of the "vision machine."

My argument, however, is that the primacy of sight produces an affect-laden illusion of overview, that is, a fallacious sense of triumphant power that is supplemented and contrasted by the paramount importance of sound and touch for the sensory experience of war. What will already become evident in this chapter on cinematic renditions of the First World War is how the Hollywood war film aims at foregrounding the expressive and thematic importance of senses other than vision when articulating the physical risk of battle. In fact, films that take the extreme battle experience of World War I as their focus establish certain audio-visual patterns essential for the Hollywood combat film of the 1940s and 1950s, as well as for the post-classical war film after the Vietnam War. Ever since dealing with the geographically specific battle space of the trenches, the genre has been constantly modeling the physical experience of narrowness, power, destruction, and overwhelming triumph or fear in attuning it to various theaters of war.

2.1 The Great War in Literature and Film

In a poem titled "Remorse," Siegfried Sassoon describes how a soldier is thrown back to his isolated physical perception of his surroundings, deprived of any sense of sight orientation. All on his own, he senses the battle space rather than assimilating it cognitively: "Lost in the swamp and welter of the pit, / He flounders off the duckboards; only he knows / Each flash and spouting crash, – each instant lit / When gloom reveals the streaming rain. He goes / Heavily, blindly on."[5]

Santanu Das, in his study on World War I literature, calls this a "phenomenological geography," "a landscape not understood in terms of maps, places and names, but geography as processes of cognition, as subjective and sensuous states of experience."[6] Indeed, nowhere becomes the notion of a measurable landscape more evident and decisive than on the battlefields of war. The strategic planning and effective progress of battle action heavily relies on the soldier's ability to evaluate and make use of the given territory. Since he is constantly forced to attune his body to different geographical conditions, his body becomes

---

[5] Siegfried Sassoon, *Counter-Attack and Other Poems*, New York 1918, 54.
[6] Santanu Das, *Touch and Intimacy in First World War Literature*, Cambridge 2005, 73.

the very site of a "re-mapping" of the battlefield. Sassoon, who happened to be an infantry soldier in the First World War himself, further writes on his experiences on the Western Front that "trench life was an existence saturated by the external senses."[7] First-hand accounts like this led geographer Derek Gregory to a close analysis of the Great War's "haptic geographies," putting an emphasis on the "slimescapes" and "soundscapes" of battle. Drawing on literature examined by Santanu Das, Gregory describes the trenches as a hybrid environment of mud, industrial waste, and human limbs, in which acoustic coordinates play an essential orientating role. Moreover, it is this muddy "cyborg nature"[8] from which the soldiers finally become indistinguishable, as their perception gradually shifts from the visual to the tactile. Here again, Das writes about them navigating space "not through the safe distance of the gaze but rather through the clumsy immediacy of their bodies."[9] This description implies that physical intimacy at war can be regarded as one major source of insecurity and fear – but it also suggests, in turn, that a distant view at the scene of battle can equally be associated with certain emotions: visual perception conveys a sense of security or omnipotence, the feeling of being able to grasp space as a whole. Taken a step further, it is even through more abstract textual perspectives on landscapes that this feeling evolves. The simplification of geography produced by maps or aerial photographs not only reproduces the safe distance of vision but also dissociates the visible from its actual appearance. Thus, used in terms of battle tactics, these texts transform incalculable nature into simple territories, creating a point of view that can only work for military strategists or outsiders *not* involved in actual battle action. What is established here is a detached perspective – the aforementioned "illusion of overview" – that is radically different from the fighting conditions soldiers are confronted with. The distant, generalizing position of military officers is always opposed to that of the individual infantryman being thrown back to his subjective sensing of the world.

It can therefore be said that the disorientation of the soldier at war, the feeling of being overwhelmed and left alone, becomes most evident through the very contrast between an apparently safe distance and the immediate physical experience of battle. And it is through this contrast that the surrounding landscape

---

[7] Siegfried Sassoon, *Memoirs of an Infantry Officer*, London 1965, 33.
[8] Using this term in "The Natures of War," Derek Gregory refers to an essay by Donna Haraway, where she calls modern war a "cyborg orgy." Cf. Donna Haraway, "A Cyborg Manifesto: Science, Technology and Socialist-Feminism in the Late Twentieth Century," in *The Cybercultures Reader*, ed. David Bell, Barbara M. Kennedy, London / New York 2000, 292.
[9] Das, *Touch and Intimacy*, 7.

is being re-mapped through the soldier's body – a phenomenological technique Derek Gregory conceives as the "corpography" of war.

The concept of (geographical) corpography underlines the idea of war as a somatic experience, for it is this fusion of physicality and space that makes bodies both vectors and objects of military violence. Predominantly, in more philosophical terms, it supports John Wylie's accounts of the body-subject in a landscape. Mainly drawing on the phenomenological takes of philosophers Merleau-Ponty and Deleuze, Wylie states that landscape is rather actualized by processes of depth and fold than simply gazed at. Thus, he argues, "exhilarating encounters with elemental configurations of land, sea and sky are less a distanced looking-at and more a seeing-with."[10] It is this affective dimension of experiencing space that is articulated through poetry and literature, as well as through film. Even more so, it is not just an affective experience lived by a certain fictional character, but is also translated into an aesthetic experience for the reader or viewer. In the very moment of film perception, the portrayed event temporally unfolds through the senses of the spectator.

As for the Great War, it is fruitful to compare exemplary Hollywood films to respective works of literature and poetry. First of all, many films (American and European) on the First World War are based on novels written by authors involved in the war. Secondly, the literary images articulated in poetry strikingly correspond to cinematic depictions of war. As Santanu Das has elaborated recently, war poems by European writers evoke a haptic sense of space, which is, in my view, also the case for American war films. The Hollywood war film incorporates the spatial conditions of soldiering to an extent that it becomes sensible as an experience of touch and being touched, which means that the intimate subjectivity we share with the protagonists evokes a tactile perception of cinematic elements, as well as the shaping of emotions specifically connected to space and sensation. Precisely this condition, albeit in a more general sense, has been outlined by media scholars Laura U. Marks and Jennifer M. Barker. While Marks, in coining the term *haptic visuality*, refers to the materiality of film as establishing "a contact between perceiver and object represented,"[11] Barker fortifies the concept of cinematic tactility by describing it as an "attitude towards the cinema" which essentially involves the body of the spectator. Tactility, then, can be grasped as "a mode of perception and expression wherein all parts of the body commit

---

10 John Wylie, "A Single Day's Walking: Narrating Self and Landscape on the South West Coast Path," *Transactions of the Institute of British Geographers* 30 (2), 2005, 234–247, here: 242.
11 Laura U. Marks, *The Skin of the Film: Intercultural Cinema, Embodiment, and the Senses*, Durham, NC 2000, xi.

themselves to, or are drawn into, a relationship with the world that is at once a mutual and intimate relation of contact."[12]

No less intimate, much of European literature on the First World War, with its highly illustrative and metaphorical rendering of war as a physical experience, articulates on a textual level what the war film's audiovisual figurations express through image, sound and movement unfolding in time. These scenes may differ from the literary original in order and emphasis but are just as intimately linked to bodily perception. In my reference to Das's work I therefore seek to point out how strongly Hollywood war films on the First World War relate to a poetic physical sensuousness that exceeds national contexts and form a universal imagery of war. Whether in Erich Maria Remarque's *Im Westen nichts Neues* [*All Quiet on the Western Front*], or in Henri Barbusse's *Le feu* [*Under Fire*], the war's effect on the senses and the physical awareness of battle plays a major role in verbalizing and connecting fragmented episodes of trench warfare and is a premise of survival. As it is stated in Remarque's novel, "a man must have a feeling for the contours of the ground, an ear for the sound and character of the shells, must be able to decide beforehand where they will drop, how they will burst, and how to shelter from them."[13] It is this knowledge and experience that war films build upon.

Shortly after the end of World War I, the conflict was cinematically negotiated within melodramatic forms, portraying families being torn apart by the war and tragic love stories. This includes Hollywood silent films such as Griffith's HEARTS OF THE WORLD (1918), THE HEART OF HUMANITY (1918) directed by Allen Holubar, Rex Ingram's THE FOUR HORSEMEN OF THE APOCALYPSE (1921) and King Vidor's THE BIG PARADE (1925). Also, with Charlie Chaplin's SHOULDER ARMS (1918) and Raoul Walsh's WHAT PRICE GLORY? (1926), there were two prominent comedy-dramas. With the exception of J'ACCUSE (1919) by French director Abel Gance, Raymond Bernard's LES CROIX DE BOIS (*Wooden Crosses*, 1932), the German WESTFRONT 1918 (1930) by G.W. Pabst, and two British films – DAWN (1928) and LOST PATROL (1929) – almost every major film dealing with events of the First World War was produced in the United States. This is due to the fact that, in the wake of war, most of the European film studios had to close down and Hollywood therefore dominated the international film market in the 1920s. Therefore, it induced what was to become the imagery of the First World War, although, according to Pierre Sorlin, these American movies "never tackled the tricky question of cause."[14] Instead,

---

12 Jennifer Barker, *The Tactile Eye: Touch and the Cinematic Experience*, Berkeley 2009, 3.
13 Erich Maria Remarque, *All Quiet on the Western Front*, trans. A.W. Wheen, London 1929, 144.
14 Pierre Sorlin, "Cinema and the Memory of the Great War," in *The First World War and Popular Cinema: 1914 to the Present*, ed. Michael Paris, Edinburgh 1999, 5–26, here: 17.

they combined "realism and melodramatic romanticism"[15] before increasingly focusing on battle scenes and soldiers' experiences by the mid-1920s.[16]

Both William A. Wellman's silent WINGS (1927) and Lewis Milestone's ALL QUIET ON THE WESTERN FRONT (1930) won the Academy Award for Best Picture. Remarkably, the latter does not deal with the American involvement in the war, but focuses on young German soldiers having to deal with trench warfare, disillusionment and human loss.

2.2 Geographies of Fear: ALL QUIET ON THE WESTERN FRONT

ALL QUIET ON THE WESTERN FRONT, as an adaptation of Erich Maria Remarque's novel *Im Westen nichts Neues*, tells the story of young Paul Bäumer who goes to fight on the battlefields of France with his fellow classmates. Remarque, in a rather fragmentary style, uses vivid synesthetic descriptions of sight, sound, touch and taste to let his protagonist reflect on the horrors he encounters "within the embrace"[17] of the front. Occasionally, he compares the front to a "mysterious whirlpool" drawing Paul into its "vortex,"[18] and a space where sensibilities are either "wiped out,"[19] or overwhelmingly intensified. Yet the film does not only adopt the subjective, intimate perspective of the original novel; it takes its corpographic impressions and experiences to another sensuous level. In addition to the then innovative technique of film sound to convey the overwhelming roar of battle, the mise-en-scène in ALL QUIET ON THE WESTERN FRONT literally *frames* the body of the soldier in relation to spatial limitations. Above all, the film shapes the bodily experience of fear and loss emerging from different structural operations.

What is most interesting about ALL QUIET is it being a U.S. adaptation of a German novel, depicting German (enemy) soldiers in an empathic way, only a little more than ten years after the armistice. The novel itself was a huge success at the time of its publishing, and is said to have caused a wave of war literature production in late Weimar Germany, mostly written by authors who

---

15 Sorlin, "Cinema and the Memory of the Great War," 17.
16 Cf. Leslie Midkiff DeBauche, "The United States' Film Industry and World War One," in *The First World War and Popular Cinema: 1914 to the Present*, ed. Michael Paris, Edinburgh 1999, 155–156.
17 Remarque, *All Quiet on the Western Front*, 62.
18 Remarque, *All Quiet on the Western Front*, 64.
19 Remarque, *All Quiet on the Western Front*, 78.

had first-hand experiences of the war.[20] Apart from that, the 1929 depression seemed to have fostered the urge of German society coming to terms with their past within the cultural and aesthetic framework of New Objectivity.[21] Nevertheless, Remarque's *Im Westen nichts Neues* was one of relatively few anti-war books compared to a large amount of German right-wing pro-war literature – with Josef Magnus Wehner even writing a "corrective" to Remarque's novel called *Sieben vor Verdun*.[22] The small number of literature critical towards the war, according to Michael Gollbach, bears several distinguishing features: above all, war is pictured here as a source of disgust, as a loss of human dignity; the soldier's psyche is characterized by disillusionment, indifference, anxiety, depression, disorientation, concern for the other, psychic deformity and lack of identity. And the enemy, finally, is regarded as a comrade of equal value.[23] Taking this into account, it becomes traceable why both Germany's Left and Right despised *Im Westen nichts Neues* in times of political polarization: socialists and communists accused Remarque of disregarding the social and economic causes of the war;[24] the Right blamed him for defaming the nation's traditional political, economic, and military institutions.[25] Under these circumstances, the book was not adapted for the screen in Germany, while it rapidly received massive international attention and German-born Hollywood producer Carl Laemmle promptly acquired the film rights from Remarque.[26] As ALL QUIET was then extensively advertised and commercially distributed by Universal, it gained a remarkable influence on the public mind "as the most powerful image of warfare in the First World War."[27] And although the film refused to take judgmental sides, it was heatedly discussed in Europe. In Germany, it was even banned for a certain time, and truncated versions were released in different countries.[28]

---

[20] Cf. Bernadette Kester, *Film Front Weimar: Representations of the First World War in German Films of the Weimar Period (1919–1933)*, Amsterdam 2003, 124.
[21] Cf. Michael Gollbach, *Die Wiederkehr des Weltkrieges in der Literatur. Zu den Frontromanen der späten Zwanziger Jahre*, Kronberg (Ts.) 1978, 203.
[22] Cf. Gollbach, *Die Wiederkehr des Weltkrieges in der Literatur*, 266.
[23] Gollbach cited in Bernadette Kester, *Film Front Weimar*, 124–125.
[24] Arnold Zweig, "Kriegsromane," *Die Weltbühne*, April 25, 1929, 598.
[25] Chambers lists Wilhelm Müller Scheld's „*Im Westen nichts Neues*": *Eine Täuschung* and Hermann Heisler's *Krieg oder Frieden. Randbemerkung zu Remarques Buch „Im Westen nichts Neues"* as sources.
[26] Cf. "Confers on New War Film," 8.
[27] Chambers 1994, 400.
[28] Cf. Pierre Sorlin, "Cinema and the Memory of the Great War," 18.

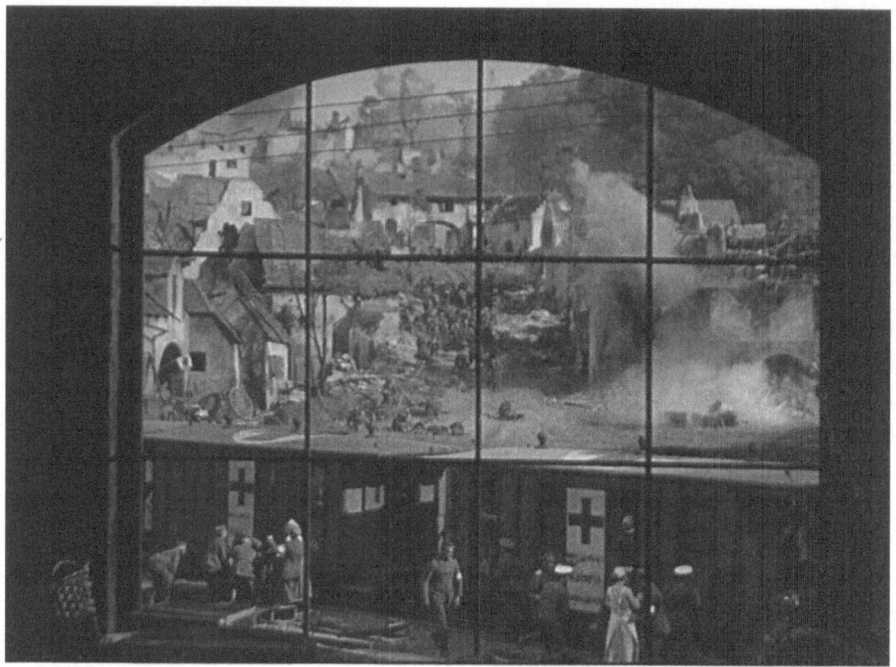

Figure 1: The window as cartographic metaphor.

But beyond establishing an iconography of the Great War, ALL QUIET, like the original novel, conveys a physical experience of war that lays the foundation for the affective dimensions of the war film genre as such. First, the film's corpography is deployed by means of contrasting near and far, stillness and movement, which can be especially observed in central scenes. When we see Paul (Lew Ayres) and his comrades arriving at a train station in the battle zone, we initially observe the scenery from a distant point of view: we look through a window, the location of which is not further deployed, that provides a safe distance to what is happening outside (see Figure 1). But suddenly, a cut takes us to the train station, where we are instantly overwhelmed by the sight and sound of bodies in motion: several regiments march across; an extreme low-angle shot shows human legs and horses ploughing the ground, more people are dashing from left to right, immediately taking cover when shells are about to hit the houses. Although set in broad daylight, the arrival of the soldiers proves to be their first heavily disorienting experience – a perceptual distortion made visible for the spectator by constantly referring to the scene's introductory window shot. It is through this contrast between distance and immediacy that we experience what Tom Conley calls "bilocation," meaning that the spectator is technically positioned both inside and outside the film. However, Conley conceives bilocation as a function of cinematic cartography. Once a map is seen in a film, it is not only a diegetic object, but also a text revealing the production mechanisms of cinema, superimposing codes on the film, which are not part of its language. As he puts it: "When a map in a film locates the geography of its narrative, it also tells us that we are not where it says it is taking place."[29] Because a map confronts the spectator with a different textual appearance and structure, the cinematic verisimilitude gets momentarily disrupted. Although this is not the case with the scene mentioned here, a similar, albeit less extreme effect can be observed: if the window is regarded as cartographic metaphor, it draws us in and out of the depicted action. As we do not even know where the camera is placed exactly, since a reverse shot is missing, we are set in an opaque space designating our distance from the action that takes place outside, and we are therefore marked as mere beholders of a moving still life. Down at the train station, on the other hand, we are part of a thoroughly chaotic atmosphere, affected by low camera angles, overcrowded medium long shots, and abrupt editing. We share the soldiers' panic about not knowing where to run and how to move. Seen in this way, the cartographic window initializes the film's corpography in marking the very contrast of embodied and disembodied perception.

From now on, we witness how the recruits physically attune to their surroundings. This becomes especially necessary and evident on their first night patrol. After having debarked a military truck and sent off to the wire, Paul and the others take a fearful look back at the vehicle – the shot that is superimposed on the very last image of the film – and march off into the night. Surrounded by fog and darkness, they are almost paralyzed, ever reaching out for Kat (Louis Wolheim), an experienced soldier in charge of the action. In the literal sense, Kat becomes someone to cling to. In a fatherly manner, he tells his recruits to align to his movements, to pay close attention to every sound they hear. As a matter of fact, sound literally substitutes sight, and in doing so, it becomes more and more related to the sense of touch. Hence, in the very moment Kat warns the boys about *seeing* shellfire, they actually *hear* it, and fall to their knees instinctively, with Paul and a comrade actually holding on to Kat. It is the starting point of experiencing battle as what Paul Rodaway calls "haptic geography,"[30] the bodily perception of space that includes locomotion and kinesthesis, and that is to be

---

29 Conley, *Cartographic Cinema*, 3–4.
30 Cf. Paul Rodaway, *Sensuous Geographies: Body, Sense and Place*, London / New York 1994.

described as a sense "spread all over the body."[31] With low visibility, navigation through space gets more intimate, and the more important acoustic coordinates become for physical orientation. Judging from first-hand accounts by WWI soldiers, Das consequentially speaks of the "haptic sound" of artillery shelling as "encasing the body," inasmuch as the soldier's tactile sense is enhanced to a synesthetic level.

Apart from the narrowing environment of the trenches, where sound in fact contributed to a strong feeling of claustrophobia, the night patrol would be another prototypical war situation in which the occurring disjunction between sight, space and danger both emerged from and amplified the mechanized nature of the First World War, where physical intimacy is to be regarded as "shield against the impersonal onslaught of the machine."[32] In contrast to the subterranean trenches, the space of the night patrol covers an uncannily dark and yet exposed terrain, and every sound is perceived as a "physical collision and possible annihilation, *as a missed encounter with death*."[33] It is this tension and threat, which is specifically conveyed in ALL QUIET's night patrol sequence. Unlike depictions of soldiers patrolling in other war films, this scene focuses not only on a "missed encounter with death" but moreover on a *first* encounter with death. The group of young soldiers is as inexperienced as it is suggestive. As they are lacking any routine, the boys engage with Kat's instructions as if they would find themselves in yet another educational situation. Coming from a lesson in enthusiasm with their schoolteacher Kantorek (Arnold Lucy), and having been disciplined, humiliated and outraged by their military superior Himmelstoss (John Wray), they now experience collective insecurity and fear. Thus, of all the authoritative attempts to transform these individuals into a uniformed group body, the night patrol is the most effective, and most affective: in describing the menacing quality of sound, Kat at the same time foregrounds its orientating potential. He acoustically imitates an approaching shell and advises: "When you hear that, down to Mother Earth! Press yourselves down upon her! Bury yourselves deep into her..." Therefore, by pointing out the importance of geographical intimacy, Kat serves as a kind of corpographic navigator. Not only that what he tells his young comrades is to re-map space through their bodies – he himself becomes the body to which the soldiers hang on to, a role model for developing their own corpographic skills. In many ways, he can be conceived as a figure mirroring and reversing the martinet trainer Himmelstoss; thus, ALL QUIET provides us with two instructors giving

---

31 Das, *Touch and Intimacy*, 74.
32 Das, *Touch and Intimacy*, 83.
33 Das, *Touch and Intimacy*, 81.

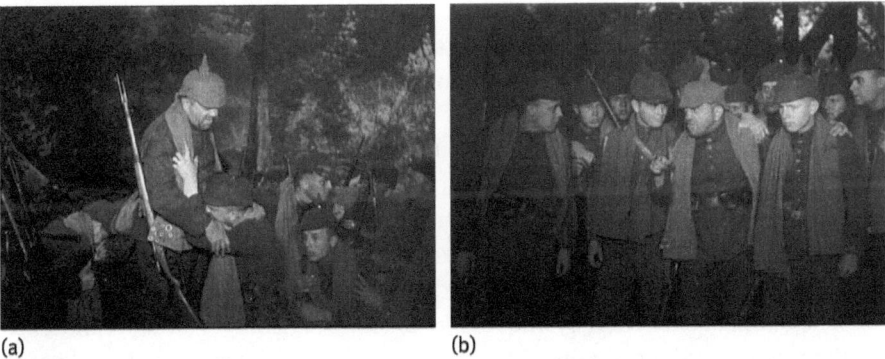

(a) (b)

Figure 2: Kat as corpographic navigator.

different forms of physical education, again contrasting distance and intimacy: Himmelstoss issues his orders without being part of the exercising group, without being actually in touch with his detachment; Kat, then again, becomes the tangible focal point of a collective objective. Seen in this regard, both of them are complementary bodies of fear, with Himmelstoss being a character from which fear and hate emerge, and Kat being a figure giving shelter when fear is overwhelming the boys. The shot of Paul tentatively reaching out for Kat, caressing his shoulder, and then grabbing it, comprises the intimate admiration of a boy for his father. Kat, in turn, in letting the young soldiers gather around him like children, pays close attention to every single one of them; not only out of care for their individual wellbeing, but to ensure the closeness of the group. Kat himself watches and touches them, making sure that he is seen and heard (see Figure 2). This informs an affective category Kappelhoff describes as "transition between two social systems,"[34] with its recurring motif of the portrayal of paternal structures within the military community.[35] But the inherent separation between masculine and feminine is blurred by the fact that Kat indeed represents both a father and a mother figure. Apart from obvious homoerotic references, his touch (and being touched) provides an intimate bond that characterizes an alternative male sociality outside

---

34 Hermann Kappelhoff, *Front Lines of Community: Hollywood Between War and Democracy*, Berlin / Boston 2018, 128.
35 For a detailed description of this pathos category, cf. also the following webpage: Empirische Medienästhetik, database "Mobilization of Emotions in War Films," "Transition between two social systems," in *Freie Universität Berlin, Languages of Emotion* (2011), http://www.empirische-medienaesthetik.fu-berlin.de/en/emaex-system/affektdatenmatrix/kategorien/uebergang/index.html (accessed March 25, 2015).

of civilian norms, as Anthony Easthope notes: "In the dominant versions of men at war, men are permitted to behave toward each other in ways that would not be allowed elsewhere, caressing and holding each other, comforting and weeping together, admitting their love."[36]

As exceptional as this form of male bonding may be in terms of gender and masculinity – what it proves on a much more fundamental level is the effect of war on perceptive orientation. The intimacy between the men leads to (and is a consequence of) an enhanced haptic perception of their environment, which lets them navigate by means of an intensified sensuousness.

The realm of smell hereby adds an "olfactory geography"[37] to this condition: terrified by the sudden shellfire, one of the boys soils himself. The fact that his wet uniform will be seen is above all supplemented by the fact that his comrades will smell it sooner or later. Moreover: "The sense of smell, unlike vision, touch or taste, is severed from its object and is a stimulus to the powers of both memory and fantasy."[38] Taking this into account, Kat's comment can be interpreted as an olfactory reaction: "Never mind. It happened to better men than you. And it's happened to me." That said, he both refers to his own memory of being an inexperienced soldier and to the present image his "children" could have of him. As embarrassing as this situation might be for the soldier – and it is even cinematically portrayed as a moment of distressing stasis – this physical incident tightens the corpographic bond between the boys and Kat.

This intimacy is conveyed through close group shots and slow camera movement – with fear emanating from an all-consuming ghostly atmosphere that fills the frame: the soldiers walk through fog and shadows, crawl forward, across looming fences, taking cover at artillery fire, merging with the churning ground. And in doing so, they regress to an almost primeval state; seen from above, they seem like squirming worms rather than men – an image that thoroughly metaphorizes their transformation from cognitively channelled human beings to bodies driven by and depending on their physical senses. Yet the loss of sight proves to be an existential experience of powerlessness. While ringing wire on No Man's Land, the group is forced to take cover from enemy fire. One soldier gets hit in the eyes and surrenders to hysteria. He rushes out of the shell hole screaming, exposing himself to heavy

---

36 Anthony Easthope, *What a Man's Gotta Do: The Masculine Myth in Popular Culture*, New York / London 1990, 66.
37 Das, *Touch and Intimacy*, 84.
38 Das, *Touch and Intimacy*, 85. Following up on that, Das illustrates the orientation provided by smell with regard to "The Night Patrol" by Arthur Graeme West: "the movements of the men are charted through the way the smell changes ..." (87).

bombardment. We can only assume that he is severely hurt because of his audible agony, for we are deprived of any clear sight of the scenery, as well. His body barely stands out against the wire and dark earth, and as he runs towards the enemy lines the camera stays static. We see him stumbling into the distance until he falls over, without being technically able to follow him. In a way, the insufficiency of visual perception – and the helplessness resulting from it – hereby finds its cinematographic double. Finally, as a cruel exclamation mark to the process of human degeneration, Kat negates the significance of this soldier's death right away: "It is a corpse, no matter who it is."

ALL QUIET is far from marking a soldier's death as heroic sacrifice for his country. Nonetheless, death is not simply treated as an incident but as a troubling process that has to be worked through by those who witness it. Death is thus negotiated in terms of how it personally affects the living. As Das writes on a war poem by Isaac Rosenberg, it is a "phenomenological unease" that "becomes the point of departure for a profound questioning of the relation" between life and death.[39] Additionally, in this process of alienation and incorporation, the boundaries between friend and enemy are blurred, if not erased. This interpretation is again provoked by the cinematic portrayal of the suffering body. In a central scene of the film, Paul hides in a shell hole while German and French regiments attack each other. From an extreme low angle, we see soldiers jumping across the hole, almost each one of them a potential enemy, a "missed encounter with death." Suddenly, one French soldier jumps into the hole; Paul reacts instinctively and stabs him. The ear-battering sound of artillery fire mutes all screams of pain, while Paul additionally covers his mouth with his hand. In that very moment, we are sharing Paul's perspective of fear and nervousness. And even with the camera reverting to a more distanced position, the act of killing is marked as something repulsive, when Paul washes the man's blood of his hands in panic. As time passes, the two soldiers are trapped in darkness, frightened by their own sensuous perception. Flares frequently light up the crater, we see Paul covering his ears, and the wounded French soldier in horror at the sight of his enemy. The chiaroscuro of the scene draws the spectator's attention to the men's faces, and the scene as a whole almost appears like a series of photographs: although it is barely divided by cuts, the rhythm of the flickering light resembles a series of shots, each one of them revealing an emotional state. This slightly expressionistic visual style stimulates the unfolding of a psychological and physiological drama. Cutting from

---

39 Das, *Touch and Intimacy*, 103. The respective poem by Isaac Rosenberg is titled "Dead Man's Dump" and mainly refers to the disturbing experience of driving over dead bodies on the battlefield.

the nightly scenario to broad daylight, mood and atmosphere have changed completely, while the on-going deafening noise of bombardment provides acoustic consistency. Paul is furious now; the dying man's heavy breathing terrifies him; he even begs him to die faster. Then again, he apologizes, but the French soldier is dead. His frozen smile is completely detached from the world he just left, while Paul desperately tries to hold on to the man's body, and to ask for his forgiveness.

A strikingly similar image is evoked in Giuseppe Ungaretti's poem "Vigil": "A whole night long / crouched close / to one of our men / butchered / with his clenched / mouth / grinning at the full moon / with the congestion / of his hands / thrust right / into my silence …"[40] The synesthetic metaphor of hands actually punching the silence describes the violent effect of a soundless body (even in the midst of the sound of battle, as in ALL QUIET). It is the frozen expression of life that gains a thoroughly haptic quality, as the witness of death refuses to let go, and literally seeks to "hang on" to life. This is the case with the narrator of Ungaretti's poem by concluding: "I have never been/so/coupled to life." And it is this overtly sensuous perspective that is established in ALL QUIET's crater sequence – an intimacy that lets Paul reflect on the lost potential of past and future. In Remarque's novel, this is once more articulated in terms of measuring space through the body, as the narrator ponders: "The dead man might have had thirty more years of life if only I had impressed the way back to our trench more sharply on my memory. If only he had run two yards farther to the left, he might now be sitting in the trench over there and writing a fresh letter to his wife"[41] Furthermore, he eventually thinks about incorporating the dead soldier's identity in order to redeem himself, to become what this man had used to be in his past civilian life: a printer (see Figure 3).

It is interesting to think about this profession standing at the very junction between touch and mechanization. Indeed, in accordance to Das, it can be said that touch and sound serve as key aesthetic modes of expression in both literature and films about the First World War. In applicable reference to the act of printing, both leave their tactile imprints on the soldier's and the spectator's sensuous perception. But on the other hand, ALL QUIET deploys another mode of perception, a machinic, industrial envisioning of war, which is the exact opposite to what Das or Rodaway describe as "haptic geographies." The film makes use of linear tracking shots and extreme long shots of the cratered battlefield to – in the words of Virilio – "fix the infinite fragmentation of a mined landscape alive with endless

---

[40] Giuseppe Ungaretti, "Vigil [1915]", in *The Penguin Book of First World War Poetry*, ed. George Walter, London 2006, 264.
[41] Remarque, *All Quiet on the Western Front*, 243–244.

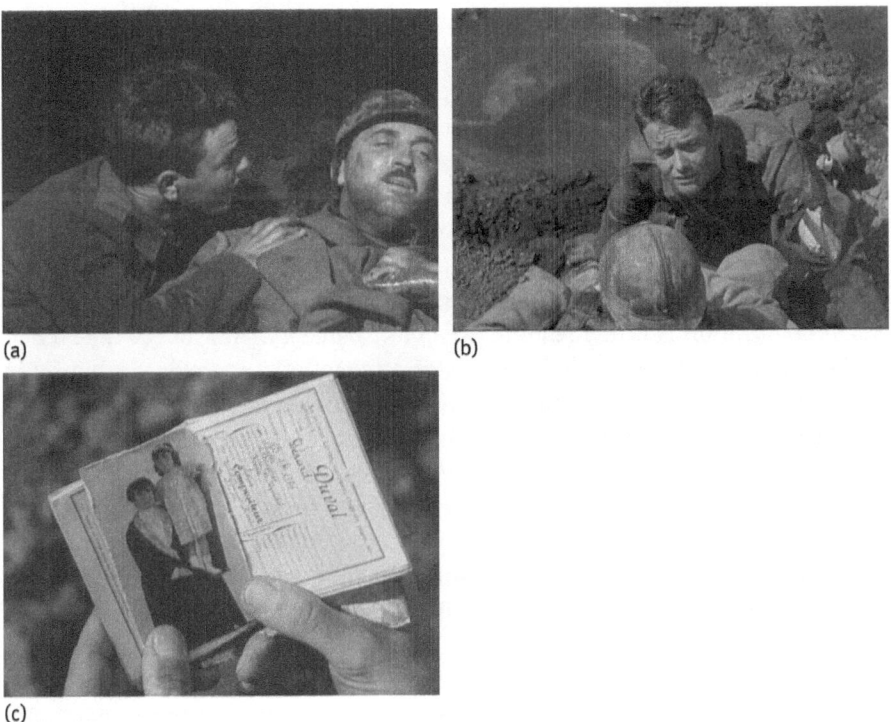

Figure 3: The lost potential of past and future.

potentialities."[42] It is here where we find what various scholars have pointed out as the main characteristic of the war film, namely the primacy of sight and mechanized vision and the difficulties connected to the demand for visual control. Then again, ALL QUIET features more than that: the haptic and the visual as two modes of expression and perception are held in tension throughout the film. This is why and how one becomes graspable as an extreme contrast to the other. Other than being a mere exception, the film thereby establishes an aesthetic pattern that lies at the heart of subsequent war films – a pattern that can be conceived as constitutive for the genre as such. While spatial distance establishes a sense of visual control and overview at certain points of the plot, it is eventually undermined by the tactile dimension of cinematic expressivity, that is, by the intimate interaction between bodies, textures, and landscapes on the level of staging. Here, in line with the theoretical approaches by Marks, Bruno, and Barker, audiovisual configurations of touch and intimacy allow for the emergence of a haptic visuality that

---

42 Virilio, *War and Cinema*, 71.

subverts the characters' optical sensorium, but also brings out other sensuous qualities of the cinematic image which the spectator is invited to experience.

The emphasis on sense experience, particularly on touch and sound here, articulates larger historical messages, in which pathos becomes a key figure of historical experience in World War I. In several scenes, the film deals with a variation of suffering; a cinematic mode of staging conveying the individual's experience of having and being a vulnerable, that is, a mortal body.[43] Here I will discuss three forms of pathos, as theorized by Kappelhoff, that are evoked in ALL QUIET. In the scene in which Paul spend the night with the man he has killed, the constellation of suffering is divided into two bodily perceptions: whereas the French soldier suffers physically, Paul articulates an emotional struggle. In his futile attempts to address the deceased man, he expresses the difficulty of coping with the irreversibility of death. Secondly, in feeling guilty, Paul questions the war's purpose, casting doubts on the authoritative institutions he is acting upon. In other words, his empathy for the supposed enemy is to be read as a "consequence of the implication in and a share of the responsibility for the suffering inflicted upon others by the military/group the soldier is part of."[44] Another aspect would be the shift from this sense of guilt, that is, the reflection on whether the soldier's actions are justifiable, to a physical outlet for him to channel these unsettling emotions. Kappelhoff speaks of the cinematic staging of "rage as the transformation of moral judgement into bodily desire and the delight in the corporeal."[45] This is less the case in ALL QUIET, where Paul's moral judgment is finally turned into disillusionment. Nevertheless, and in contrast to other war films, his "bodily desire" is evident in the intimacy with the French soldier. Here, it is not so much Paul's rage but his feeling of guilt that results in physical closeness. Very similar to Rosenberg's poem, this marks a change of perspective and affective registers, when "metaphysical and moral unrest replaces responses such as disgust or horror."[46] And it goes along with the moral alienation from the national military structures by which Paul feels exploited: "Oh God, why do they do this to us? ... Why should they send us out to fight each other?"

---

[43] This again conforms to Kappelhoff's pathos scenes. Cf. the following webpage: Empirische Medienästhetik, database "Mobilization of Emotions in War Films," "Suffering / victim / sacrifice," in *Freie Universität Berlin, Languages of Emotion* (2011), http://www.empirische-medienaesthetik.fu-berlin.de/en/emaex-system/affektdatenmatrix/kategorien/leidenopfer/index.html (accessed March 25, 2015).
[44] Empirische Medienästhetik, "Injustice and humiliation / moral self-assertion," 2011.
[45] Empirische Medienästhetik, "Injustice and humiliation / moral self-assertion," 2011.
[46] Das, *Touch and Intimacy*, 103.

Thirdly, the reflection on injustice blends over into a third category of pathos scenes that is closely related to the memory of the soldier's homeland, family, and femininity[47]: it is the return to civilian life that dominates the last part of the scene, when Paul finds out about the man's name and discovers a photograph of his wife and child. He promises to write to them in order to be forgiven, and this pledge keeps him alive in the end. More than that, it corresponds to a need for security that also represents an emotional layer for the other two mentioned pathos categories (suffering and moral self-assertion): while the suffering soldier realizes that he has been abandoned and exposed to his physical vulnerability, the humiliated soldier feels betrayed by his authorities; he turns a passive suffering into an active, corporeal upheaval, without being able to accommodate himself to a time and space outside war. Both can be found in Paul's verbal expressions and his body language, while he faces his own potential suffering through the French soldier's agony. The craving for a return to civilian life, then, is the longing for a lost innocent environment, a past that the individual soldier seeks to recover; it implies hope and motivation, but also the subliminal certainty about a life that can never be retrieved again.

All three categories mark specific stages within the "melodramatic dramaturgy" of the war film genre, while it has to be said that they cannot be differentiated as isolated figurations. Rather, the narrative constellations and affective dimensions of pathos scenes coexist and modulate each other in changing variations, which is why several categories can be detected in one scenic complex of a film. Furthermore, these underlying affective layers not only motivate and modulate cinematic emotions (unfolded by the film and targeted at the spectator), but also influence how war is felt and perceived as an emotional landscape. This classification of pathos, I would argue, draws on a specific spatiotemporal configuration, which is constantly reformulated within the war film genre: it unfolds over the duration of cinematic time, but is especially related to the affective quality of filmic space. Precisely, as the exemplary crater scene in ALL QUIET shows, the limited space of the shell hole, the intimately close camera, and the intense lighting and sound design create an audiovisual image of claustrophobia – a constellation within which the body is not only re-territorialized but *de-territorialized*. Without a geographically and historically definable place, it becomes aware of its troubled *being-in-the-world*. More precisely, the

---

47 Cf. the following webpage: Empirische Medienästhetik, database "Mobilization of Emotions in War Films," "Homeland, woman, home," in *Freie Universität Berlin, Languages of Emotion* (2011), http://www.empirische-medienaesthetik.fu-berlin.de/en/emaex-system/affektdatenmatrix/kategorien/heimatfrau/index.html (accessed March 25, 2015).

conscious body realizes its dependence on the communicative connection with its tangible environment. In addition to this elusive setting, it is because Paul loses the communicative tie to his world, because the frozen smile of the French soldier lingers on as if he were about to speak at any minute, that we share this existential irritation; we, too, get uneasy facing an image that potentially talks back at us – but refuses to do so. And here it is not simply the landscape that is remapped through the body, but moreover Paul's body that is remapped through the landscape.

A similar existential "in-betweenness" is evoked by ALL QUIET's depiction of the trenches as the Great War's most emblematic setting: located in the surrounding landscape of No Man's Land, they make up a subterranean labyrinth that positions the soldier spatially between life and death; the soldier himself becomes a spectral figure caught in the insecurity of a vulnerable and yet enclosing environment, living two extreme experiences of space, which, according to Santanu Das's reading of World War I literature would be "the claustrophobia of the trenches and agoraphobia induced by the shot-riddled space overhead."[48] Through these poles, and through this "haptic mode" of spatial perception, a so-called "geography of fear" is registered and represented, that is, "the threat of enclosure and exposure alike produces a sense of space felt as volume surrounding the body rather than as surface or distance to be covered."[49] Even more so, the trenches themselves become living beings, feeding from the soldiers inhabiting them; these men who are intimate with the earth clasping around them form a "cyborg nature" with the tangible world, becoming part of the trenches as an incorporated existential experience. Das thus suggests that trench life is peculiarly marked by the loss of visual coordinates and the primary importance of touch; that the feeling of and for distance is substituted by an immediate sensuous perception, and that two-dimensionality is in a way replaced with three-dimensionality. He underlines this conclusion in quoting an extract from Henri Barbusse's *Light*, in which the haptic threat posed by the trenches is expressed through the feeling of being continually clasped and choked by the earth.[50] What this literary metaphor in Barbusse's novel implies is the phantasm of the trenches as physical beings, closing in on the soldiers

---

48 Das, *Touch and Intimacy*, 76.
49 Das, *Touch and Intimacy*, 76.
50 Cf. Henri Barbusse, *Light*, 112–113: "We followed the trench along for three hours. For three hours we continued to immerse ourselves in distance and solitude, to immure ourselves in night, scraping its walls with our loads, and sometimes violently pulled up, where the defile shrunk into strangulation by the sudden wedging of our pouches. It seemed as if the earth tried continually to clasp and choke us, that sometimes it roughly struck us."

inhabiting them. Indeed, also cinematic depictions of the trenches seem to evoke a similar mood, only without actually picturing them as living creatures. Instead, dense image compositions, static camerawork, and medium close-ups or close-ups of frightened soldiers create the iconographic atmosphere for numerous trench sequences in WWI films. Nevertheless, the surrounding, three-dimensional presence (or rather menace) of space Das describes is exceptionally articulated in ALL QUIET: when the German infantrymen await the enemy to storm the fences dividing the battle zone, the camera tracks above and along their aligned heads looming over the dugout. Helmet next to helmet, there seems to be an infinite string of bodies crouching in the trenches, with every head marking a new link of the human chain. This slow forward motion is then crosscut with long shots of the empty plain ahead of them, which suddenly bursts open in shellfire. The approaching enemy moves from left to right, framed in high angle (and occasionally in low angle) when we get to see him from inside the dugouts. Having crossed the fences, the German artillery guns eliminate the French soldiers one after another; in the reverse shot of the firing weapons the camera races sideways on a horizontal axis, imitating the movement of the shooting gun. Along with the camera, the spectator can transform into just this gun, become one with a mechanical eye aiming at the enemy. Soviet filmmaker Dziga Vertov once described this intimate and empowering fusion with the camera as follows:

> I am kino-eye, I am a mechanical eye. [...] Now and forever, I free myself from human immobility. I am in constant motion, I draw near, then away from objects, I crawl under, I climb onto them, [...] I outstrip running soldiers, I fall on my back, [...] I plunge and soar together with plunging and soaring bodies. Now I, a camera, fling myself along their resultant, maneuvering in the chaos of movement, recording movement, starting with movements composed of the most complex combinations.[51]

Taken one step further, this description again builds the basis for another pathos scene within the war film's poetics of affect: here, the body at war occasionally charts its territory by merging its sensuous perception with a thoroughly mechanized perspective.[52] In contrast to suffering in facing his own mortality, the soldier is operating in an ecstatic mode of felt omnipotence. In becoming one with the

---

[51] Dziga Vertov, "Kinoks: A Revolution," in *Kino-Eye: The Writings of Dziga Vertov*, ed. Annette Michelson, trans. Kevin O'Brien, Berkeley / Los Angeles 1984, 11–20, here: 17.
[52] Empirische Medienästhetik, database "Mobilization of Emotions in War Films," "Battle and technology," in *Freie Universität Berlin, Languages of Emotion* (2011), http://www.empirische-medienaesthetik.fu-berlin.de/en/emaex-system/affektdatenmatrix/kategorien/kampftechnologie/index.html (accessed March 25, 2015).

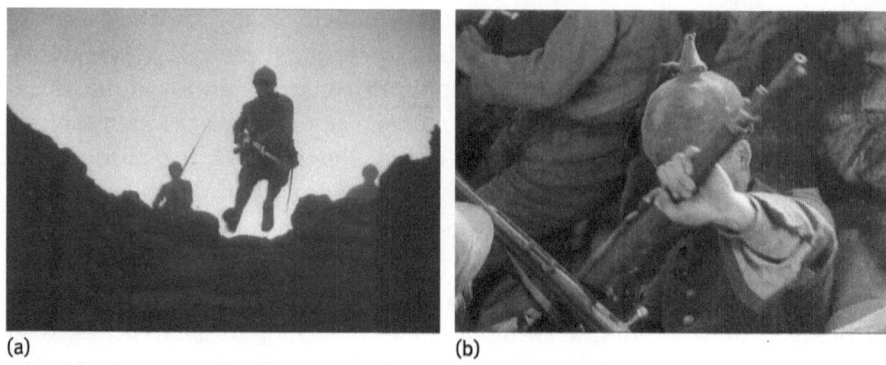

(a) (b)

Figure 4: Trapped in the trenches.

artillery gun or his rifle, he transforms into a weapon driven by a triumphant desire. Just like the mechanized tracking shots mentioned earlier, this mode accounts for the technology-based envisioning of war that stands in opposition to Das's reading of the Great War's haptic nature. The figurative metamorphosis of the soldier into a machine that Kappelhoff describes is moreover an embodiment of mechanical power. It is a recession from the physical to the automatic, which marks, like the fallacious security provided by distanced vision, a detachment from corporeal vulnerability.

While this affective notion of omnipotence definitely counts for the battle scenes in ALL QUIET, and for the trench battle in specific, again, the presumably dominant affective dimension alternates with another. In this case, it is an overt expression and experience of fear[53]: after we have immersed ourselves in that short moment of omnipotence and action spectacle, we join the camera in taking inferior positions. We are immediately thrown back to terror and fear, when the enemy soldiers jump into the trenches and stab the Germans with their rifles (see Figure 4). As it is marked by an extreme low angle, we share the perspective of the overrun trench regiment, which is – like us – trapped in the ditch without any means of escape. Inasmuch as the "kino-eye" allows us to take part in effective battle action it also enables us to engage with most uncomfortable spatial figurations from a victim's perspective.

---

[53] In terms of pathos categories, this corresponds to the category entitled "battle and nature." Cf. the following webpage: Empirische Medienästhetik, database "Mobilization of Emotions in War Films," "Battle and nature," in *Freie Universität Berlin, Languages of Emotion* (2011), http://www.empirische-medienaesthetik.fu-berlin.de/en/emaex-system/affektdatenmatrix/kategorien/kampfnatur/index.html (accessed March 25, 2015).

The camera hereby establishes a three-dimensional but narrowing battle space – a "geography of fear" – through alternating perspectives and shot sizes. As Jean Epstein would argue, it is thus not the landscape itself but above all the "dance of the landscape,"[54] its movement in terms of montage that creates a feeling of embodied experience: in the trenches of ALL QUIET, various angles set up an unstable and undefined space that is as limited as it is vulnerable; a space where protection turns into exposure, where fear is above all created by contracting (bodily) movement. That is to say, the constriction the German soldiers experience here is by no means only conveyed through static images; rather, it builds up as a spectatorial experience, as an expressive movement of horizontal and vertical camera motions that both pace out the combat zone and unhinge it. While the contrast between immovable and storming soldiers increases the tension on the level of character movement, the filmic body, too, is torn between tension and orientation: its space is constructed by and collapses again to ephemeral visual fragments. The physical and affective dimension of this sequence is therefore developed on three levels: the soldiers on screen as independent bodies are either paralyzed or racing to confront their opponent; the camera as the film's mechanical eye either imitates this stagnation or movement from an external point of view, or merges its perspective with that of the Germans; and finally, the spatial atmosphere of the dramatic conflict is exclusively articulated through mise-en-scène and montage, mapped and remapped through character movement and a cinematic body in motion. Because space and affect are thereby modulated on the basis of physical coordinates, they are mediated as a thoroughly affective sensation for the spectator.

ALL QUIET thus establishes certain patterns of cinematic expressivity that can be regarded as basic affective elements of the war film genre. With regard to these modulations of (emotional) perception it can be made clear how following war films draw on, vary and invert them in order to constantly reformulate the genre.

2.3 Images of the Paths: Stanley Kubrick's PATHS OF GLORY

One of the most exceptional attempts to reformulate the war film genre has been made with Stanley Kubrick's PATHS OF GLORY. Made in 1957 as an adaptation of Humphrey Cobb's homonymous 1935 novel, it took up the subject of the Great War when the Second World War, and with it a large number of WWII combat

---

54 Jean Epstein, "Magnification," in *French Film Theory and Criticism: A History/Anthology, 1907–1939. Vol. 1: 1907–1929*, ed. Richard Abel, Princeton 1988, 235–241, here: 237.

films, had become images of the past. Meanwhile, the Cold War had arisen as an ideological conflict revolving around the fear of unexpected nuclear destruction – a dominating subtext for many American crime and science fiction films of the time. Almost thirty years after the theatrical release of ALL QUIET ON THE WESTERN FRONT, PATHS OF GLORY echoed the events of the First World War, this time focusing on military incidents within the French Army.

In contrast to the human tragedy depicted in ALL QUIET, however, Kubrick's portrayal of WWI is not told or staged as an emotional journey, nor is it perceived through the eyes and sensing body of the recruit. Instead, through the ways somatic experience is radically opposed by analytical and symmetrical imagery, the artificiality of war, and the abstract vision of battle from a general's perspective, become graspable on the level of cinematic aesthetics. What the film thus shows is not only the dehumanizing dimension of combat per se, but also the corporeal intensity thereof – precisely by mainly withholding depictions of physical violence, only to occasionally accentuate individual acts of brutality, in turn. Therefore, identifying the corpographic elements that PATHS OF GLORY seems to lack at first glance, also helps to define the patterns and variations within the poetics of the war film genre as such.

Cobb's novel has already been described as "not fitting neatly into the American war novel tradition"[55] portraying French military superiors who force their troops to attack without any reasonable prospect of victory and sentence three of their soldiers to death for being believed to have disobeyed battle orders. Whereas most of the literature on the First World War concentrates on the balance, contrast and eventual imbalance between individual experience and the war machinery, Cobb emphasizes the overall effect of war in making use of parallel and multi-perspective storytelling. Nevertheless, the novel also encompasses highly subjective accounts of battle, describing expressionistic landscapes and physical experiences of fear, suffering and intimate closeness.[56] Kubrick's film therefore draws on a First World War novel that, being published a few years after ALL QUIET ON THE WESTERN FRONT, showed signs of stylistic shifts in the literary representation of war. But, with even greater distance to World War I, the film, in many ways, again differs fundamentally from the original novel – mostly because of its

---

[55] James H. Meredith, "Introduction," in *Paths of Glory* by Humphrey Cobb, New York 2010 [1935], xxiii–xxiv, here: xxiii.
[56] The following lines from Cobb's novel are exemplary in this regard: "The telescopic lenses seemed to spring the mass of bodies right into his face. Those bodies were so tangled that most of them could not be distinguished one from the other. Hideous, distorted, and putrescent they lay tumbled upon each other or hung in the wire in obscene attitudes, a shocking mound of human flesh, swollen and discoloured." Humphrey Cobb, *Paths of Glory*, 72.

distinctively objective and objectifying style as well as its narrative focus on the character of Colonel Dax: James H. Meredith, in his introduction to Cobb's *Paths of Glory*, refers to the film as being less complex and depicting Dax as overtly and singularly heroic, veering toward the "Hollywood Western hero morality play."[57] As much as this observation holds for its plot structure, this minor complexity, in turn, sharpens the conceptual character of Kubrick's film as an analytical work on codes of war representation as such. What is more, the apparent "Western hero morality play" he sets up has to be defined more clearly. In fact, the hero in PATHS OF GLORY is not so much Dax as a person; rather, it is "force" – in the way in which pacifist philosopher Simone Weil conceives it as a synonym for war. In an essay on Homer's *Iliad*, she writes:

> The true hero, the true subject, the center of the *Iliad* is force. Force employed by man, force that enslaves man, force before which man's flesh shrinks away. In this work, at all times, the human spirit is shown as modified by its relations with force, as swept away, blinded by the very force it imagined it could handle, as deformed by the weight of the force it submits to.[58]

Seen in this way, PATHS OF GLORY not only differs from Cobb's unconventional novel; it partially reverts to even older traditional modes of epic storytelling while at the same time marking a shift in representational codes of the First World War: whereas a significant amount of the literature, poetry and cinematic material concerning this matter puts an emphasis on the aural and tactile dimensions of war experience (as does Cobb's novel to a certain extent), Kubrick establishes with his work another sensorium that builds on almost mathematically defined coordinates of movement and the translation of power into optical constellations, turning human beings to "things."[59] By doing so, he unfolds a visually grounded reference system that connects various layers of time, space and form.

While much has been written on the significant visual style and characteristic movement patterns in Kubrick's films[60] – mostly to demonstrate how his overtly photographic style and the geometrical symmetry in his image compositions account for an exposed artificiality – numerous takes do not take into account how these operations relate to the expressive patterns of the war film.

---

57 Cobb, *Paths of Glory*, xxii.
58 Simone Weil, "The Iliad, or the Poem of Force," trans. Mary Mc Carthy, *Chicago Review* 18 (2), 1965, 5–30, here: 6.
59 Weil, "The Iliad, or the Poem of Force," 9.
60 Examples include Thomas Allen Nelson's *Kubrick: Inside a Film Artist's Maze*, Bloomington 1982, Mario Falsetto's *Stanley Kubrick: A Narrative and Stylistic Analysis*, Westport, CT 2001, and Paul Duncan's *Stanley Kubrick: Visual Poet 1928–1999*, Cologne 2003.

If we assume that Kubrick makes use of the spectator's expectations towards the iconography and modes of staging of the First World War, just to leave them eventually unfulfilled or to contrast them, PATHS OF GLORY's generic affiliation has to be differentiated. One useful approach in this regard has been made by Fredric Jameson, who calls the film "metageneric" in a way that it is not a quintessential genre film, but uses the pregiven structure of the war film as a mere pretext for its production.[61] According to Jameson, the classical "golden age" of the genre film has ceased to exist since the possibilities of individual filmmaking were blocked by the business system of film production. But still, for him, this breakdown coincides with "the moment in which the deeper aesthetic vitality of genre comes to consciousness and becomes self-conscious."[62] In other words, in exposing a genre's expressive modes of staging in a self-referential way, a metageneric film is both intertextual and nostalgic, both deconstructive and reconstructive towards its structural origins. While Jameson conceives these characteristics as two opposing but co-existing forms of interpretation, a second conceptual model poses an alternative access to Kubrick's take on the war film: the idea of "genre memory," as developed in narrative terms by Mikhail Bakhtin, most prominently in his book, *Problems of Dostoevsky's Poetics*.[63] Circumscribing ways of shaping the re-enactment of the past, this memory recalls past genre conventions while at the same time refiguring them for present use, that is, embedding them into "vibrant narratives of the present."[64] As Robert Burgoyne notes, this concept can be applied for the rewriting of cinematic genre codes within the framework of the Historical film (of which the war film forms a subgenre).[65]

Underlying both approaches is not only a specific notion of referentiality, but also a specific relation to time. If films provide a present audience with a "feeling for history," they engage present spectators with the past, thereby fusing the time of film production and film viewing with a past time the film's action is set in. In addition, they demonstrate the temporal persistence of certain representational codes by relating the present to earlier stages of genre history. But PATHS OF GLORY is not only recalling the past events of the Great War while exposing its own film form – rather, it makes time itself perceivable on various levels of sensuous

---

61 Fredric Jameson, *Signatures of the Visible*, New York 2007 [1992], 115.
62 Jameson, *Signatures of the Visible*, 114.
63 Bakhtin writes that "[a] genre lives in the present, but always remembers its past, its beginning," being "capable of guaranteeing the unity and uninterrupted continuity of this development." Mikhail Bakhtin, *Problems of Dostoevsky's Poetics*, Minneapolis 1984, 106.
64 Sarah Cole, *At the Violet Hour: Modernism and Violence in England and Ireland*, Oxford / New York 2012, 3.
65 Cf. Burgoyne, *The Hollywood Historical Film*.

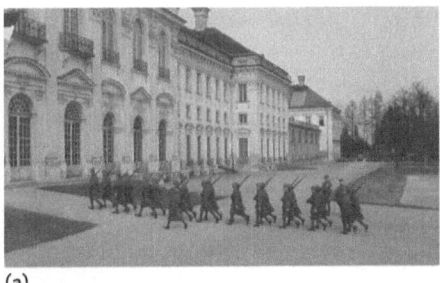 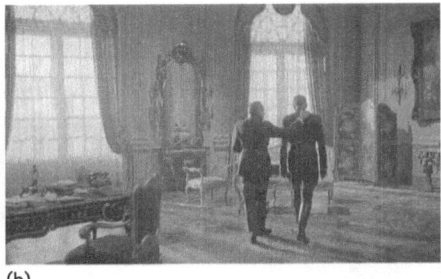

(a) (b)

Figure 5: Hegemonic space.

perception. It is the very substantiality and co-existence of temporal layers that characterize PATHS OF GLORY as a metageneric film. Regarding the cinematic corpography of World War I, it marks a representational shift from intimate and haptic modes of expression to a sensorium that translates time into eclectic optics, rhythmic sound and movement. Thereby, PATHS OF GLORY exemplifies the First World War as an allegory of cyclic violence – with the effect that not only space but also time becomes tangible as a major factor of cinematic experience.

First, with his specific deployment of visual markers, Kubrick does not simply articulate the war's crisis of vision or logistics of perception; rather, the convergence of war and cinema technology that Virilio proclaims later is used here to expose and deconstruct the optics of control within military structures as in every way physically detached functions; the (physical) perspectives of both soldiers and generals are subordinated under disembodied visual configurations of power.

In the first sequence of the film, the mise-en-scène exaggerates this notion in situating the characters within a dominant hegemonic space that seems to predate and outlast them in its all-consuming visuality. The Generals Mireau (George Macready) and Broulard (Adolphe Menjou) meet in a chateau converted into Mireau's headquarters. The interior is voluptuously decorated: high ceilings, emblazed furniture, enormous windows, paintings and mirrors indicate hegemonic power incorporated in the building's architecture (see Figure 5). The two men, walking up and down the room in circular movements, are 'highly decorated' themselves, adding another image of sophisticated cleanliness and superiority to the scene. But – and this contradicts most depictions of military briefings or meetings – in discussing their plans to attack the Ant Hill, they do not have any substantial objects of reference. No maps, aerial photographs or documents would provide an overview of the battle situation; considering the range of their decisions made, the generals' sight is literally limited and self-centered, as curtains even deny a look outside the windows.

In addition to this thoroughly confined view, the scenery conveys a highly stylized, unemotional artificiality, with Mireau and Broulard being corporeally detached from the events of war and yet themselves being (dis)placed by the dominant architecture enveloping them.

Similar to what Sarah Cole writes on the allegorical meaning of the ancestral house in Irish literature and poetry, the chateau is "a site of vexed beauty" with "no active relation to the present."[66] Its architectural structures represent a past hegemonic time that attests to wealth and power, and it is artefact of a past time that co-exists with another time of military hegemony, in which Mireau and Broulard are involved. This juxtaposition of bygone configurations of power with an actual military framework signifies the repetitive nature of a persistent force that, in its symbolic allusion, calls for an enchantment of violence.[67] The chateau as a manifestation of oppressive superiority could create the impression of the generals being powerful instances of control, of their actions being the "germinating core of rich, symbolic structures."[68] But on the contrary: the visual opulence of architecture overpowers them, and the circular movements of the characters seem to designate their imprisonment within a cyclic scheme of (military) violence. Thus, they become captives of their own visual signs of control and objects of an artificial machinery. What is made perceivable here is a figuration of "force" itself: a phenomenon that belongs to no group or person, and affects both those who are in power and those who are its victims.[69] The overabundance of the chateau, then, points to nothing more than the force's end in itself. Consequently, Jameson refers to "the beautiful" in Kubrick's work with regard to Roland Barthes' understanding of "connotation" as a signifying mechanism, "in which the language and formal categories of the medium are its deepest message, and in which the very quality of the image itself emits a meaning that secretly outdistances the ostensible or immediate purport of its content."[70] According to Jameson, Kubrick thereby enforces a "sense of cultural asphyxiation."[71]

When the film's setting changes from the chateau to the trenches for the first time, this agency furthermore sets up a binary configuration of optics and touch. While confronting the spectator with the familiar iconography of the First

---

[66] Cole, *At the Violet Hour*, 188.
[67] Cole, *At the Violet Hour*, 43.
[68] Cole, *At the Violet Hour*, 43.
[69] Weil's definition is very close to Derek Gregory's take on soldiers' bodies as both vectors and objects of military violence.
[70] Jameson, *Signatures of the Visible*, 117.
[71] Jameson, *Signatures of the Visible*, 119.

World War, the scene is yet provided with a thoroughly different framing, which transforms familiar codes of expressivity into an analytical deconstruction of the (cinematic) war machinery: we see a soldier observing the battlefield through a loophole. Here, again, sight is extremely limited, blocked by multiple planes of trench landscape, and even more narrowed by the frames of the loophole. In opposition to the immaculate chateau, the trench labyrinth is a site of dirt, inhabited by fatigued soldiers covered in mud and sweat. In this contrastingly haptic environment, General Mireau pays a visit to his men, blatantly unaffected by their condition, and always as the vanishing point of the image. Similar to the scene in the chateau, his movements seem to be presaged, mathematically clocked and calculated by the spatial authority of the camera. Mireau walks along the trenches, stopping frequently to ask some soldiers whether they would be "ready to kill more Germans?" A non-diegetic drumbeat accompanies his parade, both illustrating his metric steps on a sound level and commenting on the artificial ceremonial of the inspection.[72]

Only now the scenery becomes more corporeal and shifts from the visual to the haptic: on his way he passes infantrymen clinging to the trench walls, their bodies almost indistinguishable from the muddy sandbags; wounded men are carried away. Still, the General marches through this scene of suffering untouched – until he addresses a shell-shocked soldier: rejecting the man's behaviour, Mireau now performs the most extreme kind of touch in suddenly hitting him in the face.

Once again, different layers of time are merged here: while the non-diegetic drum beat enhances the tension and anticipation towards the climax of the scene, the encounter with the shell-shocked soldier points to traumatic past events he must have experienced. Shell-shock, in this sense, "represents an entirely different temporal schema, where the past constantly invades the present."[73] The present, finally, is then accentuated by the immediate moment of touch. Even more: in the instant of the hit, time stops. As Sarah Cole writes on a sequence in James Joyce's *A Portrait of the Artist as a Young Man* (1916), when the protagonist is beaten on the hand by his prefect of studies: "Indeed, time, space, and experience all become enfolded and massively intensified in the injuring scenario."[74]

The striking effect of Mireau's gesture is also due to the fact that it stands in harsh opposition to PATHS OF GLORY's persistent rejection of touch and sensuous intimacy. That is not to say that the tactile dimension of war is denied throughout

---

[72] Cf. Hansjörg Pauli, "Umgang mit Tönen," in *Stanley Kubrick*, ed. Peter W. Jansen, Wolfram Schütte, Munich / Vienna 1984, 259.
[73] Cole, *At the Violet Hour*, 28.
[74] Cole, *At the Violet Hour*, 10.

the film; rather, it is restrained in order to undermine the audience's expectations regarding the genre, its patterns of staging, and its affective register. Mireau's hit marks the exact opposite to the equally appalling closing shot of ALL QUIET, where Paul reaches out for a butterfly outside the trenches and gets shot. In contrast to the effect of Mireau's brutal motion, the shock here evolves from the fact that this very last touch is denied. Above all, the take emblematizes the tactile as such, since it solely frames Paul's hand as if to subsume his body under the sense and need of touch. With the respective scene in PATHS OF GLORY, again, we become aware of the two significant poles of the moment of touch: it can either be a "sign of healing, or of callous and inhumane brutality."[75] The latter is performed by Mireau as the most intimate act of violence, with his hand being a manifestation of elemental, grievous ferocity. In the words of Cole, the sense of touch, in this very moment, is falling in between places of extreme physical presence and absence: the chateau as an empty symbolic space of hegemonic power, and the trenches as a rudimentary figuration of narrowness and tense physical closeness.

Being familiar with ALL QUIET's portrayal of immediacy and physical contact, the trench sequence in PATHS OF GLORY recalls the cinematic genre memory of World War I, triggering phenomenological experiences of narrowness and anxiety. But instead of reliving these bodily states or building up geographies of fear, the film provides us with a sensuous engagement with space *and* time. It is this spatio-temporal sensorium, which precisely sensitizes us for the complex perceptive layers of audiovisual war representation.

Another example is the film's night patrol scene, which is in itself also part of the cinematic iconography of the Great War. Again, the actual absence of one or more sensuous dimensions numbs these and intensifies other senses, which is specifically conveyed to the spectator: once we watch the soldiers crawling along the cratered landscape and scouting the enemy lines, it becomes clear that not only the lack of sight, but also the lack of diegetic sound adds to the viewing experience of the scene (similar to the almost soundless night patrol in ALL QUIET). Except for the pulsating drum beat on the soundtrack, we only hear noises emerging from or caused by the soldiers' bodies: their breathing, their arms and legs sliding on the ground create an intimate perceptive connection to the spectator, who is then acoustically and visually tied to their movements. Alternating shot sizes from close to long shots, filmed from different angles, almost double the vibrant rhythm of the drums and tend to draw the spectator in and out of the action while maintaining a temporal tension. This pattern of *in and out* is finally translated to an *on and off* on another visual level, when

---

75 Cole, *At the Violet Hour*, 291.

two of the three soldiers wait for their third man to return from inspecting a ruin. Two flares brighten the scenery, which is dominated by a crashed German plane. Their light then reveals numerous corpses on the ground before the dark swallows the dead again.

Through a mode of staging known from the horror genre, where most notably the lack of sight intensifies our hearing, this sudden appearance of the visually repressed[76] has an all the more shocking effect. What is uncovered here is a heterogeneous "cyborg nature," consisting of organic and inorganic material. Here we realize the cruel "in-betweenness" of No Man's Land, which by name exceeds all imaginations of humanity, nature and belonging: a surreal hybrid of bodies and wreckage, where life and death are closely tied together.

In contrast to the night patrol, PATHS OF GLORY's attack scene foregrounds the unfamiliar effect within Kubrick's optic sensorium: amidst the kinesthetic chaos and the battering sound of shellfire, the camera maintains a sharp focus on Colonel Dax (Kirk Douglas). It follows him running across the heavily bombarded field, whistling, advising his men to keep up with him. In line with the mechanized vision set up in ALL QUIET's battle sequence, the cinematography of this scene in *Paths* is almost geometrically calculated. The camera moves horizontally in the lines of French infantrymen dashing by right in front of it. But blocking the view, they are mostly blurred due to the camera's focus on Dax as the centre of the image. At other times, we see static shots of the battleground where men drop dead and get the momentary feeling that we ourselves take the perspective of a dead or immovable soldier. Strangely, although visual and acoustic layers stimulate the creation of an audiovisual image of chaos and disorientation, the camera perpetuates an overall linear movement that refers to the film's title and main principle of staging: the "dynamization of space" and "spatialization of time," which Erwin Panofsky once defined as unique possibilities of film.[77]

The film thereby establishes an analytical space that is explored through linear movement on certain paths, which are in itself inevitable and inescapable. Moreover, as a metaphor that is connected to form and narration just as it is applicable to architecture, the word "path" is what fittingly marks this film,

---

[76] The psychoanalytical notion of repression in the horror film was mainly circumscribed by Robin Wood as an ideological reading of horror within cultural theory. See for example Robin Wood, "The American Nightmare: Horror in the 70s," in *Horror: The Film Reader*, ed. Mark Jancovich, London / New York 2002, 25–32. In terms of how sensuous or perceptive levels of a film relate to each other, repression is, in my view, to be stripped from its theoretical contexts and to be taken in the literal sense: as a perceptive dimension that is restrained or superimposed by another, only to return in an even more effective way.

[77] Erwin Panofsky, "Style and Medium in the Motion Pictures," *Critique*, Jan / Feb (1947), 5–28.

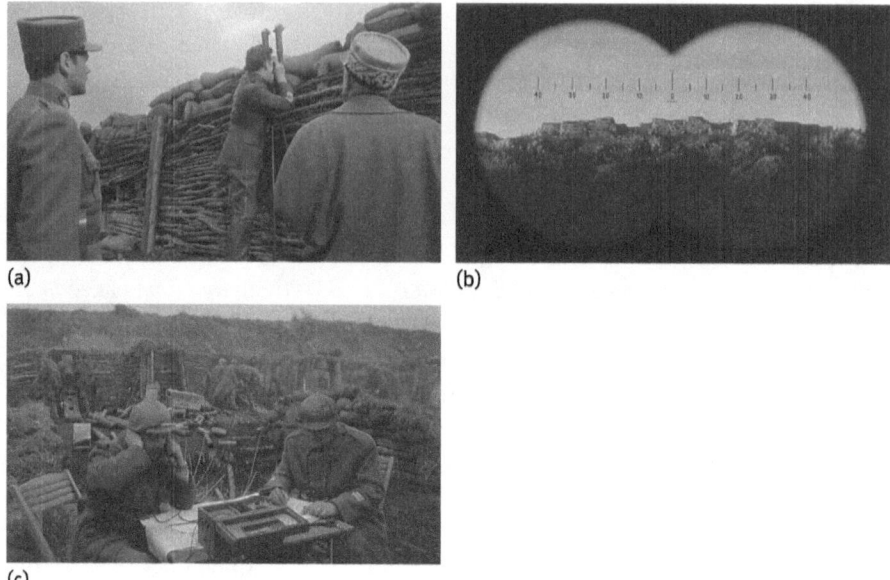

Figure 6: The calculus of war.

and film in general, as a conceptual space. According to Sergei Eisenstein, the term characterizes cinema as an

> imaginary path followed by the eye and the varying perceptions of an object that depend on how it appears to the eye. Nowadays it may also be the path followed by the mind across a multiplicity of phenomena, far apart in time and space, gathered in a certain sequence into a single meaningful concept; and these diverse impressions pass in front of an immobile spectator.[78]

In terms of space and embodiment, it needs to be demonstrated that this mode of staging differs profoundly from the performative corpography of ALL QUIET. With PATHS OF GLORY, the superior and inferior perspectives of war are less sensed and felt through human bodies, but rather dehumanized by abstract architectural constellations involving and reflecting on these bodies. Space is thoroughly measured by a disembodied camera that transforms the iconography of the Great War into analytical images of symmetry and focus, according to what James H. Meredith calls a "calculus of war"[79] that had dramatically changed in the twentieth century (see Figure 6). While Meredith refers to the radical increase of fallen soldiers due to modern war technology, Kubrick renders a new calculus of cinematic

---

[78] Sergei M. Eisenstein, "Montage and Architecture," *Assemblage* 10, 1989, 111–131, here: 116.
[79] Meredith, "Introduction," xx.

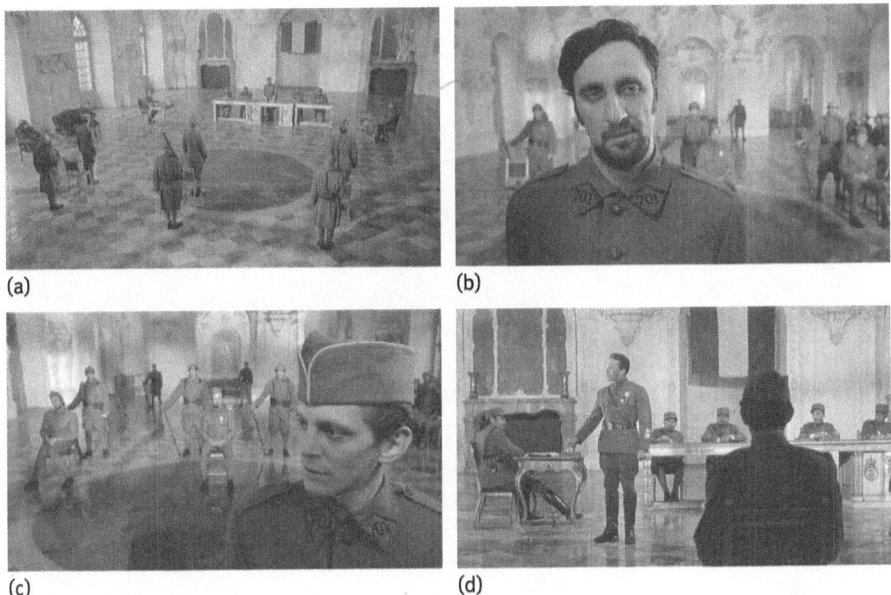

(a) (b) (c) (d)

Figure 7: The chess game of war.

warfare that clearly opposes aesthetic codes of subjective bodily experience. All the more, PATHS OF GLORY aims at the sensory experience of the spectator in both intensifying and distorting levels of perception.

This is especially demonstrated in the film's court-martial sequence which takes us back to the chateau: an exorbitantly decorated hall abounding with plastering and marble is in any case too oversized and empty to do justice to the relatively small court hearing. The latter has to be taken literally, since the resonance in the hall at times hollows the words of the speakers. Absurdly, we are situated in a room where hearing is made difficult while at the same time sound is intensified through strong reverberance. Nevertheless, the spectator's attention is drawn to the prevailing visual level, which, in turn, is heavily disregarded by the prosecutor, as he interrupts the accused Private Ferol: "The court has no concern with your visual experiences."

Just like the large rooms of the French chateau dominate the generals, designating and limiting their actions, we here again get the feeling that the involved characters are not controlling their space, but being controlled by it, "surrounded and impelled by the mechanism of their destruction."[80] They are, in relation to

---

[80] Robert Kolker, *A Cinema of Loneliness: Penn, Stone, Kubrick, Scorsese, Spielberg, Altman*, Oxford / New York 2000, 105.

the marble tiles on the floor, exposed as mere pawns in an abstract chess game standing for warfare's end in itself (see Figure 7).[81]

In fact, more than being a comment on military conflicts at the time of its release, PATHS OF GLORY reflects on the characteristics of war and the war film as an artificial construct. Its translation of power into optics, architecture and décor may in some way articulate how we understand modern warfare, but it also challenges the affective engagement we expect from the war film. Retrospectively, PATHS OF GLORY, as a metageneric film, deconstructs the very foundations of a genre that took its substantial beginnings from Hollywood productions on the First World War and was further established in the wake of World War II. In examining what seems to be missing in Kubrick's film, that is, in exploring its sensory shift from the haptic to the optic, the various sensuous features of the war film are extrapolated. As ALL QUIET shows, in line with many examples of First World War literature, these expressive modes are based on the balance, contrast and eventual imbalance between the soldier's body and the machinery of war. As it will also become evident in the following chapters, in the Hollywood war film, elements of sight, sound and touch build up sensuous geographies, which allow for the spectator to embody these coordinates as crucial part of the film experience. While this imbalance is transformed to spatialized time and to calculated geometrical movement in PATHS OF GLORY, the disparity between the illusion of overview and the actual loss of orientation characterizes the war film as such, and it is with these aesthetic configurations that the representational shifts within the genre become most tangible.

Nevertheless, what PATHS OF GLORY points out, is the paramount importance of temporal aesthetics for the analysis and qualification of expressive genre modes, be it in terms of spatial navigation, somatic experience, or, with regard to film form, related to concepts of film history and memory. Genre itself is a cyclic but transforming construct, in which not only historical developments are negotiated and reshaped, but in which the "force" of history, in this case war and violence, affects the senses and becomes a site of negotiation.

---

81 See Philippe Mather, *Stanley Kubrick at Look Magazine: Authorship and Genre in Photojournalism and Film*, Bristol / Chicago 2013, 243.

3 From Above and From Within: Aerial Views and Corpographic Transformations in the WWII Combat Film

ALL QUIET and PATHS OF GLORY are, each in its own way, exceptional representations of the First World War. As I have pointed out earlier, only a few war-related films of 1920s Hollywood (and beyond) focus on trench warfare and are often centred on tragic love stories instead. Actual battle sequences are regularly reduced to illustrative episodes building on and further shaping the iconography of WWI. In contrast to the haptic geography of the trenches, several Great War films that do concentrate on combat action deploy another, supposedly detached, battle space: the skies – a setting and cinematic point of view that would gain iconographic significance for later documentaries and feature films about the Second World War.

William A. Wellman's WINGS (1927), or Howard Hughes' HELL'S ANGELS (1930), as well as THE DAWN PATROL (Edmund Goulding, 1938) starring Errol Flynn, emphasize the audacious manoeuvres of American pilots in WWI, thereby foregrounding their individual heroic achievements and struggles. While especially HELL'S ANGELS features a dominant cloudscape staging the dramatic performance of warplanes and zeppelins, WINGS involves not only numerous high-angle shots of No Man's Land, but also offers spectacular aerial views, as we are sharing the battle pilot's perspective.

As Denis Cosgrove notes, the aerial view is distinctively "Apollonian," motivating "visions of rational spatial order to be written across the land."[1] His account is very similar to what Michel de Certeau describes as a totalizing and omniscient gaze, as an Icarian view detached from "endless labyrinths far below" – a position freeing one's body from "the mass that carries off and mixes up in itself any identity of authors or spectators."[2] One could assume that this clear distinction between distanced visual perception and physical intimacy (as exemplified with the bodily experience of the trenches) would isolate the aerial shot from any form of emotionality. But on the contrary: through the medium of film, that is, through movement, it gains a dynamic subjectivity, which initiates a feeling of omnipotence and inviolability. This, again, becomes particularly evident in audiovisual representations of war: the intangible feeling of power

---

1 Denis Cosgrove, *Geography and Vision*, London 2008, 89.
2 Michel de Certeau, *The Practice of Everyday Life*, trans. Steven Rendall, Berkeley 1988, 92.

felt above is opposed to the disorienting physical experience of the foot soldier, while it at the same time corresponds to the merging of sensuous and mechanized perception he feels when operating arms. In this regard, Teresa Castro refers to a 1918 documentary film made by the Cinematographic Service of the French Army (Service Cinématographique de l'Armée) shortly after the end of The First World War: EN DIRIGEABLE SUR LES CHAMPS DE BATAILLE shows the destroyed combat zones of Flanders and northern France, their ruined cities, villages and battlefields. Castro writes:

> If the camera angle exposes the dimension, i.e. the geographic and quantitative scale of the devastation, the smoothness and fluidity of its aerial movement represent an unquestionable source of emotion: emotion linked to the visual pleasure of discovering the earth's surface from a new and exciting angle of vision, emotion attached to the sudden revelation of the territory as yet another injured body, and 'e-motion', finally, of being able to move freely in the space–time continuum.[3]

According to Castro, these images provide us not only with a totalizing gaze. Moreover, they combine the kinetic qualities of both flight and film, providing "nothing other than a *cinematographic sensation* of the world."[4] Taking into account that EN DIRIGEABLE SUR LES CHAMPS DE BATAILLE also displays the airman operating the camera attached to the airship, Jacques Trolley de Prévaux, aerial cinematicity[5] has the potential to immediately link the spectator to what he sees, and to another human gaze sharing this sensation. Thus, it "engages with structures of affective connection and identification."[6]

The "visual pleasure of discovering the earth's surface" that Castro describes not only links to the unfolding of cinematic aerial views but can be experienced in connection to cartographic objects in general. The hubris of the mapmaker diffuses into the confidence of the map-reader in attempting to comprehend and to control a given territory. The actual territory, however, resists absolute representation, prompting a much more intuitive sensuous interaction with its navigator instead. This, in turn, is a core problem of warfare, as it sets up hierarchical contrasts between those who map certain spaces from a distance and those who in

---

3 Teresa Castro, "Cinema's Mapping Impulse: Questioning Visual Culture," *The Cartographic Journal* 46, 2009, 9–15, here: 14.
4 Castro, "Cinema's Mapping Impulse," 14.
5 I am using the term "cinematicity" to describe the intermediality of the cinematic, which, above all, encompasses changing modes of perception throughout media history. See Jeffrey Geiger and Karin Littau (eds.), *Cinematicity in Media History*, Edinburgh 2013.
6 Jeffrey Geiger, "Making America Global: Cinematicity and the Aerial View," in *Cinematicity in Media History*, ed. Jeffrey Geiger, Karin Littau, Edinburgh 2013, 133–156, here: 143.

fact fight over and through them. Here, Castro's account of the aerial view needs to be slightly modified: the "emotion attached to the sudden revelation of the territory as yet another injured body" is in fact tied to the foot soldier's perspective, as it is his vulnerable body that stands in contrast to the elevated position of the aerial view. Hence, when used in a war film, aerial views and maps mark the sites of fracture between self-confident military strategy and actual despair and disorientation in battle. They separate the perspective of generals and tacticians from the soldier's point of view. In other words, they induce and reveal an "illusion of overview" in the very moments they are proven to be dysfunctional, when they are of no use for a corpographic navigation through the combat zone.

3.1 Documenting War: The United States, Britain, and the Burma Campaign

Indeed, the aerial view became increasingly important for the Hollywood war film, particularly in form of cartographic devices. Numerous combat movies of the 1940s made use of maps as diegetic objects, or expository texts not only to provide a verifiable historical background, but also to affectively charge their stories. From the intimate and tactile setting of the trenches, and moving across the skyscapes of the Great War, the genre therefore seemed to have developed from an emphasis on the haptic to a privilege of the optic. Indeed, as I have pointed out earlier, a so-called 'crisis of vision' lies at the heart of the war film's narrative and affective structure. As the loss of sight in the chaos of battle and the invisible enemy have always been key tropes of the genre, combat films seemed to emphasize these tropes by contrastingly foregrounding cartographic aspects of vision and visibility. But this has to be relativized with regard to other elements of cinematic corpography. In order to mark the visual regime of war as fallible, the war film's optic dimension is constantly thwarted with aspects of touch and sound. Depending on the theater of war depicted, the invisible enemy is thus substituted with enhanced nature sounds, while the uncertainty about his potential presence results in intensified aural perception. Even more so, a non-diegetic soundtrack accompanying the action provides recognisable – and redundant – musical motifs.

The rapid development of sound technology from 1927 onwards enhanced the possibilities of aesthetic expression in general and thus allowed for a multisensory portrayal of war. Yet there is more to be considered in terms of genre and media history, and for what concerns history in general. By the mid-1940s, the extensive media coverage of the Second World War had produced a vast amount of intertextual and intermodal references: images and sounds shared by feature films and documentaries from different national backgrounds. Furthermore, the U.S. American cinema at that time already anticipated TV journalism while actively connecting to photojournalism – a liaison that helped in establishing and shaping the *combat film* as such. This is especially due to the fact that both the U.S. government and the *OSS (Office of Strategic Services)* sent several Hollywood directors to the frontlines to shoot documentary footage of the action taking place. John Huston, George Stevens, John Ford, Frank Capra, and William Wyler each had their own film units operating alongside camera teams working for the newsreels.[7] The production of WWII combat films, in turn, relied on the iconography communicated by newsreels and documentaries for the sake of accuracy and emotional impact.

In fact, the arrangement of intertextual references (that is, images and sounds combined) within documentary and fiction films additionally built on the public viewing experience that cinema audiences had before and during the war. As it had been conventionalized by 1935, a typical double-bill screening usually consisted of an "A" and a "B" picture, cartoons or live action shorts, coming attractions or trailers, and newsreels (while it has to be said that the production of B films decreased by the end of the 1940s).[8] Bearing this in mind, the interaction of 1940s war documentaries (especially Capra's WHY WE FIGHT series) and combat films was not only a conceptual one in terms of how the films were shown, but it was also an exchange of audiovisual patterns in their intermedial contexts. The aesthetic experience of a war film produced at that time has thus to be seen in the light of a specific historical situation, and a political discourse carried out through media. If nothing else, the cinematic portrayal of war has always been an expression of how war was mediated through cultural and discursive forms.

A particularly demonstrative example for the above stated intermedial contexts is Raoul Walsh's OBJECTIVE, BURMA! Released in 1945, it provides a specifically American perspective on the Burma campaign, a military operation conducted by allied forces between 1942 and 1945. Mainly British, Indian, American, and Chinese troops were sent to fight the Japanese in the Burmese jungle under combined command, and to supervise the construction of the Stilwell Road (named after U.S. Army General Joseph Stilwell), a supply line for the Chinese in their fight against Japanese occupying forces. Visual material of the campaign

---

7 Hermann Kappelhoff, "Kriegerische Mobilisierung: Die mediale Organisation des Gemeinsinns. Frank Capras Prelude to War und Leni Riefenstahls Tag der Freiheit," *Navigationen. Zeitschrift für Medien- und Kulturwissenschaften* 9 (1), 2009, 151–165, here: 151.
8 For further reading, cf. David A. Cook, *A History of Narrative Film*, 3rd ed., New York 1996, 301.

was later turned into two competing documentaries, a British and an American production, which, alongside Walsh's film, spawned a debate on how to portray the event in a most accurate way.

Although OBJECTIVE, BURMA! can be regarded as a quintessential text in both illustrating the controversy between fictional and documentary accounts of a historical event and in elaborating some of the war film genre's most fundamental staging patterns, it has been largely neglected in critical discussion. So far, analytical treatments by Kathryn Kane, Steve Neale and, fairly recently, Tom Conley, have either focused on the film's strategic use of communication, its distribution of knowledge among the characters, or its symbolic undertones. But, what is more, beyond these observations, OBJECTIVE BURMA! overtly demonstrates the dialectics between sound and vision that lie at the core of the war film. And it does so to the extent that it exposes both the strengths and the weaknesses of vision for representing and experiencing war. Hence, OBJECTIVE, BURMA! visibly and audibly links vision and sound to certain opposing affects – affects related to concepts of space and the body.

OBJECTIVE, BURMA! focuses on a group of U.S. soldiers led by Captain Nelson (Errol Flynn), who are ordered to destroy a Japanese radio station located behind enemy lines. Their depiction is loosely based on the story of a special jungle warfare unit known as "Merrill's Marauders," and by no means representative of the Burma campaign as such. Nevertheless, the film quickly became highly controversial in Britain, where it was withdrawn from cinemas and was not to be screened until 1952.

The British Press considered OBJECTIVE, BURMA! an offensive work of propaganda, as it did not mention Britain's major contribution to the operation, and emphasized the singular heroism of American forces instead.[9]

In the light of this controversy, the two following documentaries about the Burma campaign, THE STILWELL ROAD (1945) and BURMA VICTORY (1946), can be seen as correctives to the stance Walsh's film seemed to have taken. On the other hand, the harsh British reaction to OBJECTIVE, BURMA! reflects on the very conflict that had shaped the development of both THE STILWELL ROAD and BURMA VICTORY – two films that were initially supposed to be one joint Anglo-American production but were challenged by different national ideas and ideals, and mainly by diverging opinions on to what extent each country's achievements should be portrayed. Frank Capra, who was once more commissioned to produce

---

[9] Ian Jarvie, "The Burma Campaign on Film: 'Objective Burma' (1945), 'The Stilwell Road' (1945) and 'Burma Victory' (1945)," *Historical Journal of Film, Radio and Television* 8 (1), 1988, 55–73, here: 55.

this collaborative film, eventually concentrated on creating THE STILWELL ROAD for the U.S. War Department, while David Macdonald (producer) and Roy Boulting (director) realized BURMA VICTORY for the British Ministry of Information.[10] Both films then sometimes used the same footage, but worked it in slightly different ways. THE STILWELL ROAD, narrated by Ronald Reagan, featured many animated maps, and foregrounded the multi-national and multi-ethnic composition of the Burma campaign, despite focusing on the American air lift effort, the road-building, and civilian refugees. As a direct connection to Walsh's film, its opening credits were accompanied by the same score Franz Waxman had composed for OBJECTIVE, BURMA! THE STILWELL ROAD was not distributed commercially; this, however, was the case for BURMA VICTORY, which was not only screened in British theaters but to the American public, as well. With its release shortly after the end of the war, BURMA VICTORY became a record, a historical document, rather than a work of propaganda. As Ian Jarvie summarizes, the film "attempted to portray a complex battlefield picture, and did it less confusingly than the American effort," although bearing some amateurish re-enacted scenes. He adds that the footage was partly of poor quality, especially since "much of the spoken sound was poorly synched."[11] Nonetheless, BURMA VICTORY earned respectable critical success and wide showing, also because it was marketed as the '*real* Burma film.'[12] It was, above all, less educational than its American counterpart, and rather concerned with the soldiers' somatic experience of jungle warfare[13]. Conforming to this idea, the film contains short diary sequences foregrounding subjective accounts of physical fatigue:

> August 16th, 44. On the march at last. We wear our capes. They don't keep us dry, but make us sweat more. You can feel little trickles running down the hollow of your chest. A lot of the men have prickly heat around the waist and on the shoulders.

As a British Air Marshall suggested, *"With the Army to Victory in Burma"* would therefore have been a more appropriate title for the film.[14] It deploys the Burma

---

[10] Tony Aldgate, "Mr Capra Goes to War: Frank Capra, the British Army Film Unit, and Anglo-American travails in the production of 'Tunisian Victory'," *Historical Journal of Film, Radio and Television* 11 (1), 1991, 21–39, here: 21.
[11] Jarvie, "The Burma Campaign on Film," 65.
[12] James Chapman and Nicholas J. Cull (eds.), *Projecting Empire: Imperialism and Popular Cinema*, London / New York 2009, 59.
[13] Regarding the American involvement in the war, in turn, one is reminded of the pictures of fatigued U.S. Marines that photographer W. Eugene Smith took for Life Magazine during the Pacific Campaign (1942–45).
[14] British Air Marshall George Pirie quoted in Jarvie, "The Burma Campaign on Film," 65.

campaign as a both individual and collective endeavour, while pointing out the weariness and discomfort it involves. That is to say, BURMA VICTORY operates in far more intimate, corpographic terms than THE STILWELL ROAD. The latter maintains an idealist educational tone, especially when calling upon the soldiers' sense of duty. In one sequence, before sending a group of American Airforce commandos off to a mission, Colonel Philip Cochran (U.S. Army Air Corps) is shown saying:

> Tonight, your whole reason for being, your whole existence is gonna be jammed up into a couple of minutes, and this is gonna balance it there, and it's gonna take your courage there to bring it through. Now, nothing you have ever done before in your life means a thing. Tonight, you're gonna find out you got a soul.

Although both films comprise many maps and aerial views, the contrast between these distanced perspectives and the foot soldier's point of view becomes more graspable in BURMA VICTORY, while cartographic inserts support the thoroughly deictic character of THE STILWELL ROAD, which rather treats the Burma campaign as a strategic objective, a lesson and prime example in effective warfare.

Seen in this light, OBJECTIVE BURMA! becomes an even more interesting object of study, especially since now, in retrospect, the film is considered "very far from being the sort of flag-waving propaganda film that some critics have painted," and rather regarded as an example of the "mature combat film that had emerged in Hollywood by the end of the war."[15] For what concerns its patterns of staging, OBJECTIVE, BURMA! clearly stands in between the poetics of these two documentaries. It is both educational and corpographic, it is contrastive and ambiguous regarding its expression of sensory perception. All three films draw on the same audiovisual material surrounding the Burma campaign, whereupon OBJECTIVE, BURMA! articulates the partly conflicting circulation of images and sounds through media, and within the war film genre.

3.2 OBJECTIVE, BURMA! / Subjective Burma: The Illusion of Overview

Within the history and study of cartography, the term "mapping impulse" plays a crucial role. As John B. Harley puts it,

---

15 Chapman and Cull, *Projecting Empire*, 59.

the mapping experience – involving the cognitive mapping of space – undoubtedly existed long before the physical artefacts we now call maps. For many centuries maps have been employed as literary metaphors and tools in analogical thinking. There is thus also a wider history of how concepts and facts about space have been communicated, and the history of the map itself – the physical artefact – is but one small part of this general history of communication about space.[16]

Harley's quote contains the important observation that maps not only represent space but also embody the wider communication about space. Applied to the war film, and bearing its aforementioned referential system in mind, this cartographic embodiment would account for various levels. Firstly, the genre itself communicates the ways filmic space is established and experienced by developing and sharing similar modes of spatial staging. Secondly, in referencing war documentaries, for example, fictional war films draw on material circulating within other media forms. Here, the communication about space also encompasses a communication between different media representations and therefore constitutes a certain media cartography. Thirdly, the maps depicted in a war film could be interpreted as metaphors and tools for thinking and narrating space, as well as for designating different affective dimensions of space. Hence, in both being coded texts and establishing an affective connection to the spectator, maps form a deictic reference to what Robin Curtis calls the "origo of time-based media,"[17] a term borrowed from psychologist and linguist Karl Bühler. In his theory of language, he states that the deixis of the speech act always invokes a corporeal performance in a distinct space and time. According to this idea, the "I-here-now" of the speaker is thus to be conceived as a "tactile body image" occupying a position in relation to visual space.[18] Drawing on this argument, one could say that the somatic involvement of the spectator in the creation and staging of filmic space is just as well the effect of deictic, communicative operations. As such, cinematic mapping processes do not only demarcate where the story of a film is taking place but they also situate the tactile body image of the spectator within (and as the -reference point of) the aesthetic experience – in the sense of Conley's *Cartographic Cinema*, these processes thus constitute a "bilocation" of the spectator.

---

16 J.B. Harley, "The Map and the Development of the History of Cartography," in *The History of Cartography, Vol. I, Cartography in Prehistoric, Ancient and Medieval Europe and the Mediterranean*, ed. J.B. Harley, David Woodward, Chicago 1987, 1–42, here: 1.
17 Cf. Robin Curtis, "Deixis and the Origo of Time-based Media: Blurring the 'Here and Now' from the Dickson Experimental Sound Film of 1894 to Janet Cardiff's Installation Ghost Machine," in *Möglichkeitsräume: Zur Performativität von sensorischer Wahrnehmung*, ed. Christina Lechtermann, Kirsten Wagner, Horst Wenzel, Berlin 2007, 255–266.
18 Karl Bühler, *Theory of Language: The Representational Function of Language*, trans. D. Fraser Goodwin, Amsterdam / Philadelphia 1990, 145.

OBJECTIVE, BURMA! is in every way a vivid example for this specific cinematic "mapping impulse," as it should become clear in the following paragraphs. The film's opening credits unfold on a stylized background image showing a jungle landscape and a rising (or setting) sun covered by clouds. Battering drums, like machine gun fire, blend over to a triumphant musical theme. Then, threatening horns and kettledrums announce a written quote by General Joseph Stilwell: "I claim we got a beating. We got run out of Burma and it's humiliating as hell. I'll go over the mountains into India and rake up an army. I'll supply them there, train them, and someday I'll lead them back into Burma." Stilwell himself had re-enacted this line for an insert in THE STILWELL ROAD.[19] But without him speaking and embodying these words this time, the written quote becomes a national rather than a personal statement. What sounds like a victorious imperial ordeal, set to music by ceremonial drums and brass instruments, transforms into an act of revenge, a motivation to restore a national pride that had been hurt on foreign territory. Seen this way, the soundtrack not only anticipates the threat posed by the mission itself but also the rage sparked by its cause.

While the dramatic music continues, a series of documentary shots follows. An aerial view of the dense jungle is presented by a voice-over narrator, who, despite his serious tone, does not refrain from discriminatory vocabulary: "This is Burma, the toughest battleground in the world. Where the Japs had sealed off the Burma Road and closed the backdoor to China – a door that had to be reopened."[20] Without going into detail on the specific geographical conditions of the battle zone, a bird's-eye view of the Burma road is cut in, as well as snippets of military training units, generals and commanders conferring. A brief introduction of British General Wingate is followed by shots of important American military superiors: General Stilwell, Colonel Cochran, and General Frank D. Merrill. As the narrator points out, Merrill's soldiers "got ready to push off," while "only their top officers knew where to or what for." Then another aerial view: "One hot afternoon, a reconnaissance plane [...] scouted the Jap-infested jungle. The operation was about to begin. Its objective: Burma." Subsequently, the same aircraft transforms into an animated plane circling over a drawn map of Burma, with the camera focusing on the region of Assam, where the image finally fades into the non-animated shot of the plane landing (see Figure 8).

---

19 Jarvie, "The Burma Campaign on Film," 65.
20 It has to be said, however, that referring to Japanese soldiers as "Japs" was indeed a common idiom within the combat film. Nevertheless, the effect of a supposedly authoritative voice-over using the term is an all the more propagandistic one.

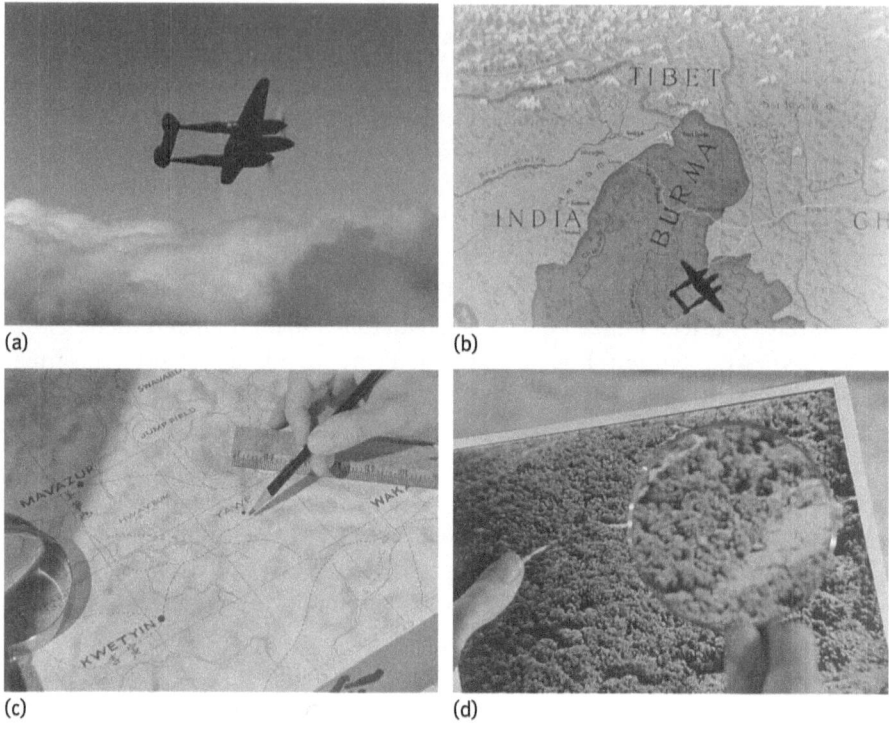

Figure 8: Scrutinizing the battle zone.

Within these one and a half minutes, the spectator has been provided with various facts and persons involved in the Burma campaign. In retrospect, however, this information is fairly superficial. We still don't know why Burma, as a "backdoor" to China is essential for the outcome of the war; we don't know how exactly the different commands and armies cooperate, either; and, just like the soldiers led by General Merrill, we don't know where or why the operation "about to begin" takes place. Furthermore, the perspective on the campaign is merely one-sided. Not only that the emphasis lies on the citation of American personnel, it is exclusively the generals' point of view we are confronted with. And it is a point of view in the very literal sense: shots of generals reading maps, generals watching their soldiers exercise, generals reading and discussing maps once more. Even if the men are shown talking, there is no sound of their voices to be heard. A sense of threat and danger pervades the tone of both voice and music, while at the same time it suggests complete control over the situation. For what concerns the content of the images, the act of seeing in order to plan the actual mission is foregrounded. Taking this notion one step further, the animated map turns the battle zone into a cartographic, projectable space that is being scrutinized on various levels.

Paradoxically, this point of view is spatially but not emotionally detached. The simplicity of a map entails both comprehension and wonderment. As Hans Speier writes on "moving maps" in propaganda films,

> [t]hey do not give geographical information, but symbolize political history and strategic events. [...] The seriousness of these abstractions in motion is strange enough to inspire awe and yet simple enough to convey the idea that strategy can be grasped by anyone.[21]

Above all, the more abstract and distanced the connection to the territory gets, the more this detachment becomes an empowering sentiment, an "objectless" sensation. This idea originates in the art movement of Suprematism, which favours abstract geometric forms over the depiction of realistic objects. In many ways, the notion of an "objectless" sensation corresponds to what Futurist painters, such as Giacomo Balla, Benedetta, and F.T. Marinetti, declared "a new reality" constituted by "the shifting perspectives of flight."[22] In their 1929 "Manifesto of Aeropainting" they voted for the artistic expression of sheer velocity, depicting a landscape that appeared to be unstable, smashed, artificial and provisional. At the same time, these parts of a landscape should "accentuate certain features of being dense, scattered, elegant, grandiose." In contrast to this impression, aerial views in films like OBJECTIVE, BURMA! or documentaries like THE STILWELL ROAD and BURMA VICTORY do not emphasize the sensation of flight as such; rather than conveying the speed of motion, they find a grandeur in the idea of overview, that is, a controlled vision and a vision of control.

In a way, the initial approach the film seems to take towards the "objective" is less object-related than perception-related. Bearing in mind that the given information in this first sequence is barely grounded on distinct historical facts, its documentary footage draws on a then familiar perception of war through media, a set-up channelling historical events into a mediated experience. A similar technique is used in Samuel Fuller's MERRILL'S MARAUDERS (1962), a later film about the Burma campaign with its opening sequence constructed as a collage of different photographic representations. Superimposed onto a coloured background image of the jungle we see a small black and white screen. Here, an array of

---

21 Hans Speier, "Magic Geography" *Social Research* 3, 1941, 310–330, here: 326–327.
22 Giacomo Balla et al., "Manifesto of Aeropainting (1929)," in *Futurism: An Anthology*, ed. Lawrence Rainey, Christine Poggi, Laura Wittman, New Haven / London 2009, 283–285, here: 283.

animated maps and footage of marching allied soldiers[23] illustrates the territorial development of the war, whereupon a voice-over introduces the protagonists of the film, who, as fictional characters, are seamlessly woven into the black and white documentary plot before the actual film proceeds in brilliant Technicolor.

What these images build on, both in OBJECTIVE, BURMA! and MERRILL'S MARAUDERS, is thus not accurate details but both national awareness and belonging, that is, the *felt* significance of America's involvement in the war – an effect Jeffrey Geiger also specifically attributes to the aerial view in U.S. wartime documentaries, which thereby visualized "rapidly changing interfaces between the individual, national and global."[24] In other words, the apparently detached (aerial) point of view OBJECTIVE, BURMA! establishes at the very beginning encompasses, speaking with Geiger, "seemingly opposed experiences of abstract distancing and emotional connection, 'objective' overseeing and embodied feeling."[25]

This literal incorporation of historical documents and perspectives eventually transforms into a process of mechanical production and effective communication. After having introduced both documentary and cartographic material regarding the Burma campaign, the fictional story does not start *in medias res*, but instead focuses in detail on the processing of photographic evidence captured by the reconnaissance plane. A close-up of the camera attached to it fades into a shot of a jeep carrying the film reel to the "U.S. Air Force Aerial Photographic Section Field Laboratory," followed by a short sequence depicting the developing of the film. The finished photos are then handed over to several military executives, before finally reaching Frank D. Merrill, the general in charge of what is now being referred to as the "Red Robin Operation." As he examines them briefly and declares the operation to be going into effect, the photos are passed on to another station of authority, where they are scrutinized again through a magnifying glass. This time, a Colonel and a Captain confer on military actions based on the analysis and interpretation of the material that has just been forwarded to them. Using not only the photographs but also maps to plan their immediate proceeding, the two men emphasize the importance of the mission they are now initiating (see Figure 8).

Both photographs and maps are thus to be regarded as means of mobilization and furthering action. More than just situating characters and spectators within a geographical setting, they implement a chain of communicative acts, setting

---

[23] At the very beginning, the allied forces of the Burma campaign are explicitly introduced (and represented by individual examples) as "our men": Irish, English, Scot and Welsh, Australian, New Zealander, Gurkha, Sikh.
[24] Geiger, "Making America Global," 138.
[25] Geiger, "Making America Global," 138.

military actions into operation. The fact of the film developing being meticulously framed in this sequence does not only highlight the structure of military hierarchy and effectiveness; moreover, along with the diegetic film reel, the fictional film, OBJECTIVE, BURMA!, is developing for the audience to see and includes them physically into this mechanical process. Furthermore, Tom Conley detects a significant representational shift within this sequence:

> Up to this point the movie has been coded as a newsreel, its grainy texture of shots 'taken' from the front [...] accompanying a voice-off telling the rough truth of the Burmese campaign. Then, at the moment it shifts from the recording of history into a dramatic re-enactment of it, at a crucial instant the photographs taken from the plane claim to be those of OBJECTIVE, BURMA! in the preceding credits and shots [...] The film develops an image of the film at the very point it [...] develops into a film.[26]

While this clearly refers to the film's self-reflexivity towards its branding as a "pseudodocumentary" feature,[27] the shift from one form of representation to another is also deployed in spatial terms. As our attention is bound to the photographic material as such, we follow its creation and its journey both vertically and horizontally, from the air to the ground, and from one station of authority to another (a direction that is in itself again vertically organized, that is, in hierarchical terms). Instead of navigating the filmic battle space through the soldier's senses, we accompany and embody the production of photographical evidence, in this case aerial shots of the Burmese jungle. Hence, we navigate with and through the mechanical body of both film and (affective) meaning production. Again, "experiences of abstract distancing and emotional connection" (Geiger) are at work here. Although we are confronted with alienating and somewhat simplistic cartographical objects, we have understood the gravity of the operation and both perceived and felt its accompanying sense of excitement and confidence in the end. The first being conveyed aurally, through the use of threatening orchestral sounds; the latter being tied to the physical behaviour of the characters, and thus shifting from technological to somatic aspects of the military body.

This body, as it is shown, demonstrates a mechanical efficiency that spans from its technical equipment to the capability of its soldiers. After hearing the general cheerfully say: "Feed your men some raw meat, we're going in," we are taken to the setting of a U.S. military camp in India, where the jeep (the scene's main connecting element) passes several soldiers jauntily playing baseball and

---

26 Tom Conley, *Film Hieroglyphs: Ruptures in Classical Cinema*, Minneapolis 2006, 91.
27 Kathryn R. Kane, *Visions of War: Hollywood Combat Films of World War II*, Ann Arbor 1982, 94.

ring toss, some of them exposing the upper part of their body, or making themselves comfortable on the side-lines. The juxtaposition of the movement of the car and the soldiers' bodies in motion insinuates a mechanization of organic structure, that is, a unity of bodies and technology. As the photographs are transported past these agile young men, we are conceiving and perceiving a sense of control and light-heartedness the sequence creates through audiovisual means.

Also in the following scene, the parallels between strict orders and playful exercise lead to a climactic figuration of assertiveness. The information about a scheduled briefing is passed down gradually as a Staff Sergeant walks by his men, watching and commenting on them jousting, riding on an elephant, bathing in the river, washing socks, seeing the dentist, throwing knives at trees, getting their hair cut, and, again, playing baseball. Since he is essentially repeating, or rather continuing the movement of the jeep in the scene before, the mechanical character of this process is taken to another level: here, apart from being one with technology, the soldiers are in harmony with the nature surrounding them. Nature, in this regard, makes up their quotidian life, their moments outside of military order within the community of the troop. This spatial differentiation of certain social situations adds to Steve Neale's mainly narratological treatment of OBJECTIVE, BURMA!: as he points out, the war film articulates certain disparities in knowledge and power between its characters, which correspond to differences in military rank. These disparities, then again, depend on formal means of motivation, narration and point of view. Along these lines, the first minutes of OBJECTIVE, BURMA!, constitute what Neale calls a "primary situation":

> Preceding the chain of events that constitutes the narrative proper, and either inferred by the spectator or directly represented, any primary situation is generally one of stability and order (however fragile), and often exists in marked and generically appropriate contrast to all that follows the initial event.[28]

The following briefing scene reinforces this impression, but not without revealing the fragile implications of this situation, which affect both knowledge and feelings connected to cartographic objects. While the short conversations between the soldiers and their superiors still seem light-hearted at first, mood and atmosphere shift from recreation to uneasiness when essential questions posed by the men cannot be answered to their satisfaction. When studying a three-dimensional sand model of the Burmese jungle, one soldier asks: "There aren't any names on the table. Where is this place anyway?" Whereupon another one says:

---

28 Steve Neale, "Aspects of Ideology and Narrative Form in the American War Film," *Screen* 32 (1), 1991, 35–57, here: 36.

"If you don't mind, Sir – how do we get back?" The responses to both questions withhold crucial information. Captain Nelson refuses to provide exact coordinates before boarding the plane taking the soldiers to their assignment (the destruction of a Japanese radio station). Secondly, the responsibility for getting them back safely is delegated to two Gurkha guides from the Burma Frontier Force, who do not speak English to "a worthwhile degree," but know the terrain extraordinarily well.

While this scene is fundamentally deictic – supported by maps, a topographical model, and a pointer which the military superiors use when talking about the objective – it fails to clarify the upcoming mission on two counts: first by withholding information for the soldiers, secondly by using specific cartographic language in referring to routes and places ("Track E," for example) unknown to both soldiers and spectators. In this regard, along with the soldiers, the audience is put into an educational situation, where they have to rely on the expertise and confidence of their instructors. Here, cartographical knowledge seems to be an exclusive privilege owned by military superiors. Only they can interpret the given coordinates or provide access to this information designating the actions to be performed by the troop. On the one hand, the separation of the group into oblivious soldiers and (presumably) knowing superiors highlights hierarchical structures within the military corps; on the other, this very separation gives way to expressions of tension and insecurity: the faces of the soldiers are full of expectation and uncertainty. Framed in low-angle shots, they are crosscut with the steady faces of Nelson and Colonel Carter. At this point the complex physical/mechanical process we have both witnessed and taken part in has come to a halt. The literal stagnation in the briefing sequence, its lack of movement, allows for the objective to "sink in." But the scene thereby focuses not only on cartographic facts about upcoming events of war but also on the negative phantasms and anxious questions this information (or the lack of information) provokes. Just for this reason, the briefing generally emphasizes the need of acquiring the scarce cartographic knowledge that is given; but what is more, it insists on the need to "get it right," as written on a blackboard in the background of the scene, to evade doubts on the part of the soldiers (see Figure 9).

As it becomes clear soon after, these ambiguities between given and processed information form the ground for one of the film's basic themes: the relation of knowledge and point of view.[29] Drawing on Kathryn Kane's observations on the opposition between technology and nature in OBJECTIVE, BURMA!,[30] Steve

---

29 Neale, "Aspects of Ideology and Narrative Form in the American War Film," 45.
30 Cf. Kane, *Visions of War*, 44–46, 51–52, and 58–59.

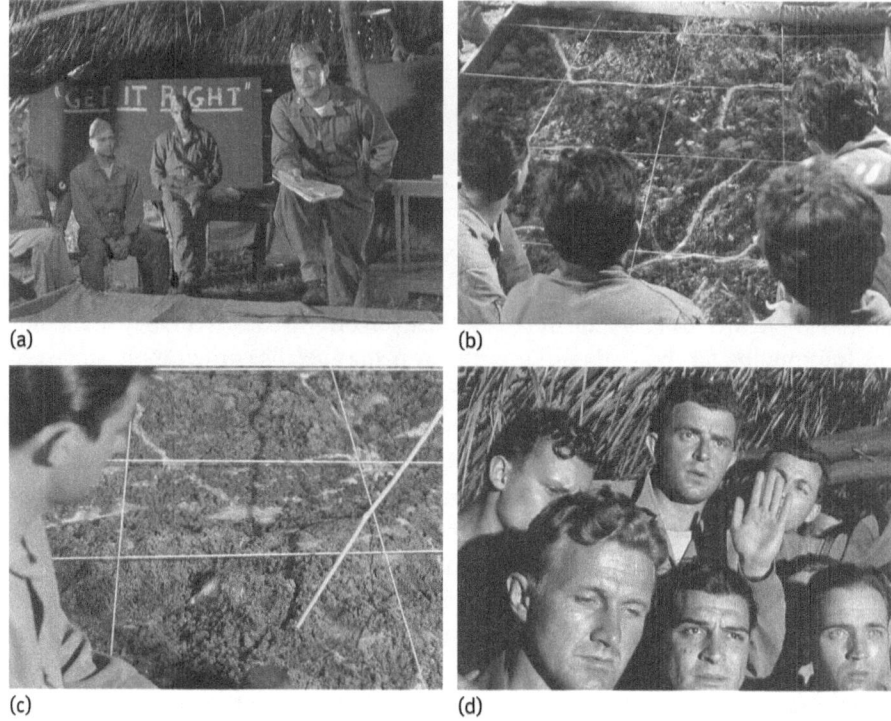

Figure 9: "Get it right."

Neale links the successes and failures of military command that are depicted in Walsh's film to respective successes and failures of communication:

> Communication in the film takes three principal forms: communication by direct aural/verbal contact (as in face-to-face speech); communication by indirect aural/verbal contact (principally radio), and communication by direct visual contact (as when the men are spotted signalling by means of a mirror and sunlight from the air).[31]

The flaws within these forms of communication are thus exposed through the disruption of both aural and visual contact. Disrupted communication, then, comprises technology as well as sensuous perception and expression. That is, eventually, it reveals the weaknesses of the military body as such, in both its mechanical and physical dimensions. Seen in this way, the briefing scene, with its contrast between exclusive, superior knowledge and signs of insecurity communicated by

---

31 Neale, "Aspects of Ideology and Narrative Form in the American War Film," 45.

3.2 OBJECTIVE, BURMA! / Subjective Burma: The Illusion of Overview — 73

the soldiers, anticipates the chaotic chains of events the film will elaborate later on – events that are heavily affected by the shortcomings of seeing and hearing and thus influence the film's corpography.

At this point the narrative perspective has changed profoundly. Coming from a confident and empowering aerial view, as deployed at the very beginning of the film, we are now sharing the foot soldier's point of view, a perception of battle from below, which is literally visualized by means of claustrophobic low-angle shots used in the briefing sequence. Reconsidering Teresa Castro's account of the aerial view's "revelation of the territory as yet another injured body," it is now the soldier's perspective that puts this vulnerability on display – exhibiting not only the injured body of the territory but that of the soldier fighting with and over it. Thus, the wounded (terrestrial) body does not lead to a "global awareness," as Geiger states for the aerial view supporting a national perspective, but it stimulates a corpographic, or somatic awareness instead, by being portrayed from a subjective, precarious perspective. In other words, the soldier's point of view deviates from what Derek Gregory calls the "cartographic imaginary" of an optical war, "entirely divorced from the corpographies inculcated by the soldiers whose bodies had to move through what they came to construe as a desperately hostile nature."[32]

In the case of OBJECTIVE, BURMA!, this somatic awareness is staged as an intensified sonic experience, thus portraying a sensorium in which sight loses its primacy to sound.[33] The controllable space of the birds-eye-view deployed in the first part of the film turns into a figurative birdcage where vision and mobility are restricted on the part of the captives (that is, the U.S. infantry men), but still leaving them to the observation and penetrating sounds of invisible enemies (see Figure 10).

When the soldiers have parachuted down to the spot from where they are supposed to head off into the Burmese jungle, darkness surrounds them, and with it various amplified sounds of nocturnal animals. Noises of frogs, monkeys and birds fill the air, as the men hastily gather their belongings and run towards the clearing.[34] Captain Nelson immediately takes a look at his

---

32 Gregory, "The Natures of War," 26.
33 As Gregory writes with regard to jungle warfare in Vietnam (a theater of war geographically comparable to Burma), "[t]hese physical sensations of exhaustion and pain were registered in a sensorium in which the usual hierarchy of senses was scrambled. As on the Western Front and in the Western Desert, sight was compromised in the rainforest. Visibility was limited by the dense vegetation and the filtered light" Gregory, "The Natures of War," 53.
34 Similar perceptions were noted in the Vietnam War. When describing his jungle experience, Larry Gwin writes about "the croaking of tree frogs, the clicking of gecko lizards like sticks of

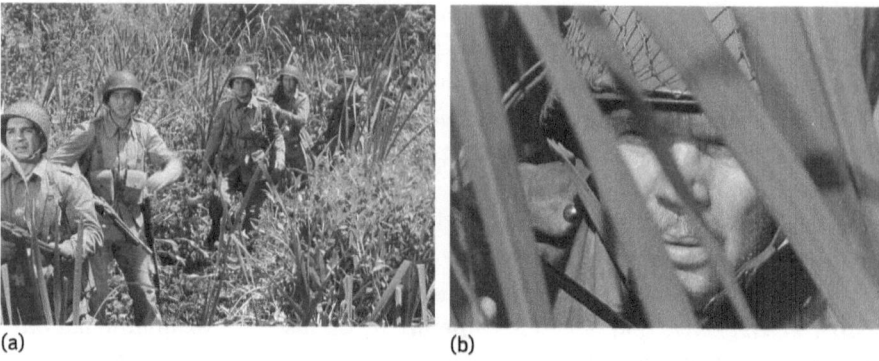

(a) (b)

Figure 10: Captives in a birdcage.

map, while bombardment can be heard in the distance. As the others quickly dig holes to bury their parachutes in, the trumpeting of elephants joins the concert of jungle sounds. The squad takes off on a track almost entirely hidden by plants and bushes, with a pounding non-diegetic soundtrack accompanying their movement.

Both visually and aurally, the jungle seems to close in on the men. They are mostly framed in high-angle or close-up shots, as we watch branches and leaves getting in their way, blocking the visual field and slowing down the march. Invisible but tangible, mosquitos distress the soldiers, while they are looking around cautiously, expecting the enemy to attack anytime and out of nowhere. Here, the camera takes an unsettling position. It is either above, or directly in front of the squad, occasionally singling out individual soldiers and their concerned faces. Moreover, the camera at times seems to be lurking next to the men, or behind them, thus establishing a voyeuristic point of view. As an uncanny, disembodied presence, this voyeuristic gaze, along with the dense vegetation, creates the impression that – if not the Japanese enemy – the jungle itself is watching them and poses a constant threat.

Quite abruptly, levels of power and visual control have shifted within the film's narrative. Whereas the jungle had been an object of scrutiny and cartographic measuring in earlier scenes, it has now turned into the observer itself – framing, analysing, and literally "mapping" the soldiers: their movements, their gestures, and their mental and physical reactions to the challenges of nature. On their way through this hostile environment, the men merely have a vague sense of

---

bamboo banging together, the drone of myriad insects, and the occasional screech of a monkey." Larry Gwin, *Baptism: A Vietnam Memoir*, New York 1999, 122.

orientation. The map provides only rough directions leading to overgrown paths, which calls for alternative sensuous coordinates. Provoked by the loss of sight, the amplified animal sounds hereby indicate both an intensified aural perception and point to devious places too dangerous to explore – places beyond the given track holding a possible threat. Sound, in this regard, functions as an immediate expression of death.[35]

Also, the fact that the soldiers advance in line points to their mutual physical dependence. As every squad member relies on the man before him in moving forward safely, each soldier becomes an element of a corpographic group body that adjusts its motion through the synchronization of individual bodies.[36] This physical closeness is expressed by means of the voyeuristic camera gaze, which not only imposes on the men, but also highlights their intimacy, their similar behavior, their simultaneity, and, eventually, their fatigue. What is more, the almost intrusive cinematography used in this scene, and more to follow, both articulates intimacy as a defense against external threats and the "intimate, intensely corporeal violation by the jungle itself."[37]

Yet, in OBJECTIVE, BURMA! and other combat movies about the Pacific War, nature seems to be characterized by mainly invisible, intangible qualities. Throughout the films the soldiers have to cope with fear induced by unseen threats, as well as with exhaustion through heat and diseases such as malaria and typhus. Examples include BATAAN (Tay Garnett, 1943), which was affectedly advertised as a story coming from "the eerie depths of a Jap-ridden jungle hell,"[38] GUADALCANAL DIARY (Lewis Seiler, 1943), and THE THIN RED LINE (Andrew Marton, 1964). One of the main physical challenges of the Burma campaign, however, is neither depicted nor mentioned at all: heavy rain. Of the 1940s war films and documentaries set in South East Asia, only BURMA VICTORY, as a British-American co-production, features the monsoon – and the serious health conditions caused by it – very prominently. In its opening sequence, rain and humidity are described as deadly forces, as "[t]he body weeps unceasingly its sweat, mildew grows on boots, and the smell of mould clings to the clothing, while thoughts of

---

35 As Frederick Downs notes, "sound was death in the jungle." Cf. Frederick Downs, *The Killing Zone: My Life in the Vietnam War*, New York 1978, 115.
36 Due to dense vegetation, patrolling through the jungle was intensely difficult. O'Brien (1975, 87), in his account of the Vietnam War, talks about soldiers following him "like a blind man after his dog."
37 Derek Gregory, "The Natures of War," in *Geographical Imaginations*, Downloads, November 2014, 1–66, here: 56, https://geographicalimaginations.files.wordpress.com/2012/07/gregory-the-natures-of-war-november-2014.pdf (accessed 7 May, 2015).
38 This quote is taken from the official trailer for BATAAN.

distance, isolation, and loneliness rise up to try the spirit."[39] Also later in the film, it becomes a decisive factor in the troop's struggle against the enemy, and in terms of their corpographic advance. In a sequence depicting a soldier writing his diary, a voice-over tells us the following: "They tell us the Japs are pulling out fast, and our job is to keep on their tail. Eight miles a day is the most we can do. Yesterday we lost a mule. He just sank out of sight in the mud."

Looking as well at first-hand accounts of the Vietnam War, many authors stress the tiring perseverance of mud wearing out their bodies.[40] The "slimescapes" of the Pacific campaign and the Vietnam War can therefore be compared and connected to the trench landscapes of World War I in building "haptic geographies." The fact that this specific tactile aspect of warfare is left out in OBJECTIVE, BURMA! strengthens the observation that physical intimacy is in this case produced by sound, rather than touch. At the same time, sound does not only oppose the sensuous realm of sight, but depends on the limits of vision in order to increase its corpographic effectiveness. Soundtrack and diegetic noises in OBJECTIVE, BURMA! both substitute and emphasize what cannot be seen to an almost synesthetic extent, that is, they make invisibility audible.

This impression is reinforced and modulated in one of the film's key scenes, in linking invisibility not only to the assumed physical presence of the enemy but also to the presence of dead or dying bodies. After the troop is split up to reach a meeting point, Nelson is directed to a Burmese village to find out that half of his men have fallen victim to a Japanese ambush. When discovering their mutilated corpses, he tries to identify them while other soldiers cannot bear the sight. For a swift moment, the camera cuts to the bodies partially hidden behind a group of trees. Eventually, Nelson finds his mangled friend Jacobs (William Prince) lying in a corner of a temple nearby. He, too, is hidden from sight, his upper body obscured by a doorframe. Seconds before his death, Jacobs refuses to be touched and begs Nelson to kill him instead. A point of view shot then shows Nelson kneeling in front of Jacobs, his face barely lit, without any reverse shot to follow; instead of seeing the victim's injured body, we hear his weak voice permeating the dark, before a last breath terminates his agony.

A similar sequence can be found in a war film released more than 60 years after OBJECTIVE, BURMA!, Clint Eastwood's FLAGS OF OUR FATHERS (2006). Here, the sudden disappearance of an American soldier on the battlegrounds of Iwo Jima becomes a traumatizing event for the film's protagonist, John Bradley (Ryan

---

39 I am quoting the voice-over narration in BURMA VICTORY here.
40 Cf. for example John Edmund Delezen, *Eye of the Tiger*, Jefferson NC 2003, or John Ketwig, ... *And a Hard Rain fell: A GI's True Story of the War in Vietnam*, Napierville, IL 2002.

Phillippe), as he keeps having flashbacks and nightmares about the incident. About one and a half hours into the film, the soldier's cruel fate is disclosed: it becomes clear that he has been mutilated by the Japanese, although his corpse is not shown (in contrast to the film's graphic images of Japanese soldiers who committed suicide in a cave). Instead, the camera rests on Bradley, whose contours are hardly visible against the dark cavernous formation surrounding him, while the silence of the moment is filled with an elegiac orchestral piece and the sound of water drops trickling from the top of the cave. As Robert Burgoyne notes for FLAGS OF OUR FATHERS, its haunting qualities emerge from a sense of being "concealed in the folds of the visible,"[41] which accounts for both the uncanny battle zone of Iwo Jima and for a false photographic history afflicting the protagonists in their later lives.

As different as Eastwood's FLAGS is from OBJECTIVE, BURMA!, both works connect in exposing specific "folds of the visible" and the fallibility of the image as such, even more so when retrospectively considering the "pseudo-documentary" opening sequence in Walsh's film.[42] What is more, while the discussed scene in OBJECTIVE, BURMA! does not reveal much about the concept of corporeal navigation through space or the flaws of media coverage, it nevertheless epitomizes the cinematic politics of the senses established in the film. In terms of physical intimacy, the denial of touch and its substitution through sound is explicitly articulated: Jacobs' "Don't touch me!" not only verbalizes the primacy of sight over tactile sensation as proposed by cinematic means, but also highlights the film's emphasis on certain *invisibilities*. Whereas the Burmese jungle seems to resist any optic scrutiny (that is, in form of photographs, maps and magnifying glasses), the images of mutilated bodies, in turn, are deliberately kept off screen. Seen this way, the film puts any sense of vulnerability entirely to the level of diegetic sound. This again supports the thesis of a somatic awareness expressed through the soldier's precarious ground perspective – an immanent sensuous awareness strictly opposed to the distanced view from above. Also, in contrasting the susceptibility of the terrestrial position with the aerial view, the latter is proven to be "never quite at the resolution or fidelity that its masters might hope for."[43]

---

[41] Robert Burgoyne, "Haunting in the War Film: Flags of Our Fathers," in *Eastwood's Iwo Jima: Critical Engagement With Flags of Our Fathers and Letters From Iwo Jima*, ed. Rikke Schubart, Anne Gjelsvik, New York 2013, 157–172, here: 161.
[42] Although one has to bear in mind that the documentary framing of the film was certainly not meant to uncover the ambiguity of media images, but rather to provide a historically valid background for the fictional story it introduces.
[43] Peter Adey, Mark Whitehead, and Alison J. Williams (eds.), *From Above: War, Violence and Verticality*, London 2014, 16.

It should not be overlooked, though, that it is here where OBJECTIVE, BURMA! also strikes an overtly propagandistic and racist note, which might or might not have been intentionally assigned to the figure of the American news correspondent, Williams (Henry Hull), who accompanies the platoon. After witnessing Jacobs' death, he gets furious about the atrocity, blaming the Japanese for being a barbaric people:

> I've been a newspaper man for 30 years. I thought I'd seen or read about everything that one man can do to another, from the torture chambers of the middle ages to the gang wars and the lynchings of today. But this ... this is different. This was done in cold blood by a people who claim to be civilized. Civilized ... they're degenerate [...] idiots. Stinking little savages! Wipe 'em out, I say – wipe 'em out! Wipe 'em off the face of the earth!

As radical as these words are, none of the characters actively agrees to Williams' rage. That is to say, none of the soldiers disagrees with Williams, either, but his monologue is eventually left uncommented. Whether this has been done on purpose is debatable, but it nevertheless points to what Jonna K. Eagle calls "strenuous spectatorship," investigating the role of the war correspondent as being both "surrogate spectator" and "heroic would-be soldier." Here she formulates the idea of the spectator's body being situated within the terrain of battle and thus combining distanced voyeurism with the risk of directly partaking in military action:

> [A]t once impervious and vulnerable, removed from the scene of violence in which he is at the same time intimately engaged [...] the strenuous spectator occupies a privileged vantage point on action alongside a fantasy of assault. Rather than being cordoned off from an embodied sense of threat, then, [...] here the spectatorial body, and the white masculine body in particular, is imagined as very much on the line.[44]

For Eagle, the figure of the war correspondent collapses the poles of spectatorship and action, that is, voyeurism and vulnerability. Thus, in terms of cartographic and corpographic perspectives, he or she embodies an objective, information-based point of view, and, at the same time, is invited to share the foot soldier's precarious experience. Yet Williams' outburst demonstrates the ultimate incongruity of these two positions, while it also shows that both points of view are not only ideologically but also emotionally charged. His rage is therefore the very manifestation – and realization – of violability, of the challenges of and for objectivity, and of a general loss of control. Moreover, the film's propagandistic implications speak for both a structural and aesthetic problem within

---

[44] Jonna K. Eagle, "A Rough Ride: Strenuous Spectatorship and the Early Cinema of Assaults," *Screen* 53 (1), 2012, 18–35, here: 18.

Hollywood wartime films of the 1940s. Since classical Hollywood cinema had been designed mainly to provide entertaining, escapist stories diverting from the realm of political commitment, this narrative had to be reworked in order to promote an active engagement in the war effort, which not always turned out to be successful.[45] Dana Polan, on this matter, states that propaganda was far from being perfected, and that many films of the period thus "reveal the incompleteness and even the structural impossibility of the project of effective wartime affirmation."[46] While it again has to be taken into account that OBJECTIVE, BURMA! had been produced and released after the end of WWII, which weakens the critical thesis of the film's predominantly propagandistic purpose even more.

If it uses techniques of propaganda, it is more likely retrospectively referring to wartime programming practices (the combination of fictional films with newsreels) than to promote a war against an ultimate enemy. In hereby amalgamating documentary footage and genre cinema, Walsh, much like Capra in his WHY WE FIGHT series, provides a media-historical frame to his film, but less to simply add a mode of accuracy or authenticity to the story. Rather, the documentary images become fictionally charged without denying their formal-aesthetic differences to the fictional film material: "both documentary and fictional footage – edited into a dense visual memory – aim at the corporeal presence of the viewers, who are given a relationship to the historical events by this documentary footage."[47]

In terms of the war film's poetics of affect, this strategy aims at the emotional participation of the spectator and thereby creates a sense of community grounded in the experience of a shared memory.[48] Moreover, for what concerns the corpography of OBJECTIVE, BURMA!, the documentary framing of the film helps in setting up the affective contrast between the aerial view and the precarious perspective of the foot soldier, between control and fear; for it is the documentary/newsreel sequence that not only conveys factual information, but forms the media-cartographic ground from which the somatic experience of jungle warfare can emerge as an all the more impactful spectatorial experience.

---

45 Cf. Dana Polan, "Stylistic Regularities (and Peculiarities) of the Hollywood World War II Propaganda Film," in *Warner's War: Politics, Pop Culture and Propaganda in Wartime Hollywood*, ed. Martin Kaplan, Johanna Blakley, Los Angeles 2004, 38–47, here 39.
46 Polan, "Stylistic Regularities," 47.
47 Empirische Medienästhetik, "A sense of community as the shared filmic remembrance of shared suffering," 2011.
48 Empirische Medienästhetik, "A sense of community."

3.3 Corpography and Conversion: FURY'S Hell on Wheels

> *This is what the LORD says: "Stand at the crossroads and look; ask for the ancient paths, ask where the good way is, and walk in it, and you will find rest for your souls. But you said, 'We will not walk in it.' (Jeremiah 6:16)*

In his study on 1940s Hollywood films, *Power and Paranoia*, Dana Polan inaugurates the term "conversion narrative" for wartime cinema, thus defining a typical storytelling mode used in genre films to promote and justify the good cause of the war. In and through this narrative, a character almost spiritually *converts* to the war and its ideological implications after having opposed or disobeyed hierarchical military structures and orders:

> [C]onversion to the mission of the combat team – and beyond that, to the war effort as organic whole – takes on directly religious meaning [...] Moreover, conversion works here by suggesting not that the meanings of engagement are imposed onto the subject from without, but that they exist rather as an inner spark that needs to be rekindled, a core of commitment that had been forgotten through cowardice or cynicism.[49]

In this regard, Polan mentions films like SERGEANT YORK (Howard Hawks, 1941), CHINA GIRL (Henry Hathaway, 1942) and CASABLANCA (Michael Curtiz, 1942), in which the protagonists ultimately act according to a national mission. What Polan describes in narrative terms can hence be formulated as a conversion to a sense of community, which is situated on the level of spectatorial experience. In line with the war film's poetics of affect, the converting protagonist of the film therefore becomes a carrier of affective modulations that shape the viewer's relation to the story. In a combat film, these figurations of conversion usually concern a young and rebellious soldier who revolts against an experienced military superior – a father figure that is eventually replaced by his young opponent, whereupon the initial order and balance of the martial society is restored.

Seen in this way, the respective conversion is not only a matter of psychological and spiritual development but first and foremost a corporeal transformation. Over the course of the film the converting rebel acquires the spirit *and* the physicality of a dedicated soldier and eventually substitutes other men who sacrifice their lives for a greater ideal. As I have described earlier, the war film genre's melodramatic journey of the soldier is marked by several stages of physical separation and adjustment: once he becomes part of the corps, he gives in to rituals of

---

[49] Dana Polan, "Auteurism and War-teurism: Terrence Malick's War Movie," in *The War Film*, ed. Robert Eberwein, New Brunswick 2005, 53–61, here: 55.

drill and group formation, feels the destructive power of becoming one with his weapon, or the vulnerability and desolation of being left alone on the battlefield.

While WWII combat films on jungle warfare in the Pacific consequently focus on the primordial fear induced by the opposition of body and nature, others emphasize the contrast of the body and technology. Following up on Das's thoughts on the "mechanized nature of the First World War,"[50] "the impersonal onslaught of the machine" against which physical intimacy provided a shield,[51] the question arises as to what extent – and to what effect – the mechanization of the body at war influences the corpographic dimension of the war film. That is, how it affects not only the hierarchy of the senses, but also the literal and intimate *conversion* from body to machine, and vice versa. As one of the most recent cinematic takes on the Second World War, David Ayer's FURY (2014), a film about tank warfare in 1945 Germany, seems to embark on this question by both foregrounding and demystifying the idea of the soldier's machinic transformation – a transformation that is by no means absolute. That is to say, rather than portraying a predominantly corporeal metamorphosis, FURY deploys an act of conversion, which not only marks a change from one physical state to another, but implies a conscious reflection on this very process and its consequences in relation to a bodily and mental commitment to war. The film's actual protagonist is Norman (played by Logan Lerman), the youngest member of an American tank crew that passes through war-damaged provincial towns and rural landscapes towards the end of war, and the end of days. As FURY's apocalyptic imagery and atmosphere suggests, his melodramatic journey not only entails his responsible commitment to the mission, and the military corps as a whole; moreover, he adapts to an environment that itself transforms into a battlefield of good and evil forces, of bodies and machines that have been involved in a process of persuasion, propaganda, and conversion. Ultimately, Norman himself becomes an active part of the machinery of war, and only the acknowledgement of, and physical adjustment to, the signs and sites of this transgressive scenario allows for an efficient navigation through the combat zone.

As we have seen with OBJECTIVE, BURMA!, the composition and deconstruction of the military's mechanical group body is one of the war film's most significant poetic figurations. Once battle technology has effectively merged with the organic structure of the corps, it is staged in direct opposition to the terrain and the nature the soldiers have to fight over and against. Defining and driving this transformation, military vehicles play an important part within the narratological, spatial,

---

50 Das, *Touch and Intimacy*, 80–81.
51 Das, *Touch and Intimacy*, 83.

and affective organization of the genre. Like the jeeps and reconnaissance planes in Objective, Burma!, other vessels like boats, aircraft carriers and tanks provide a certain point of view on the warzones they traverse. But more than being navigational tools and weapons, they are also temporary domiciles for soldiers on their way to or away from the front – they are transit spaces that enhance and at the same time limit the men's mobility, forcing them to close ranks and to cope with their individual fears. In this regard, a closer look at the Hollywood combat film reveals a general scenic pattern: several boat scenes before a beach landing, or sequences portraying soldiers on a plane about to be dropped over enemy territory develop existential monologues and arguments fortified by claustrophobic image compositions. The interior of a respective boat or plane therefore turns into a site of confession – a site of last human doubts in a process of being de-individualized and incorporated by the machine. These include thoughts about the meaning of war, or missed opportunities in a former civilian life, memories of loved ones, and, most importantly, the fear of death. The fact that this almost metaphysical constellation calls for a specific setting, however, suggests itself: among the diverse battle zones of WWII, the dense jungles and impracticable islands of the Pacific theater do barely allow for motorized transportation. Consequently, the aforementioned scenes in related war films are confined to the elements of water and air.

Films about the battles of Europe and North Africa, on the other hand, feature continuous front movements on land, either across civilized geographical areas or vast desert landscapes. Trucks and tanks are thus frequently seen, associated with both allied and enemy forces. And, as Derek Gregory notes judging from letters written by members of the American Field Service, travelling in these vehicles along the desert tracks was a "wretchedly corporeal affair."[52] Moving this close in and with their tanks, the soldiers form a technomorphic alliance, within which their bodies quite literally converse to mechanical devices. The vehicle, in turn, is oftentimes anthropomorphized to the extent that it is treated as both protective habitat and loyal companion. This might apply less to the truck, since it is not a battle craft in the narrowest sense of the term. Tanks, on the other hand, like naval vessels, carry an entire group of soldiers who share the same space and experience of battle and quotidian life.

With regard to the warship as a crucial setting of the combat film, Kathryn Kane states four fundamental characteristics that could similarly be assigned to tanks: first, "the warship encapsulates the hierarchy of all combat groups"; second, "the ship is a domicile where the occupant can identify himself as

---

[52] Gregory, "The Natures of War," 20.

a unique human being"; third, "the ship is the center of communal life for its crew"; and fourth, "an emotional bond is formed between men and ship, resulting in a mutual enrichment and dependence."[53] It is this emotional bond in particular that does also touch upon questions of intimacy, sexuality, and corpography: Zoltan Korda's 1943 combat film SAHARA, for example, tells the story of a U.S. tank crew led by Sergeant Joe Gunn (Humphrey Bogart) crossing the Libyan desert on a Sherman tank called "Lulubelle." The vessel is not only named after Gunn's beloved horse and therefore palpably compared to a reliable mount, but is constantly feminized, as well ("She's a good tank").[54] As this could be read as a somewhat psychoanalytical implication, Kathryn Kane goes on to say that, in Freudian terms, "the warship appears simultaneously and paradoxically as both phallic and womb symbol – i.e., both aggressively active and outer-directed, and secure and nurturing, inner-directed."[55] Indeed, for what concerns the contextualization of warships, planes and tanks, borders between the interior and exterior, as well as between organic and inorganic structures seem to be blurred. On a corpographic level, inner and outer movements are synchronized, while sensory perception is at the same time concentrated and isolated, bound to the physical and technological limits of the vehicle.

This being the soldier's perspective from inside a tank, a cinematic view of other war machines from the outside reveals their metaphorical connotations: Inasmuch as American vessels embody the physical and emotional desires of their crew members, enemy tanks, then again, become mythical creatures of their own, almost independent from the soldiers operating them. Examples can be found in films such as FIXED BAYONETS! (Samuel Fuller, 1951),[56] ATTACK (Robert Aldrich, 1956) and SAVING PRIVATE RYAN (Steven Spielberg, 1998). Most recently, and outside the Hollywood studio context, the common zoomorphism of military crafts has been taken to a highly allegorical level: the Russian war film WHITE TIGER (BELYY TIGR, Karen Shakhnazarov, 2012) bears the name of its ghostly protagonist, a white painted German "Tiger" tank portrayed as a dreaded and most wanted target. Regardless of its crew the tank is treated like an armoured Moby Dick, a phantom appearing and disappearing unexpectedly. Along these lines, Russian tank movement in WHITE TIGER is often depicted from inside the vehicle

---

53 Kane, *Visions of War*, 29–30.
54 Likewise, William Wyler's documentary MEMPHIS BELLE (1944) focuses on a B-17 aircraft flying missions over WWII Germany. Memphis Belle is in fact the name of the plane, which is thereby equally feminized.
55 Kane, *Visions of War*, 31.
56 It has to be said, however, that this particular film is set in the Korean War.

or filmed in a way that the spectator seems to take the tank's point of view to form an embodied mechanical counter-perspective to the Tiger's mythical presence.

This is very similar to the main battle sequence in ALL QUIET, where the viewer becomes one with the machine, sensing and navigating with the help of mechanical perception. In a way, the film thereby makes use of an immersive technique common for films about aerial warfare, and most notably known from the days of Early Cinema. Around the turn of the twentieth century, primarily linked to the touristic realm, so-called "phantom rides"[57] simulated a slow forward movement across landscapes and city centres by means of a camera attached to the front of a train or car. Since the actual vehicle was not visible in the frame, the spectators were under the illusion of magically moving into the depth of the image themselves, being both passengers and a part of the virtually travelling machine. While Tom Gunning explains that, within this configuration, the actual body of the locomotive is reduced to a phantom-like presence,[58] it is moreover the spectator who becomes a phantom body, whereby the eyes perceive the ride metonymically for the viewer's whole sensomotoric complex.[59] This aesthetic effect, often described as "immersion," is in fact a necessary condition of cinematic experience as such, as the spectator automatically adopts an external sensuous perception offered by the film to literally "dive" into the diegetic world – a situation I have explained earlier with reference to Vivian Sobchack's neo-phenomenological approach to cinema and spectatorship. Nevertheless, the theoretical concept of immersion goes beyond the illusory potential of cinematic representation. The spectator's sensuous disposition, so to say, is twofold: on the one hand, he or she is virtually incorporated in the diegesis; on the other, and in a more active way, the viewer must actively (and affectively) engage with the audio-visual image. That is, cinematic experience, in any case, implies the spectator's empathy, the ability to have a feeling for the representational space of the film, irrespective of different grades of abstraction. As a result, immersion can be seen as a process of decorporealization, while the viewer's senses are at the same time attuned to the filmic body.[60] As an equally sensory and emotional investment, the

---

57 Phantom rides were utterly popular from about 1896–1907 (cf. Tom Gunning, "The Attraction of Motion: Modern Representation and the Image of Movement," in *Film 1900: Technology, Perception, Culture*, ed. Annemone Ligensa, Klaus Kreimeier, Eastleigh / Bloomington 2009, 165–174.).
58 Cf. Gunning, "The Attraction of Motion," 170.
59 Erkki Huhtamo, "Unterwegs in der Kapsel. Simulatoren und das Bedürfnis nach totaler Immersion," *montage/av* 17 (2), 2008, 41–68, here: 54.
60 For a more detailed theorization of immersion and empathy, see Robin Curtis, "Immersion und Einfühlung: Zwischen Repräsentationalität und Materialität bewegter Bilder," *montage/av* 17 (2), 2008, 89–107.

immersive condition thus forms the ground for the affective potential of abstract, disembodied aerial views, or the foot soldier's purely somatic perspective.

This brief theoretical outline is essential to understand in what ways David Ayer's FURY both conforms to and diverges from classical immersive modes of staging that have been established within the genre. As one might expect, being a film about a tank crew fighting in WWII Germany, its focus would either lie on the thrills and confinements of technological warfare, or, in line with Kane's definition, on the emotional bond between men and machine, involving their physical and sensuous alignment with the tank. And although all this can be found in FURY, it is unique in combining these elements anew, and thereby challenging common correlations of immersion and empathy. The film inverts the aforementioned themes in order to compass a kind of "cyborg corpography," a process of physically adjusting to the navigational space of the tank. Here, as I will point out in the following paragraphs, a certain connection to Polan's "conversion narrative" can be made. In this sense, and on many levels, Fury stands in an antithetic relation to Objective, Burma!, while still working on the basis of conventional genre patterns.

Numerous Russian and Polish war films about WWII notwithstanding, American combat movies are seldom centred on tank crews and their objectives. In addition to SAHARA, ATTACK and SAVING PRIVATE RYAN (which, in its house-to-house fighting scenes, bears striking resemblance to Attack), PATTON (Franklin J. Schaffner, 1970) might be one of the few salient examples displaying military vehicles in their iconographic function of signifying allied advance movements.[61] Like OBJECTIVE, BURMA!, PATTON is a highly cartographic war film that, instead of aerial views, features numerous panoramic views and thereby foregrounds the general's imperial perspective. George S. Patton is cynically portrayed as an archaic warrior seeking to command and conquer, and, above all, to maintain his sole authority. Many scenes therefore obtain their pathos from the protagonist's obvious references to ancient Rome and several great battles of history. The film thus occasionally presents itself as a heroic tale to which it then takes up an ironic stance.

In its opening sequence, FURY, too, clearly refers to the war film's epic implications, but rather by mystifying and immediately demystifying the ethos of the noble warrior at one stroke. The scene starts with an extreme long shot. We hear the wind sweeping over a rough plain, a gloomy sun rising above the misty ground. Far back,

---

[61] In fact, it was General Patton who commanded the 2nd Armored Division, a unit of U.S. tank battalions serving in North Africa and Europe during WWII. The tank crew portrayed in FURY is supposed to be part of this division.

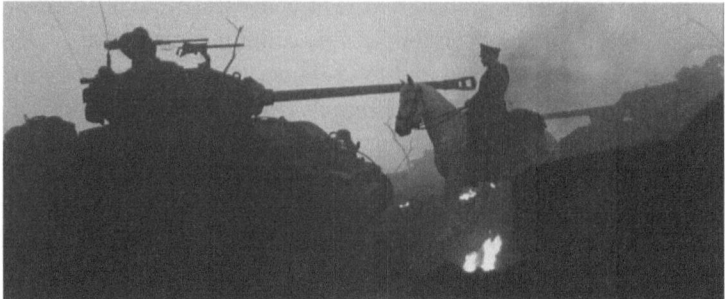

Figure 11: Cyborg nature.

a dark silhouette comes into view, growing bigger and bigger as it crosses the rocky landscape. Rhythmically whispering voices accompany its movement. Slowly the camera tracks to the left, as the figure turns sideways to reveal itself as a German SS officer riding on a horse. A close-up of the white animal's trotting hooves is followed by an establishing shot of an almost post-apocalyptic setting: the officer rides through a bizarre scenery composed of burning vehicles, wrecked tanks and dead trees (see Figure 11) – a cyborg nature in Gregory's terms, where organic and technical structures collectively shape a heterogeneous, lifeless landscape reminiscent of how Jocelyn Brooke poetically describes the remains of a tank battle near Tobruk:

> This land is hard, / Inviolable, the battle's aftermath / Presents no ravaged and emotive scene, / No landscape à la Goya. ... all / The rusted and angular detritus / Of war, seem scarcely / to impinge / Upon the hard, resistant surface of / This lunar land ...[62]

Here, Fury's mise-en-scène has a similar, nearly numbing effect, evoking a sense of trance within the maelstrom of a surreal limbo. All the more shockingly, this spectatorial state is then disrupted at a glance: as the German passes another exanimate tank, he is suddenly attacked by a soldier who pulls him off his horse and brutally stabs him – one last twist, and the stranger rips his knife out of the horseman's eye. The hitherto proud equestrian has met his disreputable end, his myth destroyed in a heartbeat.

Additionally, within these few seconds, the dynamics of power indicated in the first shots of the film have changed completely, bearing in mind that its pre-title sequence had confronted us with the following words: "In WW2 American tanks were outgunned and out armored by the more advanced German tanks.

---

[62] Jocelyn Brooke, "Landscape near Tobruk," in *Poems in Pamphlet V (1952)*, ed. John Manchip White, Aldington 1952, 360.

U.S. tank crewmen suffered staggering losses against the superior enemy vehicles." Aside from the fact that the quote mentions tanks before soldiers, it sets up the expectation that we are shortly to be presented with a powerful and fearsome German army. Indeed, the image of a lone SS officer riding across a desolated battlefield seems to implement this speculation, as his portrayal is as intimidating as it is majestic, even though his equipment (including the horse) appears to be utterly inferior compared to the armoured vehicles surrounding him. The officer looks oddly out of place, as if he, much like Patton, belonged to another time, to another war. His shadowlike presence adds to the infernal atmosphere reinforced by the mystical non-diegetic voices, and although we don't see him at close range, or take his point of view, his superiority is articulated through his elevated position and the sheer vitality and movement of his horse, distinguishing him from an apparently inanimate environment. Defeated machines mark the German's way, like inglorious trophies from a cruel fight, while a disembodied gaze is framing him, adjusting to his pace. Nevertheless, his presumed corpographic control is undermined and abruptly undone, starting metaphorically with the appearance of a cracked windshield through which we see the horseman moments before his death. Finally, the knife in his eye viciously symbolizes the loss of visual dominance and superiority. On the level of aesthetic experience and focalization, we have just been kept from tentatively engaging with, or at least following the officer's position, after having been drawn into and distracted by the sublime half-light of the setting. His death thus interrupts a certain immersive process and initiates a change in perception and perspective. What is more, in relation to the film as a whole, it is also a definite sign marking the general limits of sight and the importance of sound and the spoken word for Fury's corpography.

This modification is induced by a shift of focus to the other side, that is, to the American soldier responsible for the German's death: Sergeant Don Collier (Brad Pitt), nicknamed "Wardaddy," rests on top of his tank for a short while, then descends into the vessel. What follows is an introduction of his crew *in medias res*. Travis (Jon Bernthal), Gordo (Michael Peña), and Bible (Shia LaBeouf) each occupy a corner of the tank's internal space.[63] Despite the evident claustrophobia

---

[63] Once more, Fury conforms to the conventions of the combat film in deploying a constellation of soldiers each representing a different ethnic group and social class. For the classical war film, it is quite mandatory to emphasise every group member's individual background epitomizing a culturally variegated America (cf. Basinger, *The World War II Combat Film*). Ayer's film, however, departs from the convention in initiating amongst the tank crew members a dialogue about their origins and ending it with Travis's words negating the importance of this background: "Hey, shut up, man. Nobody gives a fuck where you're from."

expressed by means of cinematography, the sequence is composed of various cuts from one close-up and one camera position to another, with every crew member being at least partially visible in each frame. The montage thereby leaves the spectator disoriented, which is also due to the fact that the cuts are motivated by the heated argument unfolding amongst the men. As they trade heavy insults, the camera captures every emotional reaction and every hateful look adding to an uncomfortably tense atmosphere. In this regard, the interior of the tank reflects the disdainful place it is trapped in – an impression that is strengthened by an interspersed shot to the apocalyptic outside, while the crew's argument is inwardly audible.

From the very beginning, FURY therefore subverts essential conventions typical for the war film genre. As noted earlier, a certain sensuous hierarchy, the ethos of the warrior, and configurations of power are reversed immediately. On the level of spectatorship, unfulfilled expectations complicate processes of immersion, empathy and identification. Wardaddy's crew seems far from being united in the face of danger. If Kane considers the warship an embodiment of moral strength and values, nurturing and protecting the men from external threats,[64] this tank appears to nurture nothing but the dominant emotion it is named after: "Fury" is also written on the vehicle's main gun, which we get to see in a POV shot a couple of seconds after the aforementioned sequence. The movement of the tank has now become a phantom ride, a bodiless motion from one site of destruction to the next. Interestingly though, the tank retrieves a body – a body consisting of multiple male bodies, and fragmented accordingly into multiple shots: one by one, we see Bible, Gordo, Travis and Wardaddy (in the exact reverse order of their introduction) protruding from their hatches like human prostheses for their armoured vehicle. Hence, in this case, ideas of corpography and cyborg physicality seem to work reciprocally. The mechanical is not to be conceived as an extension of the human senses; rather, the human body functions as an annex, an implantation to the machine (see Figure 12). In fact, the tank moves on behalf of these bodies, and, moreover, by way of, and over other human bodies standing or lying in its way. In contrast to Kane's statement, the tank does not (or not only) nurture – it feeds from lives and emotions that are not his, channelling them into one fundamental driving force: "Fury" is thus more than a title for Ayer's film and its steely protagonist; it is the figurative manifestation of an overpowering emotion, it defines the crew's "raison d'etre."[65] And, most importantly, in its

---

64 Kane, *Visions of War*, 32.
65 Here, I refer to Kane's conclusion that the warship eventually defines its crew to the extent that it "becomes their raison d'etre" (Kane, *Visions of War*, 30).

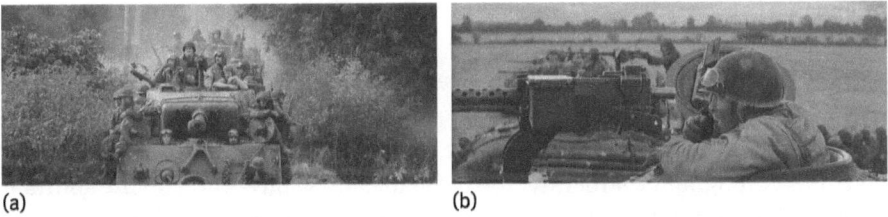

(a)   (b)

Figure 12: The body's inseparability from the machine.

inseparability from the machine, this feeling corrupts our spectatorial desire for an unconditional immersion, the desire for total transparency and the absolute embodiment of technology in such a way that we are unaware of its presence is perpetually proven to be illusory. With FURY, we are constantly confronted with the technological body, and we become *it* before it becomes us. This is also due to a restricted mobility the film makes us aware of permanently. Not only that scenes inside the tank convey an inevitable claustrophobia; what is more, the vehicle does not allow for spontaneous movement outside its walls, either: the soldiers are bound to stay on the tracks the tank is rolling on, the only exception being a fight in a beet field, where they leave their road to attack a German regiment hidden behind a treeline. Whether the more plausible interpretation of this condition would be that the men have to pursue a given, predestined way (to 'stay on track', or 'walk the line', so to say), or that they are doomed from beginning to end, is arguable. At any rate, both suggestions conform to the notion of "corpographic conversion."

If we think about Polan's definition of the war film's conversion narrative again, saying that the actual conviction to the mission of the combat team takes on a religious meaning, and, furthermore, that the meanings of engagement exist "as an inner spark that needs to be rekindled," this is exactly what happens in FURY. Only that it rather works in somatic than narrative terms. The film's main subject, or object, of conversion is a character joining Wardaddy's crew as a replacement for his assistant driver who had been killed in a past fight: as a clerk typist, only having been in the army for eight weeks, Norman resembles the typical rookie figure of many classical war films, an insecure and inexperienced boy facing the challenge of transforming into a soldier. His first task, then, is to clean the tank of what is left of his precursor, being given the advice not to get too close to anyone. Nevertheless, Norman's first encounter with the tank affects him significantly and, above all, viscerally. Scanning the interior of the vehicle, he comes across a physical relic of the dead driver: a part of his face, ripped off in an explosion. Nauseated by the sight, he leaves the tank to vomit outside, as a truck pulls up, with flowers strapped to its front bumper, and a crucifix attached to its radiator grill.

The process of conversion is thus marked by an initial sign of physical rejection before Norman returns to the tank implying to clasp his hands in prayer. Already, this short scene epitomizes the three forms of substantiality that make up Fury's corpographic structure: the mechanical, the physical, and the spiritual (as a level of conscious reflection). Each one of these forms constitutes a strong counterpart to the other, while all of them together create a corpographic trinity within which the film's excessive modes of staging are constantly manoeuvring. That is to say, as technological and technologically influenced perception is a dominant aesthetic factor, the portrayal of physical violence is equally extreme, as is the amount of religious allusions. POV shots through binoculars and crosshairs, and even the laser-like beams of bullet tracers become important elements in battle sequences, while scenes involving graphic deaths are numerous and Christian symbols omnipresent. All this adds to the impression that – for what concerns questions of representation – FURY presents much to the audience what would otherwise be located outside the realm of the visual (which is certainly a matter of advanced special effects), while at the same time depicting sight as a somewhat flawed domain for the characters. Norman has to learn that things are often not what they seem when he fails to shoot a disguised German aggressor, or when he hesitates shooting at a treeline because he cannot see the hidden enemy clearly. But over the course of the film, his actions become more and more intuitive as his sentiments become numbed towards the cruelties of the war. In the end, he is finally accepted by his fellow crew members when Wardaddy christens him "Machine" – a terminus to Norman's battle-tested conversion to the mechanical. This conversion, however, is not to be understood as a complete denouncement of human flesh and deceptive emotions. Rather than an ideal, it is a necessary somatic conformance to the rules of battle, the growing of a weapon for and a shield against the overwhelming effects of violence. In this configuration, religion or spirituality is not a justification of war that would turn it into a fight for the good cause. Building a level of conscious reflection and agency instead, religious motifs in FURY are placed between signs of physical struggle and mechanical imperfection, thus exposing unsightly aspects of warfare and spoiling any body's aspiration to simply "become" a machine. Furthermore, within the context of the Second World War, the religious layer helps to create distance, to establish a cynical perspective on American fighting on the one hand, and to demonize a distinctly futurist, or even fascist, that is, an over-aestheticization of the body on the other. On a metaphorical level, this condemnation of the mechanized soldier is also applicable to the framework of contemporary American warfare. Through the lens of WWII, the film thematizes and criticizes the constitution of the modern "cyborg soldier" that, according to Cristina Masters, represents a post-human subjectivity, wherein processes of thinking and reasoning are transferred from the human body onto technology.[66]

It cannot be denied that this notion has a predecessor in early twentieth-century art. The Futurist ideal, as formulated in early twentieth century, is aiming at achieving a non-human perfection of the male body, a beautiful unity of man and machine. However, the Futurists strictly exclude any affectionate emotions from this conception, as they would pose a threat to the flawless functionality and strength of the man-machine. Ideally, it would represent pure dynamic force and potency, as noted by F.T. Marinetti, founder of the Futurist Manifesto:

> [W]e must prepare for the imminent and inevitable identification of man and motor, facilitating and perfecting a continual interchange of intuitions, rhythms, instincts, and metallic disciplines that are absolutely unknown to the great majority of people today and are divined by only the most clear-sighted minds ... we are aspiring to the creation of an inhuman type, one in which moral suffering, generosity, affect, and love, will be abolished, poisonous corrosives that sap the inexhaustible supply of vital energy, interrupters of our powerful physiological electricity. We believe in the possibility of an incalculable number of human transformations, and we declare without a smile that wings are waiting to be awakened within the flesh of man ... This inhuman and mechanical type, constructed for omnipresent velocity, will be naturally cruel, omniscient, and combative.[67]

The combative aspect foregrounded by Marinetti partly reveals an inherent martial doctrine of Futurism, to which some fascist writings bear striking resemblance: where Marinetti places the utopia of a "multiplied man," a human being whose will is externalized by means of advanced technology, the fascist physical principle of the "man at war" is founded on the opposition between body and consciousness and on the paradoxical simultaneity of immediacy and distance. Klaus Theweleit, who formulates a predominantly psychoanalytical theory of fascism in his study *Male Fantasies*, writes:

> War is a function of the body of these men. Strangely, however, their body remains inwardly divided in the very moment in which its functioning is most intensely pleasurable. In war, the man appears not only naked, but stripped of skin; he seems to lose his body armor, so that everything enters directly into the interior of his body, or flows directly from it. He is out of control and seems permitted to be so. But at the same time, he is all armor, speeding

---

[66] Cristina Masters, "Bodies of Technology: Cyborg Soldiers and Militarised Masculinities," *International Feminist Journal of Politics* 7 (1), 2005, 112–132, here: 114.
[67] F.T. Marinetti, "Multiplied Man and the Reign of the Machine (1911)," in *Futurism: An Anthology*, ed. Lawrence Rainey, Christine Poggi, Laura Wittman. New Haven / London 2009, 89–92, here: 90.

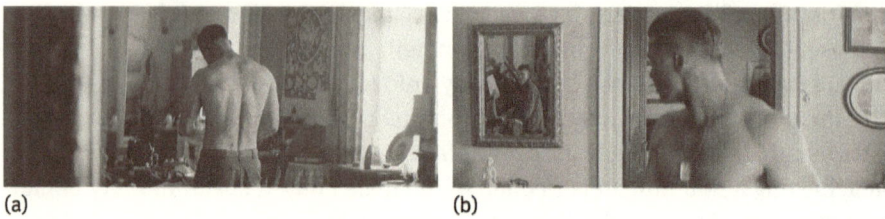

(a) (b)

Figure 13: The body as site of reflection.

bullet, steel enclosure. He wears a coat of steel that seems to take the place of his missing skin. He is collected, directed toward one strict goal; in this sense he is controlled in the extreme.[68]

Here is where FURY clearly deviates from the idea of an absolute machinic transformation: while the skin, as a natural shield, is removed in the fascist ideal of the body at war, it is clearly foregrounded in Ayer's film. Despite the graphic mutilation and destruction of enemy bodies, the display of branded skin becomes most important in a scene that marks the centre of the film – both in terms of its dramatic structure and its running time. Plot and pace of the sequence are sensibly reduced here: Wardaddy and Norman force entry to an apartment occupied by two Germans, a woman and her young cousin. What begins as a violent act turns into a slow and quiet exchange of looks, words and gestures within a temporary homely space. When Norman and the young girl start to bond through him playing a piano piece she is singing to, the sight of Wardaddy's scarred back suddenly paralyses them. In this very moment, his exposed skin designates him as a soldier whose "historical make-up"[69] has been deconstructed by nudity. Without the uniform, Wardaddy's body becomes a site of reflection; his scars both demonstrate his vulnerability and turn his skin into a physical armour shielding him from any form of intimacy (see Figure 13).

Now the apartment, which seems to have momentarily turned into a Biedermeier setting – a mannerly configuration of men, women, furniture and musical art – forms a harsh contrast to the brutality engraved on this individual body. But this paralysis, in turn, provokes another manifestation of intimacy, as Wardaddy prompts Norman to take the girl to her bedroom. Before the two of them have sex, Norman reads the girl's palm, tracing every line on it with his fingers. This

---

[68] Klaus Theweleit, *Male Fantasies, Vol. 2, Male Bodies: Psychoanalyzing the White Terror*, trans. Erica Carter and Chris Turner, Minneapolis 1989, 192.
[69] Marzena Sokołowska-Paryż, "The Naked Male Body in the War Film," in *Journal of War and Culture Studies*, 5 (1), 2012, 21–32, here: 31.

careful touch, which culminates in the physical unification of the couple, marks an appropriation of sensuality that is entirely oppositional to the rage and eventual numbness connected to the process of the soldier's mechanization.

Additionally, the second part of the scene provokes a definite rejection of the male martial body on the part of the spectator who is in this moment most aligned to Norman's perspective. As Travis, Gordo and Bible join the dinner the women are preparing, specifically Travis's rude behaviour highlights every repugnant aspect of military sociality, a certain roughness and insensitiveness expressed through violent grasps, audible chewing and spitting. By means of a time-based narrative strategy the tragic dimension of the soldiers' corpographic conversion is epitomized in this sequence. First, the turning away from the military body as represented by Wardaddy's partial nudity and Norman's sexual devotion promises a future return to humaneness. Then, the men's reflections on the horrors they had to endure in the past, Gordo's story about how they had to kill wounded horses on the way to Germany, points to the irreversibility of their brutality as soldiers. Here is where the melodrama of war finds its most poignant expression, articulating that, once body and mind of the soldier have attuned to the unforgiving conditions of war, they can never return to civil life again. In FURY, this eventual unchangeability of the hardened, mechanized body is thus framed as a questionable effect of armed conflict. Roughness and imperfection render the American soldiers as unaesthetic bellicose products, an image which is distinctly opposed to the flawless and elitist appearance of the German officer that we saw in the film's opening sequence, although it is qualified as equally disdainful.

Despite this dystopian rather than utopian portrayal of the man-machine, its constitution is at other points staged as a functional sensuous adjustment, an indispensable consequence of the soldier's actual conversion process. The fusion of Wardaddy's crewmen with the mechanical perception of their tank, for instance, results in an enhanced aural navigation for which the human voice plays a specific role, since the restricted space of the vessel only allows for a limited sight of the exterior. The voice itself pronounces the intermediate state of the soldier's body – a body that operates between human and machinic physicality. First, it operates as a means of spatial orientation: every time the crew has to face a battle, the gunners have to rely on Wardaddy's directions, which he tells them via radio communication. More than that, all crewmembers have to trust each other in coordinating their actions encompassing driving, shooting, and reloading, which also calls for concise verbal communication. That is, within this configuration, the voice, in its omnipresence and dominance, gains physical independence; regardless of the character it belongs to, it serves as primary source for information and mutual comprehension. As the film constantly cuts between different corners of the tank's interior and POV shots showing targets on the outside, the voice allows for a feeling of continuity. It is thus mostly through the authority of the voice that characters and spectators gain access to spatial information.

While in this portrayal human bodies are bound to merge with the mechanical body of the tank, the human voice is about the only element that distinguishes the men from the machine. And although they share a confined and intimate space, which often seems like a chamber play (or *Kammerspiel* in German), it is less physical contact, but rather the directness of sound creating this intimacy. It becomes an expression, a manifestation of fury, only to then turn into a comforting aftereffect of this emotion before transforming into rage again.

In sum, we can say that the film's actual protagonist, the tank, can indeed be compared to the functions of the warship according to Kane: it is an almost domestic centre of communal life, and it certainly is of emotional and corpographic value for its crew. As long as their bodies are encapsulated by their vehicle, as long as their perception is aligned with the machine, it is the tank that is physically most vulnerable – a fact that becomes most evident whenever it hits a mine and is therefore immobilized. This is when the mechanical body finds its ultimate other in a terrain turning into a touch-sensitive weapon, which implies that any movement outside the tank can lead to immediate death. But there is more about Ayer's film. The tank indeed encloses a certain military hierarchy, but any authority outside its walls is neglected. Strategic briefings are handled almost *en passant*, the typical illusion of overview turns into a disillusion from the very beginning. And as a contrast between the general's and the soldier's perspective does not exist, there is also no substantial need for maps, either. What serves as a crucial narratological turn, a point of realization in films like Objective, Burma! is a clinical and omnipresent fact in Fury: the men are doomed from the very beginning, going down the "road to hell."

Since this road is therefore predestined but not mapped out, as opposed to many classical combat films about WWII, maps do not serve as objects of historical reference or frame, either. Instead, as we have seen, Fury begins with a mythically charged long-shot following comparatively vague intertitles that rudimentally locate the spectator in time and space of the diegesis: "It is April 1945," "deep in the heart of Nazi Germany." The ending of the film, however, reminds us of traditional modes of war representation again, while once more linking them to contemporary media aesthetics – modes that almost seem like a reversal of Objective, Burma! in putting an Icarian perspective at the end of its running time: Fury's very last shot is an aerial view of the wrecked tank. While the camera circles above the vehicle, it moves higher and further away from it, enabling us to see the tank stands at a crossroad, surrounded by the corpses of innumerable German soldiers (see Figure 14). Here is where the tank becomes a last stand facing the enemy in

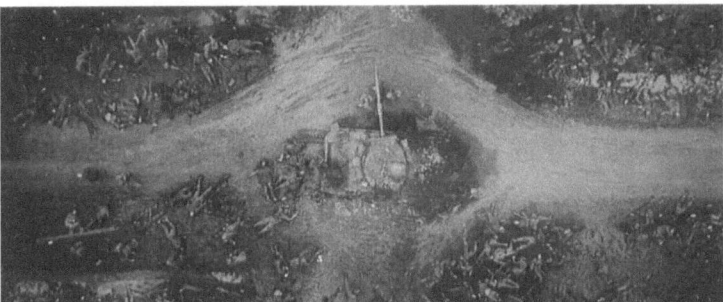

Figure 14: Ex machina.

an already desperate situation. Yet in its spiralling upward movement, the camera does not invoke a glorification of the scene, for it all the more reveals the shocking aftermath of battle. In this reading, the aerial view does not stand for visual control and an empowering national awareness, but rather puts an accusatory question mark to the topos of the martial body. Closing on the pathos formula of the abandoned warrior (the tank in this case), this last shot plainly visualizes the notion of the soldier as both an object and a vector of war. Incorporated by the tank, the soldier is a mechanical object in the literal sense, and with the vehicle being located at the intersection of several directions, it paradoxically moves everywhere and nowhere. Thus, at this point of no return, the tank is left at the mercy of both witnessing and observing spectators who eventually experience a separation from the machine. As our virtual self departs from the tank as our mechanical body, we obtain the state of a presence "ex machina" in the truest sense of the word, that is, in turning to the exact opposite of a deus ex machina, we are reminded of our status as immobile spectators, having no means of interference whatsoever. This aerial view, which is more of a satellite view in its plain two-dimensionality, deprives the scenery of any sublime affectivity and sets up a significant audiovisual contrast instead: on the aural level, intense strings and choir voices intone a powerful elegy that almost seems to bewail the analytical detachment that is expressed visually. By all means, the closing shot sets a final cartographic image to FURY's process of corpographic conversion, epitomizing every element and substantial level involved in it: the physical, the mechanical, and the spiritual.

While Ayer's film has often been compared to Steven Spielberg's SAVING PRIVATE RYAN, especially for what concerns its graphic depiction of violence, FURY's message seems to deviate from that of earlier Hollywood war films.

As Susan Owen and others have argued, American post-Vietnam war films articulate a profound trauma, which can be grasped in form of a destabilized meta-narrative of national strength and unity. Those films, then, express the soldier's difficulty or impossibility of "coming home." Referring to films such as Apocalypse Now, The Deer Hunter, or Full Metal Jacket, Owen goes on to say that, along these lines, Saving Private Ryan could be read as what she calls a "cinematic jeremiad," a visual rhetoric operating as "a corrective to contemporary conditions gone awry."[70] That is, whereas prominent Hollywood films about the Vietnam War contain and perform acts of lamentation and failed redemption, Saving Private Ryan, according to Owen, restores the "American vision of righteous destruction" by "resacrilizing" the gun – by letting the spectator share the U.S. soldier's point of view in the act of killing.[71]

In the case of Fury, however, this rhetoric seems to be missing, or at least to be inverted. The various religious allusions presented in the film do not contribute to the impression of righteous destruction, but rather complements the *physical* charge the soldier has to undertake in order to function. Epitomizing moments of reflection and resistance, through the contrast of spirituality, the gun is not "resacrilized" but desacralized. Thus, Fury refuses to restore a mythical national narrative, and instead deconstructs it. More than that: the film dismantles the body of the soldier by first merging it with and eventually stripping it from its machinic armour. As the film's final shot suggests, what remains of the tank is a corpse, a lifeless part of the soldier's body, which he has to leave behind in order to regain his human existence. The aerial view we are confronted with therefore symbolizes loss and recuperation, a complex and tragic process of a physical unification with and the necessary separation from the machinery of war. After all, and beyond national or ideological narratives, the individual soldier maintains a problematic status of being both vector and object of warfare, which affects his body and corpography irreversibly – as it is formulated in Lebanon (Samuel Maoz, 2009), a recent Israeli war film: "Man is Steel. The tank is only Iron."

---

[70] A. Susan Owen, "Memory, War and American Identity: Saving Private Ryan as Cinematic Jeremiad," *Critical Studies in Media Communication* 19 (3), 2002, 249–282, here: 250.
[71] Owen, "Memory, War and American Identity," 269.

4 Dismembering War: Touch and Fragmentation in Anthony Mann's MEN IN WAR

In the preceding chapter, I outlined how combat films unfold as narratives of corpographic transformation. In OBJECTIVE, BURMA!, for example, the contradiction between a cartography-based vision of control of the battle zone and the actual disorientation caused by the somatic experience of battle constitute a crisis of sensory mapping, the feeling of losing control over the war zone due to a profound perceptual shock. FURY, for another example, demonstrates a continuous shift between the human and the mechanical body as the individual soldier's process of becoming a functional member of the corps. With FURY's focus on tank warfare, it becomes clear that the recruit has to attune and commit to the restricted space of the military vehicle – as he must to the corps – in order to benefit from its sensory enhancements – its instruments of vision and communication, its movement, its weapons. The tank becomes both claustrophobic prison and powerful armour, both suppressing and enhancing the human body. As such, it becomes a metaphor for the soldier himself, who, to fulfil the ideal of military masculinity, has to transform into a striking weapon himself, only to realize in agony that he is still vulnerable.

Examining the physical relationship between soldier and tank as depicted in FURY is another way of looking at cinematic modes of staging what Gregory describes as the "cyborg nature" of war. What he defines as a terrain "saturated with the debris of violent conflict" might as well comprise the transformed human body that is the "cyborg soldier" – a body torn between man and machine, an object and product of military violence. As Gregory writes in his article, "The Natures of War," with regard to the mechanized warfare of WWI, "some soldiers came to regard themselves as having become as 'un-natural' as the militarized, industrialized natures in which they were embedded."[1] In his second case study on the Western Desert, 1940–43, as a major theater of WWII tank and mine warfare, this condition is foregrounded even more, while the author emphasizes that, even then, "bio-physical entanglements still remained immensely powerful."[2] Despite the effects that dry heat, sand, and dust had on the soldiers, one important aspect of the desert warzone was a tactile one: the numerous minefields covering the landscape turned it into a touch-sensitive weapon, which I already discussed within the context of FURY.

---

[1] Gregory, "The Natures of War," 14.
[2] Gregory, "The Natures of War," 14.

What Gregory thus highlights is that, through the placement of mines, the landscape transforms into an invisible enemy, hiding a potential threat under its surface. In this case the soldier's close haptic relation to his immediate environment becomes an even more delicate matter, as he must mistrust the visible landscape itself while at the same time maintaining an even more intimate contact with his surroundings in order to detect a hidden threat – a mine, for example. This intensified sensuous navigation centred on the sense of touch is also a mode of self-exploration, or, according to Santanu Das, "the making and unmaking of subjectivity through the most elusive and private of the senses."[3] Das's study of WWI poetry and literature additionally demonstrates how tightly the individual sensory experience and memory of battle is bound to spatial metaphors and figurative verbs: in *Under Fire*, Henri Barbusse, for example, writes about the "pestilent atmosphere" of the trenches: "Your hands touch only the cold, sticky and sepulchral clay of the wall, which bears you down on all sides and enshrouds you in a dismal solitude; its blind and mouldy breath touches your face."[4] The tactile perception of the combat zone described in numerous poetic accounts of the Great War articulate the attempt to position oneself within an incomprehensible environment. With regard to poetic practices as such, this tactile experience is, above all, a way of remembering the otherwise inexpressible events of war. Images of touch and space – figurations of haptic geographies – function as symbolic renderings of and somatic connections to the past, whether they are presented in literature, or film. It is important to note, however, that this way of remembering is hardly an exact representation of historical facts but a process of creating something entirely new, an artefact of its own that combines and redefines recollections of incidents, experiences, feelings in the form of artistic expression. As Gaston Bachelard writes:

> The poetic image is not subject to an inner thrust. It is not an echo of the past. On the contrary: through the brilliance of an image, the distant past resounds with echoes, and it is hard to know at what depth these echoes will reverberate and die away. Because of its novelty and its action, the poetic image has an entity and a dynamism of its own; it is referable to a direct ontology.[5]

In this sense, cinematic corpography can be seen as an aesthetic strategy to create poetic images in film, to share sensuous, spatial experiences with the spectator, and to give shape to a "feeling" for the past. The depiction of touch and intimacy

---

[3] Das, *Touch and Intimacy*, 6.
[4] Barbusse, *Under Fire*, 278.
[5] Gaston Bachelard, *The Poetics of Space: The Classic Look at How We Experience Intimate Places*, trans. Maria Jolas. Boston 1994, xvi.

in a war film can therefore be regarded as a visceral link to a specific historical ground, which gains its historical value precisely through incorporating the physical memories of individual bodies that were once embedded in and interacting with their respective battle spaces. From a phenomenological perspective, corpography would correspond to what Bachelard, in psychological terms, once defined as "topoanalysis," a "systematic study of the sites of our intimate lives."[6] And he adds: "In the theater of the past that is constituted by memory, the stage setting maintains the characters in their dominant roles."[7]

Although Bachelard locates these spatial memories that make up an individual's subjectivity in domestic places, the intimacy and sensuous intensity experienced in times and spaces of war bears a comparable "topoanalytical" potential, making the past reverberate through a character's sensorial navigation of filmic space, and through the spectator's relatable viewing experience. WWII combat films of the 1940s and 50s, however, unlike the "memory films" of WWI rememoration, are rooted in the present. Striving to render the respective battle actions depicted as historical moments of restoring or preserving old values, they show soldiers in the process of charting a presumably "savage" territory by way of corpography and symbolic acts of sacrifice for future generations (as opposed to the "lost generation" of WWI). This representational shift once again points to the fact that images of war define and are defined by our cultural understanding of war, which, in turn, is shaped by specific historical contexts.

The Korean War film, however, conveys yet another variant of the expressive themes I have charted before. As the war itself was both too close to the end of WWII and overshadowed by fears of an atomic Third World War, at least two major cultural phantasms dominating 1950s America found their way into the combat genre: techniques of mobilizing the past for the sake of stabilizing social ideas, and uncertainties concerning the immediate future. As effects of McCarthyism and the so-called "Communist Scare," as well as America's "crusade for freedom,"[8] these figurations of confinement posed existential questions that were eventually negotiated within several cinematic genres. But although much has been written on the ideological implications of 1950s science fiction, or film noir, war films of the time

---

[6] Bachelard, *Poetics of Space*, 8.
[7] Bachelard, *Poetics of Space*, 8.
[8] The "crusade for freedom" served as the central trope of U.S. Cold War rhetoric that heavily influenced Hollywood filmmaking of the time. Democracy's spiritual and material values were supposed to be spread to doubtful Americans and the uninitiated overseas. However, as Tony Shaw points out, "overt preaching had to be avoided if possible, lest it make America appear absolutist. Allegorical techniques were one way of avoiding this, by encouraging audiences to imbibe the message subconsciously" (Tony Shaw, *Hollywood's Cold War*, Edinburgh 2007, 105).

still lack critical and scholarly attention in this regard[9]. The Korean War film, so it seems, is either qualified as an annex of the WWII combat movie, or as a set of films framed by other dominant genres, for example the family melodrama.[10] Yet this hybridity of the Korean War film testifies to a general representational crisis of the early Cold War, whereby ideological uncertainties become manifest in the films' depictions of protagonists and antagonists, motifs, and attitudes toward military conflicts. Standing between genres, and, above all, standing in the shadow of the established WWII combat film, the Korean War film marks an interesting development within its own genre as it incorporates different historical reference points. This hovering between various cultural purposes and media frameworks, however, ultimately gave way to some profoundly existentialist, and overtly cynical tales of war, one of them being Anthony Mann's MEN IN WAR (1957). As I will demonstrate in what follows, the film treats warfare as a system of interacting spatial, physical and mental confinements – which not only testifies to a shift in the audiovisual representation of war in the 1950s, but also reflects on the Korean War's problematic status in American history and culture. By means of its cinematic language, MEN IN WAR articulates the corporeal constriction of its characters, and of the representation of war itself.

4.1 The Forgotten Subgenre: The Korean War Film of the 1950s

Within the context of U.S. history, the Korean War (1950–53) is also known as the "Forgotten War." Retrospectively, it might have been regarded as a less momentous conflict, as it was temporally framed by the preceding Second World War and the subsequent Vietnam War, while it has also been neglected by the film industry from the very beginning. There are, up to today, relatively few feature films about the Korean War, most of them being American B-pictures produced between 1951 and 1963.[11] Among those are two films that exploited the war's

---

[9] Notable exceptions are: Jeanine Basinger (with sub-chapters on the Korean War film in her book, *The World War II Combat Film*); Tony Shaw, *Hollywood's Cold War*; Rick Worland, "The Korean War Film as Family Melodrama: 'The Bridges at Toko-Ri' (1954)," *Historical Journal of Film, Radio and Television* 19 (3), 1999, 359–377; Charles S. Young, "Missing Action: POW Films, Brainwashing and the Korean War, 1954–1968," *Historical Journal of Film, Radio and Television* 18 (1), 1998, 49–74.
[10] Cf. Worland, "The Korean War Film as Family Melodrama."
[11] In his Korean War Filmography, Robert J. Lentz lists a total of 91 English language features released between 1951 and 2000. However, these also include many films that only partially deal with combat in Korea, or only use the war as a historical backdrop for their actual stories.

potential for visual spectacle to probe and promote new cinema technologies: DRAGONFLY SQUADRON (Lesley Selander, 1954), and CEASE FIRE! (Owen Crump, 1953). Shot and exhibited in 3D, they did not achieve a palpable impact on production or audience reception, let alone on the public recognition of the war itself.

In addition, the U.S. film industry continued to circumvent explicit portrayals of current conflicts by advocating other genres and past wars for political purposes. Tony Shaw, in his book *Hollywood's Cold War*, points out that, at the time of the Second World War, WWI had been instrumentalized for the purposes of cinematic mythmaking: Howard Hawks' SERGEANT YORK (1941) and Henry King's WILSON (1944), for example, "had mythologized Great War heroes in order to cast a positive light on the conflict against fascism."[12] During the 1950s, however, history provided an opportunity "to advance or critique contemporary political concerns on an unprecedented scale," as film audiences were "inundated with thinly and thickly camouflaged messages about the Cold War carried in movies set in the near or distant past."[13] Within the generic framework of the Western, for instance, spectators were confronted with left-wing and conservative views about the Cold War's ideological clash between East and West; Disney's films of the time were often set in the past and focused on the narrative tropes of religion, work, individualism, progress and patriotism – which was done, according to Disney himself, in order to "renew acquaintance with the American breed of robust, cheerful, energetic, and representative folk heroes."[14] Finally, and also to compete with television, Hollywood produced a large number of epic films and biblical films combining religion and history with Cold War messages.

Under these highly political conditions, war films – not surprisingly – continued to be supported by the U.S. Defense Department – a relationship fostered by the Motion Picture Production Office, which "ensured that the vast majority of these films depicted the armed forces and combat generally in a positive light."[15] If, upon revision, film scripts did not meet the Pentagon's expectations, the Defense Department could withdraw its assistance and object to the whole production. Shaw goes on to say that movies therefore "strongly endorsed the militarization of U.S. Cold War strategy in the 1950s and the development of a permanent national security state."[16]

Cf. Robert J. Lentz, *Korean War Filmography: 91 English Language Features through 2000*, Jefferson, NC 2003.
12 Shaw, *Hollywood's Cold War*, 112.
13 Shaw, *Hollywood's Cold War*, 112.
14 Shaw, *Hollywood's Cold War*, 113.
15 Shaw, *Hollywood's Cold War*, 202.
16 Shaw, *Hollywood's Cold War*, 202.

Yet at the same time this endorsement played into a general American post-WWII scepticism, a social climate of anxiety and violence. In the wake of Senator McCarthy's "Red Scare," ideological doctrines colonized American domestic spaces suggesting that Communism would infiltrate the United States, threatening the integrity of the country, and of every U.S. citizen. From an American perspective, the Korean War (1950–1953), although a large-scale military conflict with international involvement, was merely regarded as a "police action,"[17] an inevitable consequence of an already raging fight against evil political forces on multiple fronts. This simultaneous exaggeration and downplaying of the war's significance was on the one hand due to the underlying atomic threat which "necessitated keeping the war limited."[18] On the other hand, at the time the war broke out the United States was suffering a "crisis of national confidence": brought about by the burdens of globalism,[19] this crisis was addressed and processed by forms of cultural mythmaking, that is, by negotiating social and historical principles through various generic codes, while the war's progress in fact weakened said national confidence even more. Fighting Chinese Communist troops in Korea, U.S. forces had to retreat several times – a situation that was picked up in quite many Korean War films. Basinger summarizes as follows:

> In the Korean War film retreat is used as a basic story presentation, similar to, but slightly different from the old "last stand" variation of the World War II film. [...] In the same vein, the films present the new jet airplanes, the use of the helicopter, brainwashing, and the Mobile Army Surgical Hospitals (MASH units) as part of the storyline. The latter means that there are more Korean films about doctors and nurses than there are World War II films of that type.[20]

In sum, the characteristic movement for and in the Korean War film is one between the poles of advance and retreat, between raging battles and the excruciating paralysis of the wounded, between freedom and captivity. This, in turn, can not only be seen as a shift motivated by plot and theme, but also as an expression of the war film's struggle with representational codes and political stances of the time, and it is a reflection of the unpopularity of the Korean War as much as it is a turn towards the agony of the soldier as a crucial narrative point in combat movies. But, in the case of Korean War films, the heroic question of "why we fight" is often reformulated to a more existentialist "Why do we fight at all?"

---

[17] Basinger, *The World War II Combat Film*, 161.
[18] Worland, "The Korean War Film as Family Melodrama," 361.
[19] Young, "Missing Action," 50.
[20] Basinger, *The World War II Combat Film*, 161.

reverting to a message formulated in WWI films like ALL QUIET and J'ACCUSE: the final qualification of soldiers as a "lost generation."

While being products of a Hollywood-Pentagon alliance, war films of the 1950s homed in on the governing socio-political uncertainties of their time by establishing a more intimate perspective on warfare as such by foregrounding scenes of suffering and desperation, and by treating combat as a deeply unsettling, personal matter. More than simply re-interpreting past conflicts, the 1950s WWII film introduced mentally and physically tormented characters, who, although fighting for a specific country, do not seem to take any definite side in their military engagement and struggle with their own moral principles.

Robert Aldrich's ATTACK (1956), while telling the story of an American battle company fighting in 1944 Europe, gradually shifts its focus from the historical background of WWII to the hate, panic, and hysteria mutually felt by Lt. Costa (Jack Palance) and his cowardly superior, Cpt. Cooney (Eddie Albert), and thereby turns into a major psychological drama about human transgression. On a different level, THE BRIDGE ON THE RIVER KWAI (David Lean, 1957), despite loosely referring to the building of the Burma railway in 1942/43, centres on the physical and mental challenges British POWs have to endure in a Japanese prison camp – a story about the peripheral zones of war and its captives that is applicable to many wars, other times and places.

At the same time, another subset of 1950s war films, such as PRISONER OF WAR (1954) and BAMBOO PRISON (1954), openly portrayed the American experience of captivity during the Korean War. In this case the figure of the POW posed a challenge to the representation of heroic masculinity, extended by the difficulties of depicting the collaboration of American soldiers with the enemy.[21] Here the notion of brainwashing served as an important trope, as stories about mental torture in Korean prison camps filled the news. Avoiding this direct thematization, but nevertheless referring to psychological aspects of battle, Stanley Kubrick's experimental war film FEAR AND DESIRE (1953) epitomizes the theme of war as a state of mind, devoid of any specific historical context. The film, set in a fictional battle zone, begins with the following voice-over:

> There is war in this forest, not a war that has been fought, nor one that will be, but any war. And the enemies that struggle here do not exist unless we call them into being. For all of

---

[21] In sum, there were six U.S. feature films about imprisonment in Korea: PRISONER OF WAR (Andrew Marton, 1954), THE BAMBOO PRISON (Lewis Seiler, 1954), THE RACK (Arnold Laven, 1956), TIME LIMIT (Karl Malden, 1957), THE MANCHURIAN CANDIDATE (John Frankenheimer, 1962) and SERGEANT RYKER (Buzz Kulik, 1968). For further information, cf. Charles S. Young, "Missing Action."

them, and all that happens now, is outside history. Only the unchanging shapes of fear and doubt and death are from our world. These soldiers that you see keep our language and our time, but have no other country but the mind.

The grim world of war and its effects on the soldier's body and mind becomes manifest in the films' mise-en-scène – a claustrophobic cul-de-sac visualizing the protagonists' liminal moral state between civilian and military society, their paranoia and fatigue. On a sensory level, this psycho-spatial construct mainly results in a sense of compromised, deceptive vision on the one hand, and the need for the soldiers' wary yet reassuring haptic perception of their environment on the other. Only few films, however, turn this condition into a distinctly somatic (spectatorial) experience for characters and audience. Not only do the protagonists literally lose touch with the world around them, but the actual historical events the films are based on are increasingly put in the rear – so much so that the Korean War, when turned into the subject of a feature film at all, ultimately served as generic template for generic combat stories. As Jeanine Basinger notes: "In many ways, the Korean combat film is the World War II combat film set in Korea."[22] Referring to the narrative and iconographic similarities between these two generic subsets, she classifies the Korean War film as part of a "third wave" of WWII combat movies, a body of films focusing on the creation of filmed reality based on earlier films and history, with conscious use of genre.[23]

While I would disagree with Basinger regarding her overall reduction of Korean War films to rhizomes of Second World War narratives, the conscious use of genre that she mentions here is where Korean War films both conform to established combat movies and consciously diverge from them. In several cases, the central war plots were woven into genre mixtures, framed by romantic stories or elements of the family drama. Starring popular actors like Humphrey Bogart, Grace Kelly, William Holden, and Don Taylor, major studio releases include romantic elements, such as BATTLE CIRCUS (Richard Brooks, 1953), and THE BRIDGES AT TOKIO-RI (Mark Robson, 1954). While BATTLE CIRCUS did not get outstanding reviews – The New York Times called it a "dawdling and familiar personal drama" too often reverting to "pure redundant Hollywood"[24] – Robson's THE BRIDGES AT TOKIO-RI was in fact critically well received. As Bosley Crowther of *The New York Times* writes:

---

22 Basinger, *The World War II Combat Film*, 160.
23 Cf. Basinger, *The World War II Combat Film*, 140.
24 H.H.T., "Wartime Romance Flourishes in Korea," *The New York Times*, May 28, 1953.

> The questions put in this picture as to the point of the Korean war and the great personal sacrifices in it are not answered, nor are the answers sought. Its purpose is not to answer questions. Its purpose simply is to show the human and professional resolution, organization and sacrifice that prosecution of the war required. And it has fulfilled this purpose in a truly efficient and moving way. One of the best of modern war pictures is "The Bridges at Toko-ri."[25]

In his reading of TOKIO-RI, Rick Worland notes that the film in fact illuminates developments in both the war film and the genre of the family melodrama in the mid-50s. The combination of the two ultimately serves a certain political argument: more than at any point of WWII, war films had to "consistently display a much greater need to rationalize the necessity for American intervention to sceptical soldiers and their family members (acting as civilian population surrogates)."[26] Yet eventually the limited success of this effort only foreshadowed the struggle for public acceptance of another, much more actively rejected American military campaign: the Vietnam War.

The very process of forgetting the "Forgotten War" is mirrored in the fact that Korean War films seem to echo genre films about the Second World War in their dramatic constellations and battle scenarios instead of reflecting on the conflict's actual development: although it was divided into several phases, comprising military manoeuvres at sea, on land, and in the air, the films depicting the Korean War only focus on distinct events or frameworks (for instance, the fight for Pork Chop Hill, important United Nations actions and contributions, the U.S. Marine Corps' southward retreat – or "attack in another direction" – from Chinese forces) and centre on the foot soldier who, according to Robert J. Lentz, makes up "the heart and soul" of most Korean War movies.[27] In doing so, many works verbally or visually describe climate conditions the soldiers had to cope with – heat, humidity, and muddy roads. Although there had also been a phase of winter fighting in North Korea crucial for the war's strategic development, the number of productions portraying this period is relatively small. The reasons for this, however, are primarily production-related, as many Korean War films were shot in Southern California – a natural setting similar to South Korea in summer.

Yet, as a subgenre, the Korean War film is more than a mere continuation of the WWII combat film against the background of a different battle theater. Lentz also points out, that, in contrast to WWII combat films, many of the films' protagonists "face complex moral, political and military dilemmas with no

---

25 Bosley Crowther, "The Screen in Review; 'Bridges at Toko-ri' Is Fine Film of War," *The New York Times*, January 21, 1955.
26 Worland, "The Korean War Film as Family Melodrama," 363.
27 Lentz, *Korean War Filmography*, 11.

easy answers," openly questioning their deployment to Korea, their orders, and futures.[28] This aspect is an important one, as it is not only a matter of character development and dialogue, but a result of several stylistic elements and influences that make some Korean War films diverge significantly from traditional genre patterns. They are considerably less concerned with territorial advance and cartographic objectives on the part of U.S. soldiers. Rather, the battle space the protagonists have to navigate is palpably static and claustrophobic, and already visibly or invisibly occupied by the enemy – a status quo that is formulated as an irreversible condition and calls for defensive rather than offensive fighting strategies. As Lisa Dombrowski notes with regard to Samuel Fuller's THE STEEL HELMET (1951):

> With only twelve minutes of battle footage in two scenes, The Steel Helmet presents actual warfare as a sudden break in the monotony, an intermittent obstacle to the soldiers' primary goal – survival – rather than as the centrepiece of a narrative concerned with victory or defeat [...][29]

This struggle for survival suggests a poignant depiction of the individual soldier's battle against nature and his own physical limits, which in some films, results in an intensified cinematic corpography, and which found its most striking expression in Anthony Mann's MEN IN WAR: The film's pronounced corporeality, its portrayal of spatial, physical and mental confinements translates the representational confinements of the Cold War into aesthetic figurations of touch, intimacy and claustrophobia.

4.2 Forgetting to Remember: In and Out of Touch in MEN IN WAR

Similar to PORK CHOP HILL (1959) and Fuller's Korean War films, THE STEEL HELMET (1951) and FIXED BAYONETS! (1951), Anthony Mann's MEN IN WAR instrumentalizes the pressing stasis of the Korean War to create a character-focused drama rich in dialogue. But while especially Fuller's work has been discussed in depth, above all in connection with his own war experiences, Mann's contribution to the genre has been widely overlooked. According to the director himself,

---

28 Lentz, *Korean War Filmography*, 9.
29 Lisa Dombrowski, *The Films of Samuel Fuller: If you die, I'll kill you!*, Middletown, CT 2008, 43.

MEN IN WAR is one of his best works,[30] and, as Jeanine Basinger claims, one of the greatest war films ever made.[31]

The film is set in 1950 Korea, where a group of U.S. soldiers led by Lt. Benson (Robert Ryan) find themselves surrounded by Communist troops. When Sgt Montana (Aldo Ray), another American soldier who is accompanied by a shell-shocked colonel, coincidentally crosses their path, Benson confiscates his jeep and forces him to join the unit in order to leave the battle zone. Here, the ongoing rivalry between Benson and Montana causes a permanent conflict between perspectives and priorities. Ultimately, the two disillusioned soldiers have to reluctantly cooperate to survive enemy attacks. It is especially Montana, acting out of instinct and intuition, who happens to make the eventually right but morally questionable decisions, whereas the experienced Benson issues his orders mainly for the sake of authority. As the enemy is almost never visible in the film, the landscape enclosing the soldiers is all the more meticulously observed and evaluated by the two competing parties. Yet based on this Benson and Montana develop different perspectives and plans according to their respective priorities. The figure of the shell-shocked colonel is incapable of taking responsibility, or to make use of his authority. Every action therefore lacks superior qualification or sanction, and the variety of opinions and perceptions about the same natural environment results in a feeling of threat and insecurity.

Mann had made a name for himself as a director of westerns and noir films such as T-MEN (1947), DEVIL'S DOORWAY (1950), WINCHESTER '73 (1950), and MAN OF THE WEST (1958), and is known for "making the western a more psychological and overtly violent genre" by bringing "a noir sensibility to the western unlike any other director."[32] Yet, unlike the western, MEN IN WAR does not feature a vast territory to be crossed and conquered, but presents nature as a claustrophobic, deceitful manifestation of enemy forces, a scenery which is never subordinate to cartographic vision. As the film's characters have to navigate a landscape they cannot trust, they develop an intense tactile relationship to their immediate surroundings. Said mistrust, in turn, extends to a profound scepticism towards their own bodies and motivations, and ultimately reflects on the representational registers of cinema itself. Mann's heroes demonstrate how the intrinsic connection between self and world is troubled by the war as a state of emergency inasmuch

---

30 Mann quoted in Jean-Claude Missiaen, "A Lesson in Cinema," *Cahiers du Cinéma in English*, 12 (December 1967), 50.
31 Jeanine Basinger, *Anthony Mann*, Middletown, CT 2007, 179.
32 David Boxwell, "Anthony Mann," *Senses of Cinema* 24 (2003), http://sensesofcinema.com/2003/great-directors/mann_anthony/ (accessed March 25, 2016).

as they conform to the film's central dramaturgic pattern: an alternation of losing and re-establishing touch with the environment.

What these soldiers are shown struggling with is their bodies as part of and producing their sensible world. In Merleau-Ponty's words:

> Visible and mobile, my body is a thing among things; it is one of them. It is caught in the fabric of the world, and its cohesion is that of a thing. But because it moves itself and sees, it holds things in a circle around itself. Things are an annex or prolongation of itself; they are incrusted in its flesh, they are part of its full definition; the world is made of the very stuff of the body.[33]

Merleau-Ponty's idea of "flesh" and "fabric" testifies to the human subject's "embeddedness" in phenomenological, social, and historical contexts. Thus, any rupture within this fabric must result in a feeling of being "out of touch" with the world. It is this intermediary state of imbalance, of not knowing how and where to move, which is constitutive to the aesthetics of Mann's war film.

MEN IN WAR's filmic landscape facilitates what Jacques Rancière calls a "modality of the encounter,"[34] albeit in the exact opposite sense than he would have it. While Rancière, in his analysis of Mann's westerns, defines a means of building a community that is founded upon a "decision taken on the spot,"[35] MEN IN WAR is based on encounters and decisions that put the idea of a military community into question, that deconstructs and "dismembers" the corps itself – to the point where even individual bodies are fragmented. Mann's "modality of the encounter" not only affects the structure of the film's action, but also the skeletal frame of its narrative. Rancière elaborates how the director deploys two different forms of constructing "episodes" in his Westerns, one of which plays on their different intensities, the other on their similarities for the sake of continuity.[36] That is, while certain scenic compositions can only be defined through the ways they relate to one another in unfolding a dramatic story, other scenes are "closed in on themselves and yet invaded by parasite temporalities," they are "moments of rest that are anything but peaceful."[37] In MEN IN WAR, too, we find these two kinds of episodes – each one embodying and completing the film's idea of a fable, a universal tale about "men in action" who are facing danger even in moments of supposed relaxation. Another aspect of Mann's cinema described by Rancière

---

33 Maurice Merleau-Ponty, "Eye and Mind," in *The Merleau-Ponty Aesthetics Reader: Philosophy and Painting*, ed. Galen A. Johnson. Evanston, IL 1993, 121–149, here: 124–125.
34 Jacques Rancière, *Film Fables*, trans. Emiliano Battista, London / Oxford 2006, 81.
35 Rancière, *Film Fables*, 81.
36 Rancière, *Film Fables*, 83.
37 Rancière, *Film Fables*, 83.

has to be re-evaluated, however: a crucial feature of Mann's westerns that results from both their episodic nature and their respective modalities of the encounter is their ostentatious principle – how everything they show is organized around the gaze of the hero: "The hero [...] displays the constancy of someone who's completely in control of the action of the film. If he is parsimonious with his words, it is because he has made his whole body into the narrative voice that gives body to the story."[38]

MEN IN WAR is organized in a fundamentally different way. As the story does not have an outstanding hero who is in control of the action, it is the body of the film that is made into the controlling instance of the story, directing and fragmenting the bodies of both its characters and spectators. In this regard, another critic's remarks about landscape in Mann's westerns might be closer to the formal-aesthetic concept of MEN IN WAR than Rancière's observations on the director's narrative and enunciative modalities. In an article for a 1956 issue of *Cahiers du Cinéma*, André Bazin notes:

> If the landscapes that Anthony Mann seems fond of are sometimes grandiose or wild, they are still on the scale of human feeling and action. Grass is mixed up with rocks, trees with desert, snow with pastures and clouds with the blue of the sky. This blending of elements and colours is like the token of the secret tenderness nature holds for man, even in the most arduous trials of its seasons. In most westerns, even in the best ones like Ford's, the landscape is an expressionist framework where human trajectories come to make their mark. In Anthony Mann it is an atmosphere. Air itself is not separate from air and water. Like Cézanne, who wanted to paint it, Anthony Mann wants us to feel aerial space, not like a geometric container, a vacuum from one horizon to the other, but like the concrete quality of space. When his camera pans it breathes.[39]

A tale of fatal and existential decisions, MEN IN WAR's allegorical character is already heralded at the very beginning of the film, when a title card reads the following quote: "Tell me the story of the foot soldier and I will tell you the story of all wars." Two aspects of embodiment are evident here: the quote itself suggests that the individual soldier incorporates a universal war narrative (which makes men and wars exchangeable factors). Secondly, the film itself seems to address its spectator through several bodiless but helmeted heads hovering in the background of the title card and facing the camera. The simultaneous threat and shell shock they seem to symbolize is reinforced by the film's first elliptic panning shot along a site of destruction: a bombed-out jeep, smoking grasslands, soldiers

---

38 Rancière, *Film Fables*, 80.
39 André Bazin, "Beauty of a Western [1956]," *Cahiers du Cinéma, Vol. 1, The 1950s: Neo-Realism, Hollywood, New Wave*, ed. Jim Hillier, London 2005, 165–168, here: 167.

dispersed across the hollow like pawns on a chessboard. Strangely post-apocalyptic, the scenery transmits a feeling of disorientation and claustrophobic stasis that points to both the presence and absence of battle. Basinger notes that "[a]lthough *Men in War* is shot on location in a real landscape, "Korea, September 6, 1950," is a door that opens to a house of horrors, and he who enters never again knows exactly where he is or why he's there."[40] Indeed, the exterior space we are presented with seems to take the form of an otherworldly indoor structure, a spatial moment frozen in time, only coming alive through the movement of the camera, which in itself is more of a scanning motion than a firm establishing shot. The film's cinematography, in fact largely resembles the visual style of a horror thriller in setting up a play between strictly limited vision and vast, deserted spaces, a "pattern of tension and release," as Basinger calls it:

> The compositions and camera movements repeatedly reveal danger in the landscape in the typical Mann style. The audience seldom has a view of the larger landscape, but, like the soldiers themselves, is kept close in the immediate space of the conflict without knowing what – other than danger – is really out there. The film establishes a realistic sense of the ordinary man's war. He never has the big picture.[41]

The director's approach to war and the war film genre is fundamentally different from the way he stages his epic films. Mann, who had already directed part of Mervyn LeRoy's QUO VADIS (1951), later realized EL CID (1961) and THE FALL OF THE ROMAN EMPIRE (1964), where he sets up a cinematographic interplay of filmic landscapes and sheer duration to express the stories' monumental scale. In fact, it is especially the title sequence that, in relation to the voice-over introduction, builds on a spatialization and compression of time. As Tom Conley observes for THE FALL OF THE ROMAN EMPIRE:

> The effect of the long span of time denoted in the title finds the moment in which the voice-over states that it is taking place. The slow and somber panoramic conflates a long elapse of time into a crepuscular landscape that extends before our eyes. Duration is shown as protracted motion across a landscape.[42]

In the opening shot of MEN IN WAR, however, the duration of the camera's circular movement implies that the story about to unfold consists of repetitive and inescapable situations taking place again and again within the general narrative

---

40 Basinger, *Anthony Mann*, 171.
41 Basinger, *Anthony Mann*, 177–178.
42 Tom Conley, "The Fall of the Roman Empire: On Space and Allegory," in *The Epic Film in World Culture*, ed. Robert Burgoyne, New York / London 2010, 144–160, here: 148.

of war. What Mann captures in this scene is not history but the experience of the present moment in all its tactility and physicality, a "making-of-the-world."

All this is already laid out in the shot's materiality: a military jeep's corroded metal, trees and grasses slightly shaken by the breeze, different layers of smoke rising in the middle ground and background of the landscape, human figures positioned in various distances to the camera, a final close-up of a soldier whispering into his radio set behind thick blades of grass – these elements turn the site into an ostentatiously haptic scenery calling for an intensified tactile behaviour on the part of the film's characters. In numerous close-ups, the camera catches the soldiers touching and scratching their faces, magnifying their beard stubble and drops of sweat on their skin. More than being signs of fatigue these gestures and bodily reactions point to a palpable tension, whereby the surfaces of bodies and objects communicate an omnipresent unsettledness and threat characterizing both the story and the formal structure of the film.

Mann thus articulates by means of shot size and editing what is a foot soldier's elemental apprehension of the battle zone: a both necessary and precarious exploration of space. Within the context of his study, "The Natures of War," Gregory makes the point that the close tactile connection between body and landscape at once limits and extends the soldier's field of mobility. He quotes Australian author Frederic Manning, who writes about his wartime experiences in his 1929 novel, *The Middle Parts of Fortune*:

> [E]very nerve was stretched to the limit of apprehension. Staring into the darkness, behind which menace lurked, equally vigilant and furtive, his consciousness had pushed out through it, to take possession, gradually, and foot by foot, of some 40 or 50 yards of territory within which nothing moved or breathed without his knowledge of it. Beyond this was a more dubious obscurity, into which he could only grope without certainty. The effort of mere sense to exceed its normal function had ended for the moment [...][43]

Corpography, in this case, is not only a necessary strategy of spatial orientation in the event of fighting; moreover, it causes an amplification of the senses due to uncertainty, a foreboding rather than an effect of danger. The fragmentary and close framing of space in MEN IN WAR adds to the impression of constant tension, of settings that are always about to be disturbed and eventually disrupted, even when they look plainly peaceful.

A central scene of the film builds on the very interplay of tension and release Basinger ascribes to MEN IN WAR, whereby space is destabilized through a modulation of surface and depth, thereby inducing a sense of heightened corporeality.

---

43 Frederic Manning, *The Middle Parts of Fortune*, London 2014 [1929], 224.

One of Benson's soldiers, Sgt. Killian (James Edwards), goes on patrol to keep an eye out for the hidden enemy. Early on, the camera's point of view can be identified as that of Korean soldiers lurking in the grass, carefully watching Killian's every move. In addition, extreme low-angle shots frame him from below, suggesting a blind angle in Killian's field of vision, a crouching danger he literally overlooks. As he sits down next to a few blooming flowers to take a rest, the two Korean soldiers slowly dissolve from the bushes they were hiding in and make their way towards Killian, which, in broad daylight, induces a sense of horror. By means of a vectorial montage technique, an almost rhythmic pressure is now imposed on the personal space Killian inhabits: while the low-angle camera seems to close in on him in several shots, the intercut enemy soldiers are performing horizontal movements, thereby condensing the filmic space to an inescapable cage.

Killian is further shown in alternating medium shots and close-ups when he takes off his helmet enjoying the seemingly peaceful moment. The delicate flowers he picks to decorate his helmet contrast the rough thicket, which, as the enemy quietly attunes to its structure through camouflage, transforms into a thoroughly hostile texture. Single branches and shrubs occasionally block the view; dry vegetation colonizes the image. In the parallel shots of Killian, however, certain parts of his body are singled out and isolated from the surrounding landscape – especially his face and his legs as he takes off one shoe to massage his foot. Overall, the heat of the day in which he visibly finds release and relief becomes manifest in the soldier's body language – a treacherous release corrupted by the oncoming attack Killian does not expect. The fact that the spectator knows about the approaching menace creates suspense and provokes a friction between affective conditions (ease and tension) and spaces (on-screen and off-screen) – once again a collision of two diverging perceptions of the same situation, and an almost Eisensteinian effect of tonal montage. The scene, devoid of any noticeable musical score, reaches its dramatic climax when Killian is shown from behind (the enemy's point of view). The head of one Korean soldier slowly emerges from below the frame, so close to the camera that it actually fills and blurs the whole image. Here, Basinger recognizes a certain pattern used throughout the film that concerns both its narrative and editing style: huge, disembodied close-ups are always followed by moments of extreme violence:

> As the danger the men of the patrol face increases, their space decreases and seems to close in around them. They are seen cut off from one another as well as from any room in which to maneuver or escape. This use of intense close-ups increases just before moments of extreme violence, which burst out into an action sequence. In matched form, the actors seem to burst out of their enclosing frames to gain space, and thus, momentarily, safety.[44]

---

44 Basinger, *Anthony Mann*, 171.

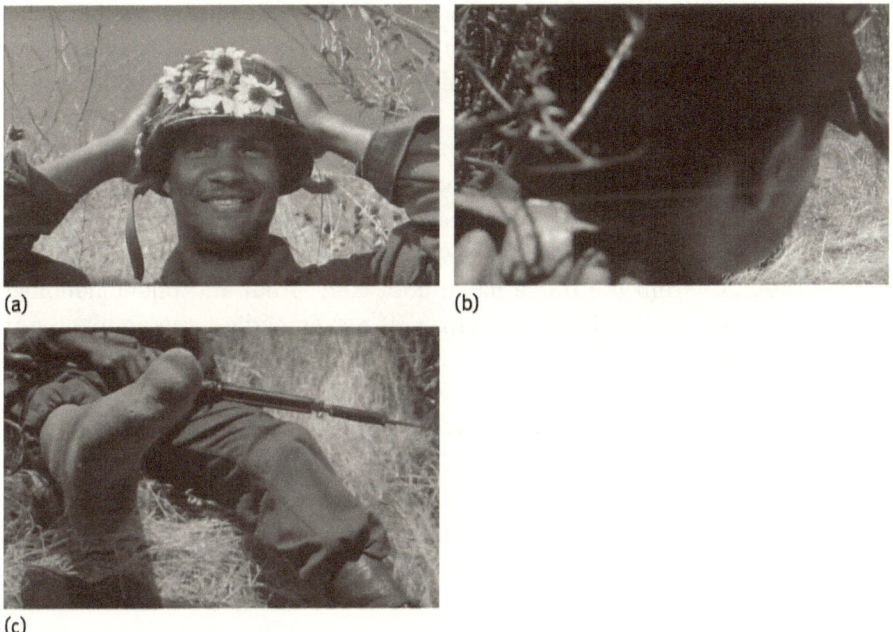

Figure 15: Killian's death.

And she concludes:

> The point is made that, during war, personal space is so limited for any one soldier that at any moment it can be seized by an alien. All any one soldier ever has is his personal space – thus the stressing of intense close-ups – but that, too, can be taken from him suddenly if he makes the mistake of relaxing and not realizing that the space around him, immediately outside his body, is full of peril.[45]

This, again, stresses the unstable relationship between the soldier's body and his environment, as well as the ever-paranoid concern about an invasion of his personal space. Killian's actual death adds to this conception, as it is technically kept off-screen. Indicated through a last close-up of his trembling and finally stiffening foot, this ultimate violent act takes no concrete shape, and instead allows for the spectator's own imagination of manifold cruelties (see Figure 15). Taking Basinger's analysis into account, the insertion of close-ups before an outbreak of violence effectively entails a juxtaposition of limited spaces – the soldier's personal space and the close-ups of his body – as what

---

45 Basinger, *Anthony Mann*, 172.

Béla Balázs would call "the film's true terrain."[46] It is this terrain, the potential of the close-up to incorporate a film's entire dramatic conflict in just one image, which is designated and navigated by means of physical coordinates. And it is a thoroughly physical field that, in Gregory's words, produces a "somatic geography."[47]

In the case of MEN IN WAR, the spectator can apprehend this intensified corporeality as an aesthetic experience which is fundamentally grounded in the film's mise-en-scène. That is, the way Mann chooses and relates objects to one another within the frame has a both conceptual and phenomenological purpose: Killian's helmet symbolizes, if not embodies, the ambiguity of war, the deceitfulness of the material world, and, as famously formulated in FULL METAL JACKET, the "duality of man." In Kubrick's film, Pvt. Joker wears both a helmet reading "Born to Kill" and a peace button, cynically suggesting what he calls "the Jungian thing," that is, the oftentimes conflicting co-existence of the collective unconscious and the personal unconscious. Indeed, as the individual soldier, due to professional duty, must act out collective ideas while suppressing his own, the symbol of the helmet perfectly articulates this antagonism in demonstrating what warfare is – and what it is not – about: although the helmet is part of a soldier's uniform, it does not guarantee protection. A sign of – rather than a shield from – battle, the helmet paradoxically emphasizes physical vulnerability, as it is often staged as a soldier's "unnatural" addendum, shielding his body but never making him bulletproof.[48] Hence, the flowers Killian applies to his helmet mirror the softness of the soldier, of the person wearing it. Marvelling at the remains of beauty in a precarious environment, Killian wears the blossoms like charms to keep off the harbingers of death and destruction – an iconic scene that not only reoccurs in several variations of the war film genre, but one that can be found in numerous firsthand accounts of battle. For his article, "The Natures of War," Derek Gregory has in fact compiled a few telling extracts from soldiers' writings about their experiences in the Vietnam War. Some of them endorse the "precious moments of relief and even of redemption."[49] in a "landscape of hopelessness."[50] As

---

46 Balázs, *Early Film Theory*, 38.
47 Cf. Gregory, "The Natures of War," 41.
48 Cf. Torsten Gareis, "Put your helmet on! Der Helm im amerikanischen Kriegsfilm," in *Mobilisierung der Sinne: Der Hollywood-Kriegsfilm zwischen Genrekino und Historie*, ed. Hermann Kappelhoff, Cilli Pogodda, David Gaertner, Berlin 2013, 345–382, here: 348.
49 Gregory "The Natures of War," 36.
50 Cf. Nathaniel Tripp, *Father, Soldier, Son: Memoir of a Platoon Leader in Vietnam*, South Royalton 2010 [1996], 68.

Gregory observes, these delineations are comparable to literary depictions of WWI in that they "affirm the stubborn persistence of a pastoral nature."[51] Author John Delezen, for instance, describes the discovery of a wildflower near an abandoned fighting hole as follows:

> I remove the sweat soaked leather bush glove from my hand and drop to one knee to touch the delicate petals. My hand is caked with slippery mud, a mixture of red dust from Route 9 and sweat; the hand seems filthy and crude against the soft purple and white flower. I decide not to touch it; I do not want to spoil this last bit of beauty and purity that has somehow escaped the Devil's grasp [...] I want to take the flower with me but it will only wither and die in the heat.[52]

Delezen's account is strikingly similar to Mann's portrayal of Killian. He, however, takes the flowers, and has to die with them, his helmet bearing his grave decorations.[53] In this perspective, the seemingly pastoral environment is already an elegy for those who fall for its apparent innocence – yet it is a poetic image for the soldier's yearning for a positive, harmonic relationship between body and nature. Ultimately, the "duality of man" translates in MEN IN WAR as formally grounded Janus face: as a duality of hard and soft surfaces, of the optical and the haptic, it becomes manifest as an engagement of visual and corporeal elements. Similar to the titular steel helmet in Fuller's Korean War film, which bears a shot hole constantly reminding its protagonist of how close he was to being killed, Killian's helmet in MEN IN WAR communicates the tight bond between life and death as much as it becomes a relic of the dead soldier himself. It is the only remnant Benson can hand over to Killian's best friend and comrade Zwickley, as a painful signifier of his absence.[54]

The case of the helmet therefore supports my revision of Basinger's quote, her reading of MEN IN WAR as a visual concept rather than a recreation of the experience of war: although there is a predominant symbolic quality and a certain iconicity about it, and although it is merely an inanimate object of steel, the helmet all the more points to the vulnerability of the living body. It is a marker

---

51 Gregory "The Natures of War," 36.
52 John Edmund Delezen, *Eye of the Tiger*, Jefferson, NC 2003, 30.
53 Such treacherous headgear, as Torsten Gareis notes with regard to the sergeant's flower-bedecked helmet in THE BIG RED ONE (Samuel Fuller, 1980), is a both a symbol and a sign of death. Cf. Torsten Gareis, "Put your helmet on! Der Helm im amerikanischen Kriegsfilm," 349.
54 The way Zwickley inherits Killian's helmet recalls a scene from ALL QUIET ON THE WESTERN FRONT (Lewis Milestone, 1930), where the deceased Kemmerich's (Ben Alexander) boots are passed on from soldier to soldier. Here, however, the boots are a definitive jinx, as they bring death to everyone who wears them.

of the war film's corpography. That the helmet literally "survives" Killian's death and finds a new body in Zwickley further speaks for the notion of "dismembrance" pervading MEN IN WAR. Killian's death is precisely not rendered as a sacrifice for the greater cause, as he himself silently disappears from the cinematic (and potentially historical) stage, and part of his military identity is given to another soldier instead. Mann's film is in this regard quite close to Fuller's THE STEEL HELMET in that it treats the helmet as a symbol of criticism, an embodiment of "collisions and contradictions." In his article of the same title, Tony Williams interprets Fuller's conception of the helmet (worn by the film's protagonist, Sergeant Zack) as follows:

> Zack is essentially [...] a war orphan, after having miraculously escaped death when the bullet ricocheting inside his helmet was jettisoned and left a scar clearly visible on his forehead. The bullet in his helmet signifies a ricochet effect that foreshadows the overarching structure of the film. Rather than representing a linear-directed odyssey that reaches a certain goal, *The Steel Helmet* announces itself as a circular exploration of the collisions and contradictions within America that may never achieve resolution. This is also reiterated in the film's final title-card, "There is no End to this Story."[55]

Analogous to MEN IN WAR's opening credits, this "story of all wars" is a never-ending one. Accordingly, the helmets in both films represent the uniformity and tragic circularity of military conflict. But what MEN IN WAR highlights is that they are also to be seen as symbolic objects exhorting the unsettling emptiness, the gap left by the forgotten soldiers of a forgotten war; despite providing protection the helmets also conceal the many untold tales of the Korean War, stories lost in public insecurities and narrative genre mixtures – so much so that the fleeting images of foot soldiers who had fought in Korea eventually found a figurative portrayal in two installations of the Korean War Veterans Memorial in Washington D.C.: instead of being displayed as photographic images, they have been sandblasted into a polished granite wall which additionally reflects the image of a second element of the memorial, nineteen steel sculptures of soldiers on patrol. Ultimately, this almost paradoxical contrast between gravity and haunting immateriality applies to many American films about the Korean War, and to Mann's work in specific. What Steven Fore, referring to THE STEEL HELMET in his dissertation, calls a "disturbing subtext" disrupting and subverting audience expectations of the war movie genre is also what characterizes MEN IN WAR as a child

---

55 Tony Williams, "Collision and Contradiction: The Steel Helmet," *Senses of Cinema* 52 (2009), http://sensesofcinema.com/2009/cteq/collision-and-contradiction-the-steel-helmet/ (accessed March 25, 2016).

of its time. It is just as much a film of contradictions, "a very nervous film, an exercise in coping with a brave new world."[56]

4.3 Vectors, Bodies, and Blind Spots

The film's "nervousness" is in fact at its peak when Mann takes his time to introduce Benson's men as a group of individuals, in a scene shortly after Killian's death, which unfolds as a cascade of scattering sounds and movements. Not only does this sequence provide further images of physical confinement, it introduces a political subjectivity which maps the soldiers as both vectors and objects of military violence, as both vulnerable bodies and as "corporate bearers of a contingent (because temporary) enmity."[57] In other words, the spatial constrictions Mann's characters find themselves in also represent their confining role as cogs of a military apparatus.

The scene develops as follows: before the unit has to split up moving through enemy fire, the soldiers take cover by their jeep, which is visually structured as a montage of several alternating close-ups showing small groups and persons: three pairs (Benson and his radio operator, Sgt. Riordan; Montana and the Colonel; two soldiers on the left), a group of three soldiers in front of the vehicle, one soldier crouching under the jeep, and Killian's friend, Zwickley, trying to find shelter in the scrubs. Deploying a pattern of action and immediate reaction, the configuration is completed by a recurring medium shot of the entire unit, and a long shot showing heavy explosions in the distance in relation to the soldiers' physical responses – ducking, wincing, their faces stricken with fear. As Benson's troop is already divided by cinematic means, the spectator must anticipate a coming decimation of the group. It is only now that Benson reads out all his men's names one by one, before he sends them off through the shelling in pairs. Up to this point most of them have remained anonymous, which adds to the impression that we are in fact watching a credit sequence halfway through the film, a delayed introduction of the characters before they are called off into the smoke, and out of the frame, into their death – a sacrifice for their country, which, apart from being a narratological consequence, would be an essential element of the war film's mythopoetics. In other words, the soldier's death is a crucial part of the genre's

---

[56] Steven James Fore, *The Perils of Patriotism: The Hollywood Film as Generic and Cultural Discourse*, Doctoral Dissertation, University of Texas at Austin, 1986, 84.
[57] Derek Gregory, "Moving Targets and Violent Geographies," in *Spaces of Danger: Culture and Power in the Everyday*, ed. Heather Merrill, Lisa M. Hoffman, Athens, GA 2015, 256–296, here: 274.

historical dimension, its modes of remembering the past, and of grounding the legitimate privileges of the contemporary western citizen. As Kappelhoff writes with regard to a central argument made by Hollywood war films, "[t]he right of the individual to life, liberty, and the pursuit of happiness, this highest value of the political community, is secured and maintained through the sacrificial death of innumerable individuals."[58]

Mann seemingly prepares the audience for this apotheosis by combining two specific factors of genre-typical mythmaking: in order for the individual soldier to become an emblem of national sacrifice and tragic loss, it takes not only his actual name marking him as a civilian member of society, but, most importantly, his face, which provides said name with a physical identity. Thus, in having called out the soldiers' names and showing matching close-ups of their faces as "symbolically laden images of sacrifice."[59] Mann builds up to a melodramatic climax, making the spectator realize the men's inevitable and cruel fate of dying young. As Burgoyne writes, "like a hologram viewed from two different angles, the soldier appears both as victim, a youth about to be subjected to a meaningless death, and as a figure of national sacrifice, an emblem of national manhood whose death serves a meaningful purpose."[60] But while this ultimate sense of what Kappelhoff calls "devotional remembrance"[61] is a fundamental aspect of the WWII combat film, it is less developed in the Korean War film as such, as the conflict itself, as opposed to the Second World War, lacked a clearly defined purpose or meaning for the American nation. With MEN IN WAR, Mann plays on the genre's notion of remembrance, but he steers it into a direction which eventually does not leave much space for commemoration, as there are no casualties at this point. Instead of focusing on the soldier's sacrifice as an aesthetic figuration to remember the past and mourn the dead, Mann distinctly locates the action in the present moment and creates a real-time experience of the depicted situation for the spectator. More than any other sequence in the film, this scene relies on sound and rhythm, which synchronize moving bodies with the scattering landscape around them like a pulse.

As the enemy fires in patterns of three, the small groups have to run in between shelling. Over the course of approximately ten minutes each pair waits,

---

58 Hermann Kappelhoff, "For Love of Country: World War II in Hollywood Cinema at the Turn of the Century," (unpublished manuscript, referenced with permission of the author).
59 Kappelhoff, "For Love of Country," 3.
60 Burgoyne, "Generational Memory and Affect," 357.
61 Kappelhoff, "For Love of Country," 3.

then dashes towards the approaching fire, thus organizing the scene's rhythm of tension and release by shifting between stasis and movement. What would have been staged and edited way more dynamically in a classical combat film is laid out here as carefully drafted temporal structure that subtly turns a situation of pressure and inferiority into an equilibrium between visible soldier bodies and invisible enemy forces. Once again, as Bazin would note, landscape is no expressionist framework, no geometric container, but a concrete quality. In this scene, it is not so much the camera that breathes when panning, but the film pulsating when cutting back and forth between the soldiers and the threat awaiting them. In the end, however, none of Benson's men falls victim to the attacks, which makes each run seem like a mere physical response to each shelling, a necessary move within a potentially lethal competition: for several "rounds," three explosions are followed by two soldiers sprinting, and vice versa, thereby establishing a rhythmical balance between bodies and explosives. Finally, the four remaining men led by Benson make their way through the smoke, slowly pushing the ponderous jeep forward. They, too, stay uninjured, which, for both the characters and the audience, is rather unexpected, bearing in mind that Killian's death earlier in the film has been embedded in a moment of supposed relaxation. In spite of this temporary invulnerability, the soldiers still serve as both objects and vectors of war. In their rhythmical relation to the exploding shells, Benson's soldiers are rendered equal to destructive objects of warfare while they simultaneously function as targets in the line of fire. At the same time, in pushing forward and provoking additional bombing, they are one driving factor in a clash of antagonistic forces.

MEN IN WAR not only negotiates the war genre's characteristic dramatic conflicts on the level of dynamics and duration; more importantly, in each episode of the film, they become manifest as embodied experiences. The trope of the invisible enemy, the precariousness of quiet moments, the frightening tension and pressure of battle, as well as the opposition of human bodies and nature can be described as crucial elements of Kappelhoff's pathos scenes – as arrangements of narrative constellations and distinct affective qualities that both relate to the film's aesthetic deployment of somatic experience and address the spectator as expressive movements. Consequently, a later sequence of the film articulates on a purely physical level what is set up as a cartographic conflict in the classical combat film: the generals' perspective, the feeling of control connected to maps and military tactics, is replaced with a disorienting battle situation that calls for corpographic navigation instead.

What is scrutinized and fragmented in MEN IN WAR is not the Korean landscape but the soldier's body in relation to its natural environment. While Jean-Luc Godard once condemned the film's visual style as a recession of Mann's art "towards a purely theoretic schematism of mise en scène,"⁶² it is this schematism which makes up the director's unique cinematic way of interweaving textual and corporeal elements, a technique that enables both a navigation *through* and *of* the body. Although he does not directly mention MEN IN WAR, Willemen describes Mann's style as "cinematic writing" by means of camera movements, light, colour, the inscription of figures into landscapes, and multi-levelled deep-focus compositions – a writing that would generate images "echoed or re-doubled by the thematic structures of the plot."⁶³ This observation is very similar to Rancière's thoughts on the director's episodic style in that it acknowledges how each image serves as a miniature for the film's theme. However, Willemen's further elaboration on Mann's style underlines and enhances what Godard devalues as "theoretic schematism":

> The image and the figure in it are simply to be looked at, to be enjoyed as pure pictoriality. While the following drama generates the rationale for changing the images, the image-track itself provides endless variations/elaborations of that initial picture. When it has run the entire gamut available in the genre, the film closes with a return to that first image, not to stop the flow, but to reactivate it as a loop.⁶⁴

As for what concerns MEN IN WAR, and the concept of genre in general, Mann demonstrates how genre itself is created and developed as a loop of plots and iconographies. Once this idea is brought to the surface, little formal and narrative inconsistencies suffice to put a genre's established formula into question.⁶⁵ Willemen's reading marks a shift in critical analysis of Mann's work insofar as he focuses on the director's visual style as opposed to an auteurist interpretation based on thematic consistency. But the foregrounding of correlations between spectacle and theme in Mann's films is only one way to reframe them analytically, as it neglects the affective and somatic underpinnings of his cinema. The argument Willemen makes is that, in Mann's work, vision is a theme for itself which is pivoted on the look at the male figure: "The viewer's experience is predicated on the pleasure of seeing the male 'exist' (that is, walk, move, ride, fight) in or

---

62 Jean-Luc Godard, "SuperMann: Man of the West," in *Godard on Godard*, ed. and trans. Tom Milne, New York / London 1972, 116–120, here: 116.
63 Paul Willemen, "Looking at the Male: Anthony Mann," in *Framework: The Journal of Cinema & Media* 15–17, 1981, 16.
64 Willemen, "Looking at the Male," 16.
65 A similar observation has also been made for Fuller's THE STEEL HELMET. Tony Williams writes: "Not incidentally, *The Steel Helmet* was directed by an actual combat veteran of the previous conflict refusing to "retread" conventions but instead ruthlessly exposing flaws within the combat genre and the America he dearly loved." Cf. Williams, "Collision and Contradiction."

through cityscapes, landscapes or, more abstractly, history."⁶⁶ However, Willemen goes on to say that this look produces an anxiety rooted in the images themselves, and expressed through fragmented lighting, bizarre camera angles, or contorted landscapes. This in fact supports a reading of MEN IN WAR as a vehicle for both the socio-political climate of his time and its immanent struggle with (or against) generic conventions. Yet, what Willemen does not mention is that anxiety, as an aesthetic emotion, exceeds the politics of looks and representation – it is an affective experience tied to the films' interlocking of space and body, that is, its corpography. What is more, the pleasure of looking at the male is further troubled in the case of MEN IN WAR: the soldiers do not *exist* in history but the viewer rather watches them *disappear* in the blind spots of history – a fundamental reversal of the war film's pathos of remembrance.

Combining these different levels of anxiety with the combat genre's politics of the body, one could argue with Robert Burgoyne that the process of disappearing into history alludes to the war film's notion of "the body at risk." With regard to Kathryn Bigelow's THE HURT LOCKER (2008), Burgoyne writes:

> Although the spectacular and harrowing combat scenes of previous war films – the night patrol and the trenches, the bombardment and the assault, the mass choreography of battle and the gruesome intensity of individual combat – are missing, the film nevertheless defines the drama of the body at risk in a way that reinforces the traumatic cultural history embedded in the genre. The film's almost anthropological interest in violence as a form of embodied experience and imagination begins to read as a traumatic acting-out.⁶⁷

In MEN IN WAR, this anthropological interest comes out strongest when the actual risk the soldiers' bodies are put into is emphasized through tactile (camera) movements and an intimate cinematography, when they are shown shifting and crawling through a compressing natural environment. Such a scene is the forest sequence (halfway into the film): the camera remains in a lower position, condensing the space in which the soldiers can move, and literally visualizing the cumbersome march they have to undertake – above them shady tree tops, below them bumpy soil and dry leaves, around them ashy logs as sallow as the men themselves. One of the soldiers, Sgt. Lewis (Nehemiah Persoff), suddenly trips over a root and makes an accidental yet vital discovery: carefully examining the ground with his knife, he detects a mine hidden under a layer of leaves. Benson, who rushes to the spot immediately, uncovers the explosive device – we see a close-up of his hand brushing away the leaves

---

66 Willemen, "Looking at the Male," 16.
67 Burgoyne, "Embodiment in the War Film," 15.

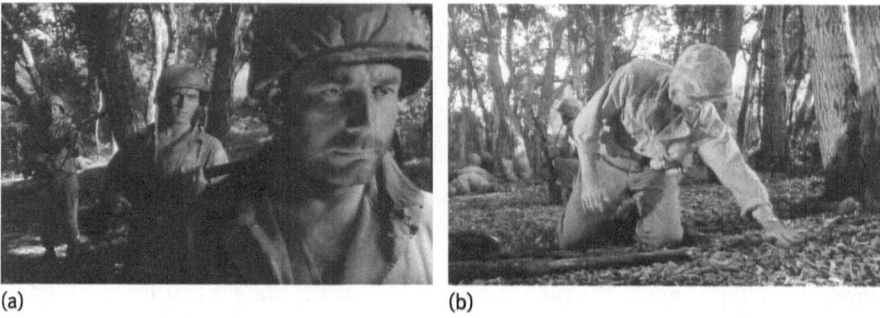

(a) (b)

Figure 16: Intimate cinematography.

around the detonator. Of all narrative episodes MEN IN WAR comprises, this scene, and this moment in particular, might be the most haptic one. It epitomizes, in its general pace, mood, and spatial framing, how a battle zone turns into a touch-sensitive weapon. What it highlights is the fundamental perceptual change and loss of control that takes place when a soldier is deprived of his trust in his natural surroundings. In his Vietnam War memoir, *A Rumor of War*, Philip Caputo explains how mines and booby-traps turned "an infantryman's world upside down":

> The foot soldier has a special feeling for the ground. He walks on it, fights on it, sleeps and eats on it; the ground shelters him under fire; he digs his home in it. But mines and booby traps transform that friendly, familiar earth into a thing of menace, a thing to be feared as much as machine guns or mortar shells. The infantryman knows that any moment the ground he is walking on can erupt and kill him; kill him if he's lucky. If he's unlucky, he will be turned into a blind, deaf, emasculated, legless shell.[68]

It is this impending obliteration of the senses that motivates a war film's intensified rendering of sensuous perception. The mined forest in MEN IN WAR in fact causes an amplification of the characters' vision, hearing and tactile sense. After the first mine has been detected, word about it spreads from one soldier to the next (see Figure 16). The men form a line into the depth of the image, and, without any physical movement, the whispered "mines" measures the filmic space acoustically, incorporated again and again by another soldier. Each man's reaction to the information is clearly visible – their worried faces, their gulping, their nervous gestures. In an outbreak of hysteria, Lewis runs all the way back, past his comrades, and is ultimately hit – and killed – by a mine.

---

68 Philip Caputo, *A Rumor of War*, New York 1977, 288.

In what follows the film takes its time studying the soldiers' cautious movements, and especially the landscape around them, as Montana expresses his feeling of being watched. The camera scans the canopy of treetops above them and finally focuses on a trunk next to the troop. Almost merging with the bark, a hand becomes visible. It belongs to a Korean soldier perched on the tree's main crutch, ready to jump down. When he does so, the haptic tension between the soldiers and their environment bursts out in another energetic movement. Up to this point, Mann has operated several formal strategies to make nature and human enemy seem indistinguishable from one another. With the Korean's attack on Montana, however, he also activates a level of moral judgment. That is, the question of trust and mistrust in nature thus becomes a question of trust in a fellow human being and is once again negotiated via the "modality of the encounter" – an encounter between enemy soldiers, and between Benson and Montana as competing decision makers. Their differences then become insurmountable towards the end of the film, when Montana impulsively kills three soldiers who pretend to be American but turn out to be Korean enemies. Benson condemns him for shooting without having seen their faces, whereupon Montana replies: "I can smell them." It is here where sensuous intuition and inhabitation of space takes a questionable racist turn, which is immediately rejected by Benson: "God help us if it takes your kind to win this war." Out of a certain political ideology, this "kind" commissions their sensory compass not to navigate through perilous territory, but to follow and destroy the physical traces of the Other – a tipping point where corpography as a way of apprehending the war zone changes into turning the enemy into a lower life form, and to the intention of deliberately transforming militarized nature into an imaginative geography where survival is substituted by cold murder (as confirmed by the family photo Benson pulls out of the dead Korean soldier's pocket). Montana has become a warrior who cannot be resocialized, a man who cannot return to civilian life because he "literally fuses with his desire to fight."[69]

In the end, the film offers no possible future nor a space "beyond" the final battle zone. When two of Benson's soldiers look out for Korean gun posts in the distance, the camera zooms in on a cliff without actually revealing the enemy's identity. Furthermore, there is not a single reverse shot that would represent the opponent's point of view, or a somewhat omniscient position, which would help establish the space given. The camera thus disables a clear orientation within the area and instead puts an emphasis on the limited view of Benson's men without ever really subjectifying it. More than just adopting the soldiers' perspective, the

---

[69] Cf. Empirische Medienästhetik, "Injustice and humiliation / moral self-assertion."

camera frames their bodies up close, almost besieging them and diminishing their free moving space. Finally, in an intricate montage of even more spatially restricted shots, not only the image space itself is condensed to a minimum, but a concrete "off" seems to be missing completely.

It is here where MEN IN WAR truly becomes an anthropological study, a film that employs the body of its characters and its own body as an aesthetic construct in order to perform a calculated revision of warfare. It seems that the film itself, rather than its director, analyses the inner and outer spaces of battle by dissecting their respective ambiguous layers, by laying bare their tactile qualities and object relations. This is what ultimately makes up its universal narrative, a tale of the foot soldier, as it repeats itself from war to war. In Mann's case, the Korean War itself conforms to its reputation: the "Forgotten War" is not *re*membered – it is *dis*membered, stripped from concrete historical references in the very moments a historical context is suggested. By alluding to and cutting off certain staging patterns known from classical war films, MEN IN WAR translates the very process of forgetting into its own cinematic language. Thus, despite Mann's experience and expertise in directing historical films, his war film is far from being epic, and barely historical in the narrower, topical sense, as it is not putting its plot in any palpable relation to the Korean War, or to any verifiable event or sources connected to this conflict. Although one could argue that many war films are in fact merely loosely based on actual historical events, they still embrace and work on the mythopoetics of war as both crisis and necessity of nation building (as has been demonstrated in the preceding chapters). MEN IN WAR, on the other hand, focuses on the individual body as not being part of a national goal and community, but as a body struggling with existential anxieties, confinements, and instabilities that prevent the combatant from taking sides – as it is torn between being a vector and an object of warfare.

Although the highlighting of sensory experience beyond vision is not unusual for the war film, Mann's reinterpretation of generic codes through emphasizing the soldier's corporeal interaction with a surrounding "trickster nature"[70] is not only a way of mapping cinematic space; it also reveals the ambiguous nature of Hollywood's genre system at the time of the Cold War. The implicit yet schematic foregrounding of this metaphor makes the Korean War fade into the background of its political and cultural implications. Similar to the film's beginning, which, according to Basinger, opens the door to a house of horrors, its ending opens the door to oblivion, to a Dantean circle, where the remains of war and its combatants only prevail in the memory of those who

---

[70] Gregory, "The Natures of War," 4.

knew them in person. "I remember men I knew, men in war," as the lyrics of the credit song tell us. The only remaining connection to the past established in and through the film is a corpographic one, the physical contact between body and space, whereas the narrative frame not only stays behind, but turns into a symbolic specter haunting its own genre.

5 Uncharting Territories: The Vietnam War's Shattering of the Senses

After a major decline in the production of films about the Korean War, the American combat genre notably reverted to cinematic treatments of WWII, foregrounding significant European battle scenarios. In contrast to the small number of "A-Movies" concerning Korea, the 1960s saw the production of many American and British war films starring renowned actors and directors, which now focused on the distinct perspective divergence between generals and foot soldiers, but putting both into a defined, mapped-out historical framework.[1]

Meanwhile, however, another much more controversial war was raging in Southeast Asia – a conflict that, similar to the Korean war, had been justified as a necessary means of preventing the spreading of communism according to the so-called "domino theory." The Vietnam War as the first thoroughly televised military conflict (which is why it is called the "living room war") became fertile soil for the American "home front" which eventually turned its dubious nature and questionable outcome into a public matter. On a par with (often graphic) reports from Vietnam were images of student movements and civil rights protests that provoked divided opinions about, and incongruent perceptions of, the war. Nevertheless, or rather because of this, Hollywood strictly avoided the topic (an exception being John Wayne's THE GREEN BERETS from 1968), until late-1970s war films like THE DEER HUNTER (1978), GO TELL THE SPARTANS (1978), THE BOYS IN COMPANY C (1978), and APOCALYPSE NOW (1979) eventually broke the silence about combat in Vietnam.

Ultimately, the at times confusing heterogeneity of the media landscape would motivate a refiguration of the senses into unexpected and unbalanced zones, a disenchantment of war and its representational codes. War had become a state of self-reflection, a condition of rethinking one's position in and relation to the world, whether for the combatants themselves or the distributors and consumers of battle images, as they all belonged to a generation influenced by what was beginning to develop into a military entertainment complex. Less a side-effect of postmodernism and more a phenomenon of post-WWII media practices, the perception of war in the 1970s was built upon viewing habits and generic stereotypes perpetuated through television culture – a condition which in fact complicates the question of representation, and of both sensuous and cognitive apprehension

---

1 This becomes especially evident in THE LONGEST DAY (Andrew Marton et al., 1962).

in the first place. As Philip Beidler (rather cynically) notes, the "sense-making faculties" of the generation fighting in Vietnam had been informed by

> Golden-age TV: cartoons, commercials, cowboys, comedians and caped crusaders, all coming across together at quantum-level intensity [...] child-world dreams of aggression and escape mixed up with moralistic fantasies of heroism beleaguered yet ultimately regnant in a world of lurking, omnipresent dangers and deceits – in sum, a composite high-melodrama and low-comedy videotape of the American soul.[2]

Following this statement, not only the U.S. soldiers deployed to Vietnam, but also those who wrote and made movies about the war simply had to take to an extreme the American experience of unreality and discontinuity which was made up of "isolated individuals, victims of a culturally conditioned alienation, estranged from external reality, from history, and from binding values."[3] Consequently, the films about Vietnam are not, or not only, to be conceived as renditions of the experience of disillusionment and disorientation in battle; rather, as I will argue, they articulate – in hyperbolic sounds and visions – how this disorientation is both a result and a symptom of media representation in the first place. More than any other earlier representations of combat, these films cannot be measured against the reality of war, as this reality itself had already been a thoroughly mediated experience.

It would seem logical to conclude that such history of media(ted), representation would alienate audiences from images of war rather than facilitating an intense sensory experience of combat. However, with regard to the media landscape surrounding the Vietnam War, the technological complexities and the transformations of narrative structures in 1970s popular culture, this conclusion would be a quite reductionist one. When Michael P. Clark, for instance, in his Benjaminian take on the Vietnam War, elaborates how visual media tend to reduce the physical immediacy between the representational artefact and the presence of the body,[4] his thesis actually obstructs any way of analysing the war film's affective and somatic registers. As Michael Wedel notes, post-classical war films in fact confront the spectator with the violent power of military technology, pushing the limits of subjective physical experience and breaking the rules of narrative continuity.[5] The fact that these films deviate from conventional codes of media representation is thus not to be mistaken with a sensuous distance from

---

[2] Philip D. Beidler, *American Literature and the Experience of Vietnam*, Athens, GA 1982, 11.
[3] James C. Wilson, *Vietnam in Prose and Film*, Jefferson, NC 1982, 101-02.
[4] Michael P. Clark, "The Work of War after the Age of Mechanical Reproduction," in *The Vietnam War and Postmodernity*, ed. Michael Bibby, Amherst 2000, 17–47.
[5] Cf. Wedel, "Körper, Tod und Technik," 83.

war in their patterns of staging. On the contrary: Benjamin's original conclusion that the mechanical reproduction of images would instil a false sense of omnipotence in their recipients[6] is precisely what is at stake in Vietnam War films, as it is in earlier combat movies. That is, the suggested omniscience that, according to Benjamin, is rooted in visual media's alteration of the viewer's relation to spatial distinctions corresponds to war cinema's "illusion of overview," which intensifies sensory perception rather than diminishing it. Yet, the typical Vietnam War film never sets up a contrast between continuity and chaos, or between cartographic and corpographic perspectives, in the first place. As I am going to show in this chapter, both THE BOYS IN COMPANY C and RESCUE DAWN as unique examples of American war films about Vietnam (and divided by almost thirty years), reject the aerial perspective as a signifier of overview and omnipotence, and instead assign their spatial coordinates to the senses of sound and touch from the very beginning. In doing so, they do not only respond to an overstraining of the senses through the chaotic, graphic, and often contradictory mediation of the war (as has been a common argument in the academic discourse), but they also turn against the media's partial attempt to justify and oversimplify military action in Vietnam. As in many other Vietnam films that treat war as a complex experience processed from within, sound and touch play a crucial role in both RESCUE DAWN and THE BOYS IN COMPANY C, countering the image as a signifier of visual apprehension and meaning.

5.1 Shattered Senses

The resolute rejection of cartographic narratives and objectives gives way to the Vietnam War film's discontinuities and forms of sensuous excess – a development originating in the many transgressions that were brought about by the war itself as shaping and being shaped by a mediated experience, or, in the words of Timothy Corrigan: "In both the war and its media coverage, the unique horror is the drama of contingencies, of the unpredictable violations of boundaries and spaces."[7] However, this overall excess can only be described as such if it articulates a turning against a certain order of representational codes, which in the case of Vietnam had been set up by television programmes and conventions of classical genre cinema – something Thomas Doherty refers to when he exemplifies

---

[6] Walter Benjamin, *Illuminations*, trans. Harry Zohn, New York 1969, 223.
[7] Timothy Corrigan, *A Cinema Without Walls: Movies and Culture After Vietnam*, New Brunswick, NJ 1991, 46.

Kubrick's FULL METAL JACKET as a "Vietnam War film in its mature stage, a stage whose distinguishing quality is its reliance on cinematic, not historical, experience."[8]

In fact, against the popular assumption that the Vietnam War was depicted in a thoroughly critical fashion, or as a nearly unfiltered stream of uncoordinated images, there is evidence that over a considerable period of time the central television news networks were quite affirmative towards America's military invention and tried to fit the war into a narrative framework. My own research on Vietnam news coverage in the U.S. has led me to believe that visual reporting on the conflict oftentimes even conformed to an affective logic known from the Hollywood war film. An exemplary analysis of late 1960s news material from television networks ABC, CBS, and NBC[9] revealed that several news items referred to certain "pathos scenes" constitutive for the war film's poetics of affect: scenes of battle and nature juxtaposed with images of suffering, movements of group formations and everyday military life – dramatic textures illustrating the soldiers' routine and ordeal along the vectors of camera movement and montage.

A possible explanation for this can be found in Daniel C. Hallin's empirical study on 1960s and 70s TV news coverage, *The Uncensored War*, where he confirms that the ideology of objective journalism as well as the intimate connection between the media and the American government kept journalists from being invariably critical towards the war. So-called "investigative journalism" only emerged anew as a post-Watergate phenomenon, and, according to Hallin's data, critical media treatments of Vietnam visibly increased only when public dissent became a dominant news topic.

While American television networks effectively acted upon the stability of the government, the U.S. Department of Defense, in turn, acknowledged the media's role in shaping political attitudes by producing educational programmes about the war. For example, a series entitled THE BIG PICTURE was both shown at public screenings and on public television[10] in order to sell a "modern, progressive and

---

[8] Thomas Doherty, "Full Metal Genre: Stanley Kubrick's Vietnam Combat Movie," *Film Quarterly* 42 (2), 1988-89, 24–30, here: 24.
[9] Here I am referring to archival research I have conducted at the Television News Archive in Nashville (Vanderbilt University) in 2012.
[10] THE BIG PICTURE was shown on more than 320 television stations in the United States and 40 stations overseas. To provide adequate distribution on this scale, films were rotated among stations. Despite these primary showings, secondary showings were available for Army Command Information Programmes, public schools and organizations. Individual episodes of THE BIG PICTURE served as a supplement for talks, presentations, or training sessions (cf. Jeffrey Crean, "Something to Compete with 'Gunsmoke': 'The Big Picture' Television Series and Selling

forward thinking" Army to American viewers.¹¹ Having first aired in 1951, THE BIG PICTURE continued to fashion itself as a marketing tool for U.S. military efforts, and operated on a constantly increasing budget to gain the status of a competitive entertainment programme. The 30-minute training films about Vietnam, some of them featuring actors like Robert Mitchum and John Wayne as guest narrators, relied on maps, quotes and historical facts in order to contextualize the war within the United States' causal – and fateful – genealogy of political struggle. Senator William Fulbright would later resentfully describe them as an indoctrinating series "glorifying the Army" and taking "an approach to the complexities of today's world that is oversimplified and one-dimensional."¹²

Obviously contrasting the growing number of unfiltered images of war, the pronounced cartographic view deployed by media formats such as THE BIG PICTURE might help to explain why later Vietnam films vehemently refused to incorporate functional maps and coherent topographical structures into their portrayals of battle, especially since the conflict itself was anything but controlled or mapped out in terms of clear frontlines. Due to the fact that the war's omnipresence in the media could not compensate the patent absence of something like a bigger picture, many Vietnam War films, by undermining the codes of the classical combat film, problematized the nature of war as a conglomerate of constructed images as well as the failure of these images to communicate the actual experience of battle as a dissociation of the senses. By formal means, and in the spirit of television and New Hollywood aesthetics, post-classical Vietnam war films each deal with a certain partitioning of sensory layers into sound and/or vision, or establish a complex sensorium which does not allow for a clear distinction between these layers. Each mode serves to create an experience of war as an "alternate reality" (to quote James Lastra), which adds to the already alternate reality of film as such. In doing so, most Vietnam War films unfold hyperbolic spaces of military excess and disorientation without ever offering a way out, or a solution to the problem of wartime disillusionment. In effect, most Vietnam War films, regardless of their individual aesthetic features, not only unmask but reject the aerial perspective, tracing the illusion of overview to the very roots of the military – and cinematic – apparatus.

Time and again, such observations have been made about films like Coppola's APOCALYPSE NOW, with James Lastra, for instance, writing that "[it] encourages

---

a 'Modern, Progressive and Forward Thinking' Army to Cold War America," *War & Society* 35 (3), 2006, 204–218).
11 Crean, "Something to Compete with 'Gunsmoke,'" 204.
12 J. William Fulbright, *The Pentagon Propaganda Machine*, New York 1970, 69–71.

us to reflect on the interpenetration of the apparatuses of human sensation and of cinema –to ask how the advent of sensory technologies has altered our understanding of human experience."[13] More than merely engaging with post-classical directives, APOCALYPSE NOW indeed explores a new cinematic sensorium in which sound and colour merge into a trance-like projection, a journey into a territory impossible to grasp but to be experienced in optic, haptic, and acoustic terms. This again corresponds to actual reconnaissance methods during the Vietnam War, which, according to Virilio, often turned out to be a search for traces rather than an observation of concrete targets:

> Objects and bodies were forgotten as their physiological traces became accessible to a host of new devices – sensors capable of detecting vibrations, sounds and smells; light-enhancing television cameras, infra-red flashes, thermographic pictures that identified objects by their temperature, and so on. When time-lags were lost in real time, real time itself broke the constraints of chronology and became cinematic.[14]

Both affirming and countering Virilio's notion of cinematic time is the unusually slow pace of quite many Vietnam War films. While also featuring jarring battle scenes and plotlines of soldierly maturation (as typical for the war film genre), they also deploy a somewhat contemplative and elegiac mode in terms of cinematography and sound. One might think of the trance-like states of APOCALYPSE NOW, or the pastoral American mountainscape in THE DEER HUNTER, and, above all, of Samuel Barber's "Adagio for Strings" as melancholic leitmotif in PLATOON (Oliver Stone, 1986). Again, all of these seem to suggest a loss of physicality, with bodies and objects moving into oblivion. Yet, the fact that these examples come across as modes of almost meditative reflection does not break the sensory ties to what they seem to alienate us from. Culminating in Stanley Kubrick's FULL METAL JACKET, crucial moments of death and destruction (such as American soldiers dying in sniper fire) are presented in slow motion – a cynical means to simultaneously distance the spectator from acts of violence and recuperate the physical dimension of war as an aesthetic experience.

Sean Cubitt, who describes slow motion as a camera effect that reveals what Walter Benjamin conceives of as "the optical unconscious,"[15] identifies the paradox arising from this condition:

---

13 James Lastra, "Film and the Wagnerian Aspiration: Thoughts on Sound Design and History of the Senses," in *Lowering the Boom: Critical Studies in Film Sound*, ed. Jay Beck, Tony Grajeda, Chicago 2008, 123–138, here: 127.
14 Virilio, *War and Cinema*, 24.
15 In his book, *The Cinema Effect*, Cubitt contrasts several theoretical approaches to slow motion, specifically focusing on Stephen Prince and Paul Seydor's respective takes on violence in the

Aestheticizing, in this context, would represent the removal of the action from the embodied senses – of pain, of empathy, of anger or disgust – and its sublimation as vision, optically stripping the event of consciousness. Subjectivizing, by contrast, reanchors the shock of violence, but in the body of an onlooker.[16]

In FULL METAL JACKET, the slowly fading figures and the blood splashing graphically from their lethal wounds, their extreme gestures in the agony of dying, become a work of art that requires aesthetic distance. But at the same time, they are profoundly visceral. Not only does this complicate the role of the body in war films, but it also makes it more difficult to find an adequate nomenclature for the excessive style of certain Vietnam War films – and it explains why many scholars have focused on singular examples, rather than extrapolating aesthetic principles that connect even the most outstanding films. When it comes to APOCALYPSE NOW, again, opinions differ as to whether the film would aestheticize the violence depicted, or rather numb the senses of the spectator. Lastra even goes so far as to compare APOCALYPSE NOW to the Wagnerian musical drama, "born of a desire to provide a total and totalizing sensory experience,"[17] which results in an experience of "blinding anesthesia."[18] He concludes:

> Put briefly, *Apocalypse Now* tries to show that the impulse toward prosthetic sensory experience is primarily an impulse to create a substitute, compensatory world, where fullness and apparent perfection strive to replace the world of actual experience with a better, more consoling, and more oblivious one. Here, to sever sound representation from a documentary function [...] is not a simple technical decision designed to allow for better sounding recordings, but a technique of anesthesia, of refusing the meaning of what one experiences. To feel oneself the hero in one's own personal movie (skiing, surfing, killing, dying), it seems to say, is vastly preferable to acknowledging one's complicity in the messy worlds of politics, war, and the media that enable them.[19]

---

work of director Sam Peckinpah. Prince argues that slow motion, as established in Peckinpah's 1969 Western, THE WILD BUNCH, unveils the "metaphysical paradox of the body's enhanced cinematic reactions during a moment of diminished or extinguished consciousness" (Stephen Prince, *Savage Cinema: Sam Peckinpah and the Rise of Ultraviolent Movies*, Austin, TX 1998, 60). Following Seydor, on the other hand, slow motion "distances us from the action by aestheticizing it" (Paul Seydor, *Peckinpah – The Western Films: A Reconsideration*, Urbana, IL 1997, 190) while, at least in Peckinpah's case, "the slow-motion shots are almost always held to a particular, often subjective, point of view that is clearly, if implicitly, identified as such in and by the film" (Seydor, *Peckinpah*, 191).
16 Sean Cubitt, *The Cinema Effect*, Cambridge, MA 2004, 207.
17 Lastra, "Film and the Wagnerian Aspiration," 127.
18 Lastra, "Film and the Wagnerian Aspiration," 128.
19 Lastra, "Film and the Wagnerian Aspiration," 136–137.

The notion of film as a substitute world is not new, especially when we think of Cavell's "automatic world projections"[20] However, Lastra's focus on sound design opens up new perspectives on certain changes in cinema's audiovisual representation of war after Vietnam. He makes an important point earlier in his text when he explains in which way exactly APOCALYPSE NOW corresponds to the perceptual effects of the musical drama:

> On this account, the musical drama responds to the shattering of the human senses into discrete and disconnected zones, by providing an arena within which they appear to reconnect. As such, it takes its place within a broader explosion of phantasmagoria of many kinds, each corresponding to the individual senses, which no longer cohere in a total system.[21]

Thus, while I would hesitate to apply the term "anesthesia" to the functional structure of other post-classical war films, it is nevertheless the notion of "blinding" and the "shattering of the human senses into discrete and disconnected zones" that, in my view, not only characterize APOCALYPSE NOW but the Vietnam War film as such, and that complicate its already distinct relation between cinematic space and bodily perception. Not always are these shattered senses reconnected on the level of aesthetic experience, but they are nevertheless affected in unusual and unbalanced ways. Even the slow-motion sequences in FULL METAL JACKET do not solely operate on the level of decelerated visible movement; rather, their disturbing effect stems from the juxtaposition of retarded and real-time sounds within a montage of slow-motion and real-time images. Furie's THE BOYS IN COMPANY C does not take this confusion to a stylized extreme; what the film achieves, however, is to unsettle the conventions and expectations linked to sensuous perception. Deliberately exposing the flaws of vision, it puts an emphasis on equally erratic verbal communication and ambiguous sounds that serve as vaguely reliable coordinates in a chaotic theater of war.

5.2 THE BOYS IN COMPANY C: Sonic Envelopes and Aural Traces

Somewhat surprisingly, even if much has been written on Vietnam as an either postmodernist or trauma-related critical point in the cinematic representation of war, the analysis of interrelating soundscapes and image spaces in Vietnam War films turns out to be rather sparse. If at all, scholarly work in this regard again concentrates on

---

20 Cf. Stanley Cavell, *The World Viewed: Reflections on the Ontology of Film*, Cambridge, MA 1979, 146.
21 Lastra, "Film and the Wagnerian Aspiration," 131.

APOCALYPSE NOW, although many key aspects of Coppola's film design offer valuable clues to other war films of the late 70s and 80s. Thomas Elsaesser and Michael Wedel, for instance, formulate a striking statement on the sonic spaces of APOCALYPSE NOW, which could serve as hypothesis for several Vietnam films:

> This tropical-tropological space of hyperbole, in which to see no longer means to know, is only possible because *Apocalypse Now* so radically reverses the conventional hierarchies of image and sound, desubstantializing the image, destabilizing ocular perception, and treating sound as a physical substance. [...] In contrast with this materiality, the visible world is not only deceptive but textured like an easily torn fabric [...] The worlds of sound that Willard encounters are not only blind but blunt, where communication either overshoots its target, or turns solipsistic and self-enclosed. Hence the need for a third space, for a soundscape that Chion calls 'emanation speech': speech not meant to communicate significant action, but merely to represent the aural traces of a body.[22]

On the one hand, these aural traces refer to the specific function of voice-over narration deployed in many Vietnam War films; on the other hand, they also describe a certain way of navigating through cinematic space that articulates the soldier's disillusionment, his perception of intimacy, and his desperate situation of being abandoned by optical power (that is, both by his sense of vision and by technological devices of visual control). But while making the audience sensuously relate to these exceptional circumstances, some films reverse the usual hierarchical order of sight and sound to such an extent that the audience becomes aware of the extreme otherness of war, and of the ways it is communicated through certain shifts within the filmic form. THE BOYS IN COMPANY C is one striking example, even though it does not operate with opulent visual tableaus or avant-gardist soundtracks. Perhaps in subtler but no less effective ways, the film subverts the military's symbolical, symmetrical, and cartographic structures for the benefit of a predominantly aural corpography – a conception of space in which acoustic elements expose and underline the limits of vision.

Initially criticized by reviewers for its rehashing of WWII combat film clichés, Sidney Furie's THE BOYS IN COMPANY C was later appreciated for its portrayal of racial issues and its change of attitude towards the war.[23] But although it was

---

[22] Thomas Elsaesser and Michael Wedel, "Apocalypse Now: The Hollow Heart of Hollywood," in *Joseph Conrad on Film*, ed. Gene Moore, Cambridge 1997, 151–175, here: 169–70.
[23] Cf. for example Brian J. Woodman, "Represented in the Margins: Images of African American Soldiers in Vietnam Combat Films," in *The War Film*, ed. Robert Eberwein, New Brunswick, NJ 2004, 90–114. Cf. also Roger Ebert, "The Boys in Company C," February 24 (1978), http://www.rogerebert.com/reviews/the-boys-in-company-c-1978 (accessed December 10, 2016).

one of the first American post-Vietnam war films that saw a theatrical release, and the first after John Wayne's THE GREEN BERETS to show actual combat in Vietnam, it is today mainly referred to as a prefiguration of FULL METAL JACKET – both films not only share a similar plot structure but also feature R. Lee Ermey playing an unforgiving drill instructor. Another striking resemblance is their detailed depiction of military training, which describes the individual recruit's troublesome physical adjustment and submission to the corps. Moreover, in the sense of Lastra, the first scenes of both THE BOYS IN COMPANY C and FULL METAL JACKET develop a cinematic choreography of military order as a re-modeling of human perception. In this regard, they do not yet differ profoundly from the basic dramatic principles of classical war films. Similar to many briefing scenes in earlier American combat films, for instance, the initial drill sequences of both films are very much in line with the war film genre's poetics of affect. They show the formation of a group body as the very state of a military body-in-being, where choreographed movements are orchestrated by the barking voices of the drill instructors. As a matter of fact, the expressive quality of the voice is negotiated in many films about the Vietnam War, its status varying from time to time, and from film to film. Alluding to style and dramaturgy of the film noir and the American detective film, works like APOCALYPSE NOW, PLATOON, or FULL METAL JACKET feature a structuring voice-over by means of which their respective protagonists reflect upon their actions and purpose as a soldier. This mode of reflection can either take on a melancholic, ironic, or fatalistic tone. In each case, however, the voice is located on a contemplative meta-level of the film, temporally and spatially detached from the events depicted. Yet, these events themselves can depend upon the corpographic character of voices. Especially in THE BOYS IN COMPANY C, it becomes evident how movement in space is initiated by, organized around, and restricted to, vocal orders. This, in turn, resounds in the visual composition of many training shots: in order to emphasize the physical separation of the recruits and their drill sergeants, the instructors are often only seen from behind while they shout at the soldiers. The sequence thereby sets the tone for the incongruity between vision and sound that pervades the film's following scenes in Vietnam.

The shaping of the military body marks a decisive point within the melodramatic figuration of the soldier: it leads up to an overall imago of power and control, before it transforms into the agony of vulnerability and powerlessness. Yet in any case, physical drill and optical superiority make up the ritualistic foundation and desired destination of every military objective, and, finally, determine the self-consciousness of every soldier. From a psychoanalytical perspective, Swiss ethnologist Mario Erdheim writes accordingly about the inscription of military rituals into cultural formations of male subjectivity: "The military is an illusion machine of a specific kind, which essentially produces the construct of masculinity."[24]

With regard to the Hollywood war film and its pathos scenes, in turn, Kappelhoff draws on Erdheim when he describes the soldier's illusion of an amalgamation with the invulnerable and immortal military corps. This corps is in fact a topographical arrangement of bodies, actions and relations that articulate the individual (and vulnerable) male's embedment into a network of strictly hierarchized symbolic significance.[25] Thus, what Kappelhoff eventually describes as an "illusion of overview" does not only relate to conflicting spatial points of view within the "military dispositive,"[26] but also to the figure of the soldier as a body at risk. Kappelhoff's analysis of FULL METAL JACKET centres on the argument that the ritualistic extinction of the individual body in favour of the military corps eventually transforms the soldier's elementary fear and pain of self-loss into violent rage.[27] However, in FULL METAL JACKET, this transformation can only be performed in all its extremity because all characters are thoroughly de-individualized from the very beginning – they all seem to have lost their past before it even came into being (a figuration of destructive masculinity that we see in many of Kubrick's films).

THE BOYS IN COMPANY C operates on the same assumption, spending a few minutes lingering on some of the characters, their social ties and backgrounds, only to stress the unavoidable tragedy of their lives as soldiers. The future recruits are shown sitting in cars, having their last talk with their loved ones. The restricted space of the car forms a both visual and sonic envelope that lets us concentrate on their conversations and their way of speaking, down to their pronounced Texan or New York accents. After the boys have left their vehicles, they line up to take the military oath, and an eager recruit's voice-over introduces each one of them to the audience by just mentioning their name and place of residence before we see them getting transported to the receiving barracks. And when they are finally sent off to get their heads shaved, the subtle brutality of this process is not so much evoked through repetitive patterns in image composition and montage (as in Kubrick) but rather through the piercing sound of the electric shaver which is amplified to an unnaturally high volume – while we see the anxious faces of those waiting in line for their haircut.

---

24 Cf. Mario Erdheim, *Psychoanalyse und Unbewußtheit in der Kultur*, Frankfurt a. M., 1988, 336.
25 Cf. Kappelhoff, *Front Lines of Community*, 323.
26 Cf. Florentina C. Andreescu, "War, Trauma and the Militarized Body," in *Subjectivity* 9 (2), 2016, 205–223.
27 Cf. Kappelhoff, *Front Lines of Community*, 323.

This is in fact where THE BOYS IN COMPANY C differs considerably from FULL METAL JACKET. In contrast to Kubrick's film, which, despite its showcasing of popular songs as an alienation effect, sound is here designed to have a more striking impact on characters and spectators. That is, acoustics always seem to colonize the foreground of the cinematic image – whether in the form of voices, sounds, or music – while never successfully reaching into the depth of the image space. It almost seems as if they were not thoroughly "magnetised" or "absorbed"[28] by the image, never really creating a unity of sound and vision.

Conforming to Corrigan's observation, the argument that several Vietnam films seem to employ popular music to reflect on the war as a historical crisis or rupture,[29] THE BOYS actually features one central sequence in which a certain song, actor Craig Wasson's "Here I am," precisely marks this rupture by both controlling and unhinging the space-time of the diegesis: a helicopter soars over a few soldiers' heads, while we hear the lyrics "Uncle Sam, I'm in Vietnam. It's a jungle, it's a prison." The non-diegetic music then forms a sound bridge to shots of other soldiers gathering on a hilltop, and listening to a sergeant's speech about savings bonds. Here, the volume of the music notably decreases, giving way to the sergeant's voice, only to take over again and underline a single soldier's anxious look at dead comrades in body bags who are taken off a truck in the background. Finally, the source of the music is revealed: two marines sit in front of a stack of ammunition boxes, one of whom is singing and playing the guitar – surprisingly, we only realize in retrospect that he has been visible almost the entire time, a nearly unnoticeable figure in the left-hand corner of the image.

The amplification of the song not only seems to detach sound and voice from their physical source, but it creates a contingent sonic space which frequently re-arranges the given image space. Only the song itself navigates from shot to shot, while the characters themselves remain immobile and bound to their "prison space." The music first communicates rather independently with the scene's elements of action before becoming anchored in the diegesis. Until then, however, it functions like a "spatiotemporal turntable" in the sense of Chion, enjoying "the status of being a little freer of barriers of time and space than the other sound and visual elements."[30]

---

28 In *Audio-Vision*, Chion writes that the image "magnetises" sound in space; that is, the spectator automatically localises acoustic sources within the image, rather than acknowledging their physical source off-screen. Cf. Michel Chion, *Audio-Vision: Sound on Screen*, ed. and trans. Claudia Gorbman, New York 1994, 69.
29 Corrigan, *A Cinema Without Walls*, 41.
30 Chion, *Audio-Vision*, 81.

Throughout the film this acoustic envelope finds visual support in poignant close-ups, medium close-ups and low-angle shots that draw the spectators into the intimate (sonic) space of the protagonists. But although the foregrounding of talking, screaming, or whispering voices implies a more or less immediate perception and understanding of words, communication in THE BOYS is rarely effective. First, conflicts between the soldiers are hardly solved on the level of verbal argument. Moreover, war is still raging in the background as an open or hidden threat. We see helicopters flying by, soldiers marching or waiting for an order, distracted from the enemy who then opens fire on them. Several motifs add to this conception: the repeatedly inefficient radio communication, the ironic voice-over commentary, even the impassive helicopters suggest that visual control is suspended by aural traces which, in turn, are not the solution to the problem of disorientation, but rather articulate this problem in the first place. Taken one step further, the attention drawn to the film's acoustics not only emphasizes physical intimacy over visual authority – these acoustics simultaneously seem to compete with image spaces and landscapes demanding our attention. Thus, while maintaining to affect the spectator in terms of sensuous perception, the film's acoustic and visual layout provokes a rearrangement of sensory hierarchies. This, in turn, does not just serve the purpose of denouncing the primacy of vision, but it is a way to highlight an overall destabilization of the senses through the medium of war. Ultimately, war is here delineated not (only) as a conflict of nations and bodies, but, on an experiential level, as a battle of the senses.

5.3 Off-screen Monstrosity

A defining trope for THE BOYS IN COMPANY C as a whole, the recruits' deployment to Vietnam is in fact a grim portrayal of various interfering competitions: despite the film's climax, a seemingly harmless but ultimately lethal football game against a team of South Vietnamese civilians, every battle action is also part of a body count mission, a quest for a high score in enemy killings. However, it is hardly the (dead) body of the enemy we are confronted with; rather, we follow the common American soldier into a zone of permanent threat and insecurity. In contrast to many other Vietnam War films, this zone is no dense jungle landscape but a network of plain roads, open hillsides and rice paddies in broad daylight. Navigation through this environment becomes a matter of uncomfortable self-exposure, a problem of (not) seeing and being seen. Although the depicted landscape indeed suggests a sense of overview, the potentially controlling gaze is frequently disturbed by blocked views. With the camera always being a bit too close to the soldiers, the film's mise-en-scène emphasizes their facial expressions, gestures, and conversations, and still fragments their bodies.

As a result, sounds and images seem to form a strange alliance throughout the film. Dialogue and acoustic traces evoke and express anger and fear as main affective qualities of THE BOYS IN COMPANY C without always revealing the visual sources and/or effects of these emotions. Compared to other genre films about jungle warfare, the omnipresent but invisible enemy is in this case not embodied by formations of nature; in fact, the enemy seems to have become a disembodied idea colonizing the covert space beneath the image surface, a force infiltrating the frame from the outside.

Halfway through the film, this notion is made plain on the level of expressive movement: we follow a group of soldiers marching through a rice field. Their chatter is drowned by the sounds of splashing water with the camera positioned at waist level, which lets their lower bodies uncannily disappear into the off-screen space below. Thus, it is especially the invisible realm of sound that harbours danger for the men wading through the paddy. One of the soldiers eagerly explains to a fellow Marine how rice fields are engineering marvels: "They terrace the land, so that the water flows evenly from one paddy to the next, to the next, to the next – like this whole valley was one giant fountain." Just this principle is then applied to the scene's image composition and dramatic structure. We cut from one pair of soldiers to another, overhearing their talks about heavy rifles and letters from home while they climb over several banks. As the camera tracks along their path, the dynamic image space itself becomes a cascade moving towards the figure of Washington (Stan Shaw) who walks at the forefront. We finally see him freezing in a low-angle shot, when he hears a second pronounced clicking noise, the first one merely being the clicking of another soldier's camera. This second noise now motivates the camera to tilt away from the ridge in the background in order to frame Washington against the cloudy sky, making him a physical monument isolated from the surrounding landscape of war. Through a close-up of his foot from above, it quickly becomes clear that he has stepped on a mine about to explode upon his next move. While the mine is not visible at any point, it still seems to "look" at Washington from below and becomes one with the camera. Moreover, the camera itself turns into a weapon – an analogy also suggested through the indistinguishable clicking sounds.

The squad leader tells the others to back off as Washington, although still alive, is a "dead man." And it is only now that we get a reverse shot of the scene which appears to be strangely idyllic despite its hidden threat. Devoid of visible enemies or stifling vegetation, the rice field's sole indicator of menace is the sound of water and tripwire. These acoustics contribute to a certain interplay of tension and release which is realized on a kinaesthetic level. The overall

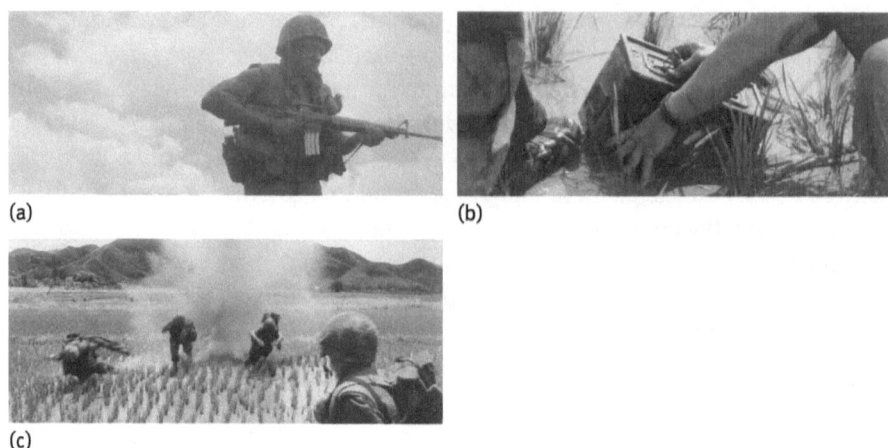

Figure 17: Hidden threat.

horizontal movement performed by each pair of soldiers, contrasted with the persistent sense of invisible underwater depth and occasional upward movements executed by the camera, translates into a wave-like expressive movement, a temporally structured figuration which culminates in the explosion of the mine – that is, the very fountain one of the soldiers has been talking about earlier (see Figure 17).

This not only testifies to a dissociation of sensory layers typical for Vietnam War films, but also to a different kind of cinematic speech that not only illustrates but structures the scene and its spatiotemporal dynamics as such. While Chion distinguishes between textual, theatrical, and emanation speech,[31] the audiovisual gestalt of the mine scene seems to arise from a combination of the first two modes. Here, spoken dialogue is theatrical insofar as it has a dramatic and affective function (it articulates the soldiers' fears and worries), and it is textual in that "it has the power to make visible the images that it evokes through sound,"[32] that is, the image space becomes the terraced field that is being talked about.

An accentuation of the invisible, in turn, occurs in later sequences, pronouncing the limitations of the filmic image itself in an almost anecdotal manner. The film's rather short scene of a beach landing is as much a reference to classical combat movies about the Pacific War as it is a striking counter image

---

31 Cf. Chion, *Audio-Vision*, 169–178.
32 Chion, *Audio-Vision*, 172.

to Apocalypse Now's Wagnerian depiction of a Vietnamese surfing beach. Significantly, the scene follows a shot of two body bags reading "remains non viewable" and starts with a minesweeper getting stuck in the sand, which forces the Marines to take cover on the shore. Up to this point there is no reverse shot of the grove the soldiers are supposed to take – only two supervising soldiers are shown in conversation, occupying the foreground of the image, while three powerful yet immobile military vessels seem to waver in the background, and the narrator's voice-over drowns out half of the words being said. A helicopter hovers above the sea, waiting in position, but not able to provide a view of the situation, let alone the enemy. Whereas in Apocalypse Now the helicopter squadron literally sweeps the shore like a wave of furious Valkyries, this lone Huey seems incapable of moving beyond the grove, or, in other words, beyond the image frame. Even when the leading sergeant orders Washington to scout the surroundings with him, we get to see nothing but treetops framed in a medium-close shot. Demonstratively, every act of seeing is verbalized instead of being performed by the camera: "Keep your eyes on the treetops, I'm gonna watch the ground," followed by one of the soldiers on the beach marvelling at the grove's beauty, which is never translated into cinematic views: "This is nice, sir, I wanna take a picture." It is Alvin (James Canning), the young and naïve narrator whose clicking camera frequently unsettles and destabilizes the film's visuals, constantly confusing the characters' and spectators' sensuous apprehension of acoustic sources and spaces. Having caused uncertainty about the position of a mine earlier, he now provokes an enemy reaction from within the image: before Alvin gets to take a photo, his motif, one of the palm trees, shoots back at him. While this is a common way of staging the invisible enemy in war films, it is significant to note that, for The Boys in Company C, the same pattern does not serve any narrative purpose. Although the enemy fire is answered by heavy shooting on the part of the Marines, there is no visible evidence of enemy casualties. Instead, the scene's impromptu ending comprises of Alvin being carried away by the now mobile helicopter. Here, the physical experience of battle is not as much connected to bodily movement as it is linked to war as an always mediated experience, with a seemingly harmless and distant image (in this case the motif of the palm tree) attacking its beholder. It is the complexity within the audiovisual representation of war that therefore comes to the fore without actually clarifying the situation represented.

Thus, tumbling the hierarchy of senses in its navigation through the battle zone, The Boys in Company C immediately counters any possibility of overview by letting sound undermine vision. Not only is this aspect one of many conflicts featured in the film, but it also demonstrates how sensory instability becomes a main principle of the Vietnam War film as an aesthetic and somatic experience.

5.4 Rescue Dawn: Into the Abyss

As typical for the Hollywood Vietnam War film, this "battle of the senses" must involve the collapse of sensory and cognitive orders. The overwhelming disorientation conveyed in Apocalypse Now, Platoon, or Casualties of War (Brian De Palma, 1989) is not just a poignant continuation of WWII depictions of jungle warfare; as has been demonstrated in Kappelhoff's empirical study of the Hollywood war film's poetics of affect, the increased presence of fear and horror in Vietnam films implies a simultaneous decrease in pathos scenes about military power structures.[33] Hence, the conventional formation of a group body as one of the war film's central narrative tropes is foiled by the subjective experience of battle and nature – an experience that revolves around the existential fear of losing oneself in chaos and agony.

Almost thirty years after The Boys in Company C, and part of another small wave of Vietnam War films in the early 2000s,[34] Werner Herzog's Rescue Dawn resumed to a purely existential rendering of jungle warfare by foregrounding the absolute consummation of control through the forces of nature, and through the experience of captivity. Despite the significant fact that Rescue Dawn was not only produced and released a long time after the first films about combat in Vietnam, but also after 9/11 as another major turning point in the audiovisual representation of war, it can still be said that it continues the tradition of the post-classical (Vietnam) war film to drastically reformulate generic conventions. While nature has always played an important role in Herzog's feature films and documentaries, Rescue Dawn's focus on landscape as an "inner world of affect"[35] draws on traditional patterns of the war film genre in recreating a somatic reality that is endured by its protagonist and sensuously apprehended by its spectators. What is more, the film symbolically negates the controlling perspective of the aerial view by centring on an American pilot in captivity and

---

[33] The diagram showing the temporal arrangement of pathos scenes in Apocalypse Now, for example, reveals the dominant presence of category three, "battle and nature" which is closely linked to the affective dimension of horror, fear, and enmity. Cf. Freie Universität Berlin, database Empirische Medienästhetik, http://www.empirische-medienaesthetik.fu-berlin.de/en/emaex-system/affektdatenmatrix/diagramme/diagramm_apocalypse_now.html (accessed December 10, 2016).

[34] Among those films were Tigerland (Joel Schumacher, 2000), a film strongly referring to Full Metal Jacket in its portrayal of military training, and We Were Soldiers (Randall Wallace, 2002), based on Hal Moore's book, *We Were Soldiers Once... And Young* (1992).

[35] Eric Ames, "Herzog, Landscape, and Documentary," *Cinema Journal* 48 (2), 2009, 49–69, here: 53.

graphically depicting his excruciating escape through the Laotian jungle. In contrast to THE BOYS IN COMPANY C, RESCUE DAWN does not so much focus on sound as it highlights the intensified haptic apprehension of nature. In fact, due to its subject, the existential struggles of an American POW, the film is rather quiet as it stresses moments of anxious silence in order to occasionally juxtapose them with outbreaks of rage and violence. While the jungle prison, in Craig Wasson's song "Here I am," has merely served as a metaphor for the soldiers' harrowing experience in wartime Vietnam, it is now a literal prison in Herzog's film. Being in captivity, as an existential and cinematic condition, forces a reduction of vision, movement and verbal communication, which, in turn, calls for the sense of touch as an instrument of both communication and orientation.

RESCUE DAWN is based on the true story of Dieter Dengler, a German-born U.S. fighter pilot who got shot down during a mission in North Vietnam in 1966. Having crashed near the Laotian-Vietnamese border, Dengler was soon captured by Pathet Lao troops and turned over to the North Vietnamese Army. After six months of torture, he escaped fighting his way through the jungle for 23 days and was eventually rescued by a U.S. Air Force squadron. Prior to this, Duane Martin, a fellow American prisoner who had accompanied him, had been decapitated by a villager. Dengler thus became the first American soldier to survive and escape imprisonment during the Vietnam War.

A few years before RESCUE DAWN got released, Herzog had already made a documentary about the airman: in LITTLE DIETER NEEDS TO FLY (1997) Dengler himself shares his thoughts and memories with the audience, even recreating his experience as a POW on a trip he took with Herzog to Thailand and Laos. Interestingly, both feature film and documentary not only convey a strong sense of loss and torment – they also emphasize Dengler's fatal naïve recklessness as a synecdoche for American hubris in Vietnam *and* a premise for the pilot's survival. As written on one of the title cards initiating RESCUE DAWN, "[i]n 1965, few people believed that the still limited conflict in Viet Nam would turn into full scale war." This is followed by grainy slow-motion footage of fighter planes dropping napalm bombs on Vietnamese villages, intensified by a mystifying orchestral soundtrack, and turned into a mesmerizing vision of destruction. Herzog had used the exact same images (albeit underscored with different music) in the prologue of LITTLE DIETER, both times intentionally referencing the famous opening sequence of Coppola's APOCALYPSE NOW, in which a wall of palm trees is bombed and bursts into flames. In RESCUE DAWN, after showing more footage of a jet landing on an aircraft carrier, Herzog's fictional take on Dengler starts with a military briefing which – not accidentally – recalls equivalent scenes from TOP GUN (Tony Scott, 1986). Although Scott's film is neither set in Vietnam nor primarily deals with actual combat experience, it nevertheless blends in the contemporary spectator's genre memory of earlier combat and action movies, setting the mood for an expected and exciting adventure unfolding over the course of the film. More than simply developing a sense of control (which would conform to the war film's basic affective structure), the briefing scene in RESCUE DAWN takes on a frivolous tone when the pilots are shown watching and ridiculing an actual military training film offering advice on how to survive in the jungle.

Said training film, too, is featured in LITTLE DIETER, after Dengler is shown demonstrating his actual survival techniques that he had employed during his escape.[36] Here, similar to one airman in RESCUE DAWN's screening room, Herzog's voice-over comments ironically on the film's unrealistic assumptions about a stranded soldier's skills and equipment:

> Back in the mid-60s, American strategic thinking was turned against Russia, so all survival meant survival in Russia and Siberia. A jungle war didn't factor much in their thinking, and that's why their instructional films look somewhat funny [...] Of course our man immediately comes across heart of palm, the film hints, as easily as in the supermarket [...] But now this is very odd: What, for God's sake, is our man signalling so frantically to the helicopter right above him?

On a meta-level, Herzog once again unveils and underlines the very pretensions and absurdities of militarist ideology that had already been pilloried by Coppola and Kubrick in their Vietnam War films (and even earlier by the original novels these films are based on). Yet, in direct comparison to works such as FULL METAL JACKET, both LITTLE DIETER and RESCUE DAWN contrast their rather light-hearted display of irony and cynicism with either re-narrated or visualized accounts of torture and pain. As becomes clear over the course of the two films, these words and images form a shockingly grim antipode to the pilot's radical enthusiasm, eventually illustrating how Dengler simultaneously incorporates the fallible hubris of the airman *and* the agony of the disillusioned foot soldier. At the end of RESCUE DAWN, he is physically broken but happy about being reunited with his comrades, and with a military group body that presents itself as a community of loving brothers. In LITTLE DIETER, the aged Dengler is shown marvelling at endless rows of discarded planes, still pondering about the miracle of flying, clearly constructing his own, at times euphemistic, reality.

In an earlier episode of the documentary, Herzog's voice-over finds equivalent words when describing the pilot's bombing experience in Vietnam:

---

36 It is important to note, however, that this specific training film, according to LITTLE DIETER, was made in 1967, while RESCUE DAWN is supposed to be set in the year 1966.

But from the air, Vietnam didn't seem real at all. For Dengler, it was like a grid on a map. He had suddenly found himself not only a pilot but a soldier caught up in a real war. But even though it was real, everything down there seemed to be so alien and so abstract. It all looked so strange, like a distant, barbaric dream.

Ultimately, this barbaric dream is effectively realized in RESCUE DAWN, after Dengler's crash is literally staged as an allegoric fall. Before he gets shot down we can see him flying, sitting in the cockpit of his plane. A little boy with an umbrella is painted on the aircraft's exterior shell – in fact, it is "Der fliegende Robert (Flying Robert)," a character from a classic German children's book called *Der Struwwelpeter (Shockheaded Peter)*. In the book, Robert is punished for wandering around in stormy weather instead of staying at home. As a consequence of his bold disobedience, he is carried away by the wind and disappears forever. Dengler, one must now infer, is about to be punished for "having his head in the clouds," for not considering the implications and severe consequences of flying a war plane. And indeed his perspective suddenly changes from the controlled vision and power of the bomber (here, Herzog inserts images that allude to the bombing footage used at the beginning of the film) to the exposed and inferior perspective of the bombed. As the plane smashes into a paddy field, the camera spins for a second; then, from various angles, we see the wreck burst into pieces.

Perhaps intentionally, Herzog not only continues to re-imagine ideas of superiority and barbarism, but he also expands this reconceptualization to certain phantasms of German culture (which, considering Dengler's and Herzog's German background, seems only consistent). Here, the explicit reference to "Flying Robert" is but one example. Even more ostensibly, as the film evolves, Herzog contrasts scenes of extreme corporeality with images of majestic nature that allude to conceptions of the sublime in German Romanticism in that the director's cinematic landscapes are designed to externalize specific emotional states.

While obvious connections to Romanticism have already been made in scholarly literature about Herzog,[37] it is his underlying sense of irony that has to be emphasized in this regard. Timothy Corrigan, for instance, attributes a "regressive irony" to Herzog's work, a quality that positions the spectator "on the edge or at the brink of an acquisition of the world through images themselves."[38] This regressive irony can also be attributed to our corpographic apprehension of Dengler, as played by Christian Bale in RESCUE DAWN. The character's almost

---

[37] Cf. for instance Brad Prager, *The Cinema of Werner Herzog: Aesthetic Ecstasy and Truth*, London 2007, or Laurie Ruth Johnson, *Forgotten Dreams: Revisiting Romanticism in the Cinema of Werner Herzog*, Rochester, NY 2016.
[38] Timothy Corrigan (ed.), *The Films of Werner Herzog*, New York / London 1986, 16.

infantile perception of the spaces of war (hence the allegorical hint to Flying Robert) abruptly turns into disorientation, and finally into a re-orientation through his bodily senses. It is pointed out early on that the flight into Laos will be his first mission; however, he doesn't take the various preparing briefings seriously (obviously there is no personal physical connection to what is being shown on maps and in training films), nor does he seem to realize that he is about to take part in battle action – shortly before Dengler boards his plane, he forms a semi-circle with his fellow pilots, heads against the wall: "This is what we were doing as kids when we were out for mischief."

Dengler's eventual subordination *and* resistance to the forces of nature therefore designates an affective convergence of sublime transcendence with embodiment. As Eric Ames observes, "[e]ven when the condition of irony is made explicit, there remains an intensity that wells up in the spectator when confronted with Herzog's landscapes […]"[39]– landscapes that are not to be understood in any geographical sense, but rather as "inner worlds of affect."[40] In RESCUE DAWN, said inner world finally emerges towards the end of the film, when Dengler, after a long time in captivity, physically engages with the jungle he tries to escape from.

Prior to this final segment, however, Herzog deploys an intense cinematic interplay between moments of stagnation and forced movement that sensuously align the spectator to Dengler's experience. His captors rush and push him through the green, passing by villages and hiding from patrolling American helicopters. We see Dengler tied up, either while standing, running, or lying on the ground with his arms and legs stretched out. While occasionally framing the surrounding jungle landscape in panoramic shots, the often hand-held camera also begins to close in on Dengler, joining his captors in guarding him and watching his every move. Any sense of visual orientation, for prisoner and spectator alike, appears to be deactivated as the film offers no way to look beyond the jungle and paths have already been laid out by Pathet Lao (their leader accordingly wears a pin-up shirt reading "Follow Me"). Yet, in subsequent scenes, the camera and the filmic body itself seem to occasionally change allegiance: when Dengler is shown being humiliated and tortured, we frequently share his perspective through POV shots and subjectified aural perception, that is, we even sense his momentary deafness when close gunshots are fired at him. Being drawn in and out of Dengler's point of view, the spectator not simply "relives" or embodies his perspective but also experiences how the scene establishes a dynamic image of obtrusion,

---

[39] Ames, "Herzog, Landscape, and Documentary," 61.
[40] Ames, "Herzog, Landscape, and Documentary," 53.

resistance, and forced movement in its composition of different image perspectives, acoustics and temporalities.

Finally, the time the film devotes to its portrayal of the prison camp unfolds as an intimate corporeal experience in which levels of sound and touch are foregrounded. Dengler and his fellow prisoners become visibly fragile against the background of their claustrophobic huts – their bare, emaciated chests, their pale faces marked by hunger, thirst, and fear are always in the centre of the image, while their hands and feet always about to be mutilated through scratching and crawling. Just like they are not allowed to move freely, the spectator cannot look away from their suffering. What is more, as the men are forced to whisper in order to evade punishment from the guards, the audience is also drawn into the captives' intimate sonic space – here, the spectators virtually become prisoners themselves in not being able to see or hear beyond the sensory restrictions of this audiovisual image.

All in all, the prison camp represents a miniature of the war film's sensuous dimensions without ever openly recalling images of battle. The figure of the POW, however, recalls a certain type of cinematic experience, namely both the depiction of prisoners in a subset of Korean War films and one Vietnam War film in particular: THE DEER HUNTER contains one specific sequence (a rather short war episode in comparison to the film's emphasis on pre- and post-combat action) where the imprisoned American soldiers, despite being locked up in a cage surrounded by water and rats, have to play Russian Roulette to entertain their captors. Through mise-en-scène and camera work, the scene conveys an unsettling tension and sense of suffocation, which is only released and rebuilt by single gunshots. A similar effect is achieved in RESCUE DAWN, when Dengler and other inmates find a way to escape and shoot some of their tormentors. Yet a comparable suffocating density only emerges later during Dengler and Martin's odyssey through the jungle: first, the camera regularly performs a vertical or diagonal downward movement and literally dives through layers of vegetation when panning from the treetops to the two men making their way through the bushes; second, the men themselves are frequently caught up in downward motion (they are almost washed away by a mudslide, then carried downstream lying on a raft, and nearly drifting off a waterfall); finally, alongside an overwhelmingly rich colour palette and amplified sounds of nature that create a mesmerizing jungle atmosphere, the weight of air and water emanates from within the images – so much so that they produce a paralysing impression of suffocation and drowning. Beyond the dense humidity, Herzog's portrayal of nature becomes intensely haptic in that it formally puts tactile motifs and situations to the fore: on the level of cinematography we see close-ups of touch-sensitive plants and leeches feasting on Dengler and Martin's skin; in terms of editing,

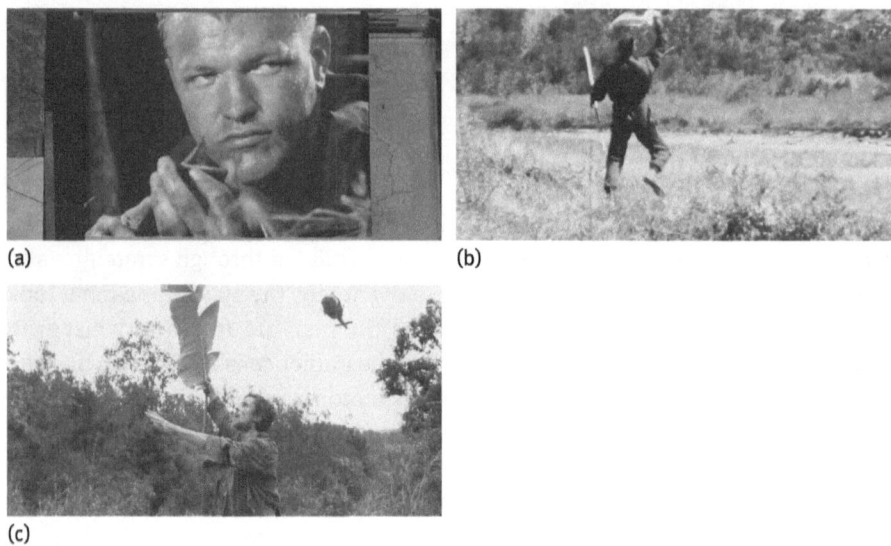

Figure 18: Re-enacting survival.

we are presented with serene images of crops cross-cut with shots of their trembling bodies. Thus, under the surface of war, and far from any encounter with human enemies, every action performed has become an act of pure endurance. Adding to the expression of irony in Herzog's work, Dengler now finds himself re-enacting the same survival techniques from the training film he once made fun of (see Figure 18).

Not only does Herzog thereby resort to fighting with and becoming nature as a common trope of Vietnam War films, he is in fact much closer to actual accounts of Vietnam veterans, as summoned by Derek Gregory in his article, "The Natures of War." Gregory himself nominates the "intimate, intensely corporeal violation by the jungle itself" as the soldiers' biggest concern and fear.[41] In this context, Frederick Downs speaks of subjugation to the forces of nature:

> Up ridges, down ridges, over ridges, wading through rocky streams, hacking at jungle growth, breathing in and hopefully breathing out some of the constant bugs that continuously swarmed around our heads, watching our skin as it quickly deteriorated from the numerous bites, scrapes, cuts, tears, thorns, and other abuses of the environment that attempted to beat our bodies into submission.[42]

---

41 Gregory, "The Natures of War," 33.
42 Downs, *The Killing Zone*, 110.

Furthermore, both Nathaniel Tripp[43] and Ed Delezen describe the need to attune their senses to their environment, to become part of the bush as a strategy to survive in the jungle. The latter accordingly writes in his war memoirs:

> When moving, the only way to pass through the vines is to become a vine; it is impossible to push through the jungle, forcing, fighting, and struggling. The bush must be negotiated with and each vine must be silently dealt with as an individual. Stealth and quiet is all that prevents our destruction from the ever-present enemy.[44]

Although engaging with these experiences so significant for the Hollywood war film, RESCUE DAWN nonetheless "recasts the genre via its protagonist."[45] Dengler represents a fallen hero, a tragically fatuous figure enchanted and then let down by military technology, conforming to what Michael Herr casually writes in *Dispatches*: "Airmobility, dig it, you weren't going anywhere. It made you feel safe, it made you feel Omni, but it was only a stunt, technology."[46]

Granted that Herzog's film and Furie's THE BOYS IN COMPANY C do not share the same production context, they have in common that they employ modes of staging that accentuate the disorientation and sensuous recalibration brought about by both the war and its media history. While THE BOYS puts an emphasis on the refiguration of sensuous hierarchies through sound, RESCUE DAWN counters the ideal of overview and military superiority with extreme physical duress, this time imposed on the figure of the fallen pilot. In doing so, both films rely on the spectator's cinematic experience and genre memory to eventually recombine the codes of classical war films towards yet another deconstruction of overview.

The destabilization of the senses through disorienting sounds and images both articulates and provokes a disturbance of sensory, cognitive, and ideological systems that underpin the war film. More concretely, these shifts within the aesthetics and poetics of the genre lead to a reconfiguration of the war film's affect economy – towards a persistent dominance of uncertainty, fear and horror that is connected to all levels of cinematic staging. Such changes conform to a conception of space in which acoustic elements not only expose and underline the limits of vision but also subvert the military's symbolical, symmetrical, and

---

43 Cf. Tripp, *Father, Soldier, Son*, 147.
44 Delezen, *Eye of the Tiger*, 37.
45 Jaimey Fisher, "Demythologization and Convergence: Herzog's Late Genre Pictures and the Rogue Cop Film in *Bad Lieutenant: Port of Call–New Orleans*," in *A Companion to Werner Herzog*, ed. Brad Prager, Malden, MA 2012, 208–229, here: 213.
46 Michael Herr, *Dispatches*, New York 1977, 13.

cartographic structures. Both THE BOYS IN COMPANY C and RESCUE DAWN show that, especially in the wake of the Vietnam War, representations of military conflict have continued to negotiate a specific sensory condition of modern warfare arising from the antagonistic relationship between technology and nature, that is, between their visible and invisible effects, the different proximities, distances and spaces they produce. The films exhibit an excess of immaterial traces, of sensory coordinates, that never guarantee to reveal their physical sources but still facilitate an intensified affective experience of combat in a reversal of sensuous hierarchies.

6 Zero Dark Thirty: Corpographies of the War on Terror

> [T]he past can be seized only as an image which flashes up at the instant when it can be recognised and is never seen again [...] To articulate the past historically does not mean to recognise it 'the way it really was' ... It means to seize hold of a memory as it flashes up at a moment of danger.
>
> Walter Benjamin[1]

In his article for *Cinema Journal*'s dossier on "Fifteen Years after 9/11," Fabrizio Cilento notes that "post-9/11 cinema marks a distinctive period in U.S. film history and is based on an imaginary of hidden global networks, potential threats, and exposure to random acts of violence."[2] Thus, recent and ongoing military conflicts have ceased to revolve around combat scenarios as numerable and predictable manoeuvres within the scope of certain battle tactics. Moreover, modern warfare, and the audiovisual representation thereof, is concerned with the underlying mechanisms and technologies of violent outbreaks and acts of terror. According to Cilento, films such as Rendition (Gavin Hood, 2007), In the Valley of Elah (Paul Haggis, 2007), The Hurt Locker (Kathryn Bigelow, 2008) and American Sniper (Clint Eastwood, 2014) "refrain from a simplistic reconstruction of events and are mainly concerned with producing what does not immediately appear on the surface."[3] In fact, what is actually produced by the films Cilento defines as the "ultraprocedural subgenre" of contemporary cinema is a distinct affective quality, both a replication and transformation of the "shape of our fears,"[4] of the paranoia and insecurity connected to the simultaneous ubiquity and invisibility of modern warfare. As Cilento adds, rather than being limited to cold digital aesthetics and pragmatic narratives of information tracking, post-9/11 movies remarkably "walk the razor's edge between the two poles of human emotion and soulless proceduralism without completely falling for either of them."[5]

One reason for this, I would argue, lies in the films' corpographic dimensions, their overt disjunctions of sight and sound which applies to both geographical and data spaces, and which becomes especially evident in the visibilities and

---

[1] Benjamin, *Illuminations*, 255.
[2] Fabrizio Cilento, "The Aesthetics of the Procedural in Post-9/11 Cinema," *Cinema Journal* 56 (1), 2016, 131–136, here: 132.
[3] Cilento, "The Aesthetics of the Procedural in Post-9/11 Cinema," 132.
[4] Cf. Stacy Takacs, "The Changing Shape of Our Fears," *Cinema Journal* 56 (1), 2016, 124–131.
[5] Cilento, "The Aesthetics of the Procedural in Post-9/11 Cinema," 134.

invisibilities generated by another ultraprocedural film, Kathryn Bigelow's ZERO DARK THIRTY. Ultimately, the negotiation of what can and cannot be seen is most interesting for a close analysis of this film, as it relates to the much-discussed media coverage of 9/11 and the phantasms and memories of terror it produced. The "peak of visibility" reached through the intensive mediation of the event was followed by an "ocular regime of denial, erasure, and incredulity or invisibility"[6] which is a decisive factor within ZERO DARK THIRTY's corpography of dissociated sound and vision.

One of the official trailers for the film not only introduces its theme, the hunt for Osama Bin Laden and his assassination, but renders its plot as a corpographic journey through potential war zones that, in contrast to conventional combat movies, are no designated areas of artillery battle; rather, these zones reach into the realm of everyday (city) life and are characterized by the undifferentiability between enemies and allies, terror and security, or even between surveillance and invisibility as conditions of quotidian actions.

The camera seems to dive into the depth of the image through several layers of clouds, passing by the logos of production companies *Columbia* and *Annapurna*, whose names are being crossed out with a black marker in the moment they become visible. But while these institutional sources of image production are eradicated, neither the marker itself nor the hand holding it is to be seen. A new, disembodied agency takes control over what the spectator gets to see, which turns out to be an externally controlled and mediated perspective – one surface after another is being unravelled: beyond (or rather below) the clouds a satellite image of Manhattan comes into view. And more than just being an image, the satellite view is a moving map. The camera zooms in, the image rotates, a few large pixels clouding the skyline visualize the digital rendering process. A black dot appears on the spot on the map where the World Trade Center's twin towers used to stand, marking the beginning of another pen line moving along the cityscape. We see the silhouette of the film's female protagonist, Maya, her shadow reflected on the glass of a framed American flag. The heads of terrorist suspects, shown as negative prints, are now superimposed onto various buildings along the moving line, which crosses out their eyes while it proceeds.

What the trailer presents is a complex layering of mediated views: not only does it play with images and imaginations of the past (of 9/11 as a media event, and of the people and organizations behind it) – it frames the present as a time of constant observation and mobility, as a time haunted by the digital ghosts of the past that vanish before they can be materialized. By means of presenting and

---

6 Cilento, "The Aesthetics of the Procedural in Post-9/11 Cinema," 131.

instantly erasing figurations of agency, the trailer seems to conceal and reveal what Anne McClintock calls "established circuits of global imperial violence that now animate the war on terror" on the level of image production.[7]

So far this seems to illustrate how the War on Terror unfolds as a series of investigative operations articulating – and already being a symptom of – a sociopolitical crisis of vision. Yet the trailer's aesthetic composition not only refers to an optical sensorium: as a graphic intertitle invites us to "witness the greatest manhunt in history," a throbbing electronic swell underpins the persevering threat, alternating with helicopter-like synthetic patterns. Like an alarm signal, or a "drumbeat for war,"[8] the low, distorted sound announces every new tagline, every new set of letters overlaying the traces left by the black marker. Finally, these letters, too, get painted over, and satellite views are frantically cross-cut with dramatic images and sounds of vehicles, clicking guns and explosions. The CIA's quest for "targets" is further shadowed by ghostly figures and uncertainty about their identity in a race against time until, after a final satellite image of Bin Laden's compound, the film's title appears, virtually being "uncrossed," as three black lines give way to the words "Zero Dark Thirty" in bold capital letters.

More than merely setting up and processing a plain metaphor for the film's advertised "uncovering" of the true story behind Bin Laden's assassination, the trailer thus sets the mood for the overall audiovisual dynamics of ZERO DARK THIRTY as a cartographic and corpographic composition where space is navigated and destabilized through conflicting sensory and technological perceptions on the levels of sound and image.

6.1 Echoes of Terror: Black Screens and Black Sites of 9/11

The fact that ZERO DARK THIRTY heavily relies on the sensuous, imaginative, and affective potential of sound to enable a phenomenological experience of cinematic space already becomes manifest in the film's opening sequence. It begins with an intertitle reading "The following motion picture is based on first-hand accounts of actual events." While this is not unusual for a film dealing with an

---

[7] Cf. Anne McClintock, "Paranoid Empire: Specters from Guantánamo and Abu Ghraib," *Small Axe* 13 (1) 2009, 50–74, here: 52.
[8] This both recalls and reverses what Andrew Jacobs of the *New York Times* has once written about the city's anti-war sentiment after 9/11: "The drumbeat for war, so loud in the rest of the country, is barely audible on the streets of New York." Andrew Jacobs, "Peace Signs Amid Calls for War," *The New York Times*, 20 September (2001), http://www.nytimes.com/2001/09/20/nyregion/peace-signs-amid-calls-for-war.html (accessed 5 December, 2016).

historical topic, the way this introductory line relates to the following moments turns out to be more than a justification of the plot, or a claim for authenticity. More than obviously referring to the lethal hunt for Bin Laden as "actual events," ZERO DARK THIRTY first confronts us with the actual events of "September 11, 2001," as it is indicated by another intertitle. We are presented with actual sonic accounts recorded on that day, but left without any corresponding images. The film hereby problematizes the politics of memory associated with 9/11 by alluding to the simultaneous (visual) absence and (acoustic) presence of its victims which generates an auditory space of memory.

It is through the analysis of the film's various presences and absences on the level of sensory, and embodied, perception that we can make this connection in the first place. In providing us with sonic accounts of 9/11, the film's opening designates an auditory space within which sound's "double nature as text and force"[9] comes to the fore: the black screen gives way to the rhythm and echoing pulse of the various acoustic traces that form a haunting driving force for the ZERO DARK THIRTY's following narrative, resonances of the past that inform our paranoid perception of cinematic space, that is, our constant anticipation of violent outbreaks.

In a very literal sense, the film's exposition forces the spectators to be an audience in being able to hear but not to see: a black screen successively fills with various distorted sounds – radio messages and phone calls. A few information fragments about flight "United 93" (one of four hijacked planes of 9/11) are followed by a women's voice: "I think there's mace... We can't breathe... I don't know, I think we're getting hijacked." Then the voice of a young man: "Hey Mom. I'm sure you've heard that a plane crashed into World Trade Center I." These words lead over to a whispered "I love you" and "Goodbye," before we hear another man screaming as a building collapses. A desperate cry for help, then the focus shifts to another woman calling an emergency hotline in New York: "Are you gonna be able to get somebody up there? ... We're on the floor and we can't breathe. I'm gonna die, aren't I" – "No, no, no, stay calm, stay calm..." – "It's so hot, I'm burning up..." – "You'll be fine, we're gonna come and get you. Can anyone hear me? Oh, my God..." The voices and random noises occasionally overlap and reverberate in the darkness, until they fall completely silent.

With no apparent connection to the film's plot about to follow, the seemingly effortless composition of this opening both refers to the problematic representation of 9/11 as media event and to the complex layering of sensory coordinates in

---

9 J. Martin Daughtry, "Thanatosonics: Ontologies of Acoustic Violence," *Social Text* 119 (32:2), 2014, 25–51, here: 30.

ZERO DARK THIRTY. While reminding us of various media responses to the attacks, the black screen especially recalls the famous black cover for *The New Yorker*'s September 24, 2001 issue: more than a plain black image, the cover (designed by Art Spiegelman and his wife, Françoise Mouly) featured the all-black graphical outlines of the World Trade Center serving as absolute negative spaces against a slightly lighter black background. Obviously articulating the horror and grief connoted with 9/11, and raising the general question of such an event's representability in general, the image bears another quality which might be best described as *haunting*. The silhouettes of the twin towers emerge from the darkness of the image like ghostly shadows of the past, creating their very own negative space, a gap demarcating a site of traumatic memory. In the same manner, journalist William Langewiesche delineates the actual collapse of the towers in his book, *American Ground*: "For an instant, each tower left its imprint in the air, a phantom of pulverized concrete marking a place that then became a memory."[10]

It is in fact this quite literal idea of negative space which also informs the opening sequence of Bigelow's film. That is, against some writers' assumptions,[11] I would argue that the audio recordings cannot simply be reduced to being a legitimization of torture practices, or an impulse for the film's causal logic of events; they set the ground for a procedural narrative within which every character, in a paranoid sense, acts upon the affective charge of the invisible, in a cultural and quotidian environment where the physical pain of others inscribed into images of the past has come to haunt our perceptions of the present. In this logic of affect, the mode of the procedural, and the way it deploys a navigation through instable spaces and transitory places, represents the frantic attempt to move through and beyond a shattered past and present in order to regain control over the future – an attempt that is realized not only as a narrative development but also as a corpographic process affecting the senses. And if Cilento writes that ZERO DARK THIRTY's strategic "black sites" would give audiences "an illusion of dominance, control, and empowerment,"[12] it is important to note that, with regard to the poetics of the war film, this illusion in fact remains a deception.

---

10 William Langewiesche, *American Ground: Unbuilding the World Trade Center*, New York 2002, 3.
11 See for instance Manohla Dargis, "By Any Means Necessary," *The New York Times*, December 17 (2012), http://www.nytimes.com/2012/12/18/movies/jessica-chastain-in-zero-dark-thirty.html (accessed December 3, 2016); Guy Westwell, *Parallel Lines*, New York 2014; Steve Coll, "'Disturbing' and 'Misleading,'" *New York Review of Books*, February 7 (2013), http://www.nybooks.com/articles/archives/2013/feb/07/disturbing-misleading-zero-dark-thirty/?pagination=false (accessed December 3, 2016).
12 Cilento, "The Aesthetics of the Procedural in Post-9/11 Cinema," 133.

The audiovisual composition of ZERO DARK THIRTY's first two minutes is crucial for this conception. Not only do we not see any familiar visual footage of the terrorist attacks – the widely-circulated images of the twin towers being crashed into and collapsing; moreover, we are being related to multiple individual experiences of fear, panic, and claustrophobia that designate the virtual "other side" of the day's mediation – the perspectives of the victims of September 11 that could not be recorded on camera. Instead, the visual point of view we are denied here turns into what Lisa Purse would call an "aural close-up"[13] of men and women in agony, and without any sense of orientation. While their voices thereby seem physically closer to the viewer, even though they are filtered through telephone lines, they also evoke vague images of separate spaces, moments, and scenarios: the situation aboard flight United 93 on the one hand, and of people trapped inside the burning World Trade Center on the other. Yet, in their specific arrangement, they meld into one, albeit destabilized, acoustic space – a kaleidoscope of visceral chaos. Therefore, it is much more what *cannot* be seen on, or what disappears from, the surface of the image which is constitutive for both the political paranoia rooted in the event and the ways it has been portrayed in the media, and which also defines the importance of sound for cinematic renditions of the War on Terror.

As for many U.S. network news broadcasts, numerous eyewitnesses that were called in (while live footage of the World Trade Center was shown) actually described what they heard and sensed of the incident before finding words for what they saw: the sound of a plane swishing by, of something like a sonic boom, the shattering explosion, shock waves, emergency sirens. Soon speculations about the size of the first plane arose, cumulating in the assumption that it even could have been a missile that hit the North Tower. Langewiesche, too, recalls: "When the Twin Towers collapsed, on the warm, bright morning of September 11, 2001, they made a sound heard variously around New York as a roar, a growl, or distant thunder."[14] While it is apparent and comprehensible that the first crash happened too fast and suddenly to recount it in visual terms, the many phone conversations with witnesses provided first-hand coordinates *exceeding* the optical register for a spatial and sensory description of the situation in downtown Manhattan – communicating an apprehension of place and events based

---

13 Purse refers to the opening scene of UNITED 93 (Paul Greengrass, 2006), in which we hear one of the 9/11 hijackers praying in Arabic before being provided with any visuals. Cf. Lisa Purse, "Working through the Body: Textual-Corporeal Strategies in United 93 (2006)," in *Film Moments: Criticism, History, Theory*, ed. Tom Brown, James Walters, London 2010, 159.
14 Langewiesche, *American Ground*, 3.

on affective bodily experiences. Furthermore, they distinctly opposed the more or less static aerial views of the twin towers by mapping out a dynamic ground space that did not exactly complement the incomprehensible images of the destruction above but vocalized the perplexity caused by what could be seen on the air.

Consequently, the constant levelling of information and emotion Cilento mainly attributes to the "ultraprocedural film" also applies to documentary accounts of 9/11. Guy Westwell, for instance, describes the opening sequence of Étienne Sauret's WTC – THE FIRST 24 HOURS, which features "locked-off" shots of the World Trade Center's North Tower being hit by the first plane and collapsing, as follows:

> [T]hese shots are denotative, objective, unflinching: seeming categorical statements of fact. The decision not to edit from one view of the event to another – and thereby establish some form of continuity – leaves the offscreen space resonant and encourages the viewer to search for a suitable framework other than that provided by the mainstream media. Second, the titles are followed by handheld shots taken by Sauret in the aftermath of the attacks [...] These shots are tentative, uncertain, thoughtful and quiet. There is no commentary, only the ambient sound recorded with the image. At regular intervals – almost as if offering a pause for thought – the sound drops out. This has the effect of aestheticizing the image for a moment before, as the sound returns, the evidential nature of the footage once again comes to the fore.[15]

What Westwell does not describe is Sauret's decision to occasionally insert black screens while leaving the sounds of each previous shot audible. This way the faint rotors of helicopters circling the World Trade Center, the sirens and horns of fire trucks, police cars and other vehicles almost seem to resound like abstract cries for help, mechanical counterparts to, and echoes of, the victims' phone calls used in ZERO DARK THIRTY. However, this technique only further stresses Westwell's argument about WTC's oscillation between "evidential" and "contemplative" shots. Also, it demonstrates that ZERO DARK THIRTY's mode of the procedural is not only a mandatory aesthetic feature of post-9/11 cinema but of an overall negotiation of perception, emotion, and history in the wake of the attacks, and across different media forms – a negotiation grounded in the ways the disruptive sounds and images of 9/11 implemented a prevailing sensory and cultural disequilibrium in contemporary society.

Thus, as the following analysis of Bigelow's film will demonstrate, this imbalance becomes graspable as an aesthetic concept, as an affective conception of dissociated visual, acoustic, and spatial components. This will lead once again to Cilento's essential observation on the ultraprocedural subgenre as represented

---

15 Westwell, *Parallel Lines*, 21.

by films like Rendition, In the Valley of Elah, Standard Operating Procedure (Errol Morris, 2008) and Fair Game (Doug Liman, 2010), or by TV shows like Homeland (Showtime, 2011–2015): "What is remarkable is how the dry, analytical, and detached aesthetic that permeates the directorial style clashes with the affective charges of the inflammatory issues of the so-called War on Terror."[16]

6.2 Behind the Surface

A little more than two minutes into the film, the black screen of Zero Dark Thirty's opening is replaced with a low-angle shot of a perforated panel sheet ceiling: "Two years later." A ray of light falls through a hole pointing to the next intertitle, "The Saudi Group," while we hear the violent opening of a door to one of the film's "black sites," in this case a room in which an Al-Quaeda prisoner named Ammar is tortured. This transition has provoked various critical responses reprimanding a suggested "cause and effect relationship between the void of September 11 voices and the lone man strung up in a cell,"[17] or the fact that it "elides two years in which […] critique, contradiction and political struggle were predominant in the wider culture, especially with regard to the War on Terror and the legality of the use of torture."[18] While Zero Dark Thirty's depiction of torture practices is certainly highly problematic in itself, a closer look at the film's formal structure reveals that both the violence inflicted upon others and the draining effect of a dissociated logistics of perception (as described by Virilio and Pisters) define two poles of paranoid disorder, an affective climate very conscious of – that is, founded on – post-9/11 political debates. If the procedural form of Bigelow's film seems to advocate a simplistic and jingoistic causal logic, this logic itself illustrates the interlocking of several meticulous methods of communication, documentation and investigation in the War on Terror – resulting in a narrative built on uncertainty and fragile facts and figures.

With the opening scene as emotional and historical reference point, Zero Dark Thirty elaborates on paranoia as an affective experience of instability on all levels of cinematic form, rather than just providing a fixed psychological mind-set or background atmosphere for the film's plot. Ways of navigating filmic space thus become profoundly confused by what Hauke Lehmann, within the context of New Hollywood cinema, has called a "dissociation of the spectator,"

---

[16] Cilento, "The Aesthetics of the Procedural in Post-9/11 Cinema," 133.
[17] Dargis, "By Any Means Necessary."
[18] Westwell, *Parallel Lines*, 173.

an affective strategy of transgression, disorientation, and disintegration that has changed the poetics of genre cinema and continues to influence the films of today.[19]

As I have argued before, this shattering of the senses is not only an effect of the New Hollywood, or of new technologies mapping out a more complex cinematic sensorium; it is also rooted in a politics of conflicting images that places the body of the spectator in an uncomfortable position between immersion and detachment – a battle of sensations that, since Vietnam, and especially since 9/11, has been epitomized by images of modern warfare. With regard to the relationship between contemporary genre cinema and military conflict, this condition has meanwhile problematized technologies of perception in a way that, for the spatial poetics of war-related films, fear and horror have become inseparable from other major dimensions of affect, creating corpographies of fragmented spaces and senses. This, in turn, seems to be a consequential evolution of the Hollywood war film which, as Kappelhoff observes, has always featured expressive modalities that strive for unsettling the spectator's perception, above all by evoking an invisible threat outside their field of vision.[20]

This again corresponds to ZERO DARK THIRTY as a procedural that carves out the traumatic and somatic effects of the War on Terror. Here, invisible threats are posed by both technological networks and violent outbreaks off-screen (oftentimes directly related to the film's protagonist, Maya). First, according to Steven Shaviro, the film features a "numbingly anonymous" but highly immersive environment of Big Data and "instantaneity (the annihilation of duration) mediated through video screens and telecommunications technologies"[21] – an information circuit ending in itself for the sake of precision and data collection. But it also represents a sensuous matrix of which the perceiver himself/herself is part – in Shaviro's words: "an ultimately asubjective or more-than-subjective atmosphere of affect."[22] Throughout the film, the visual field is simultaneously obstructed, scrutinized, and analysed; shots are composed of multiple planes, competing surfaces that deeply unsettle the image and its spectator. Figures in the foreground are oftentimes out of focus and at the same time obscuring what is happening in

---

19 Cf. Lehmann, *Affektpoetiken des New Hollywood*, Berlin / Boston 2016, 1–53.
20 Cf. Kappelhoff, *Front Lines of Community*, 124.
21 Steven Shaviro, "A Brief Remark on Zero Dark Thirty," *The Pinocchio Theory*, January 18 (2013), http://www.shaviro.com/Blog/?m=201301 (accessed June 5, 2016).
22 Steven Shaviro, "Kathryn Bigelow," *The Pinocchio Theory*, March 10 (2010), http://www.shaviro.com/Blog/?p=862 (accessed June 5, 2016).

the middle ground, while other characters are partially masked by fences, blinds, and similar architectural structures.

In one scene, for instance, Maya's car is held up and searched at a checkpoint in front of the American embassy. The film's perspectives change frequently from close-ups to medium long shots, from Maya's POV from inside the car to what seem to be multiple observatory gazes from outside (which, in turn, are never assigned to a specific character). As every shot is only a few seconds in length, and each cut to a new camera position breaks up any sense of spatial continuity, we are not able to orientate ourselves within the area of the checkpoint, nor are we given the opportunity to follow every action to the very end: the movement of a large mirror below the car, the opening of the trunk, a look at Maya through the windshield – all these are interrupted by cuts, blurry objects, or reflections, exposing (and concealing) one visual layer after another. Once inside the building, Maya is further scrutinized; we see her on a surveillance monitor next to a guard x-raying her suitcase. This image composition in fact epitomizes what Lehmann would call the "dissociation" of the spectator: still empathizing with Maya in experiencing the uncomfortable closeness and simultaneous fragmentation of her surroundings, the monitor set-up also puts her in the position of an x-rayed object that we are watching without ever fully "embodying" the camera gaze.

ZERO DARK THIRTY thereby articulates a general desire to look behind the surface, which is shared by the film's protagonists and its audience (see Figure 19). This technique, however, also demonstrates the impossibility of fulfilling said desire, as the images develop a technological, procedural life of their own, rather than serving any relatable character. However, what Shaviro calls a "more-than-subjective atmosphere" neglects Maya as an important – and ambiguous – focal point of the film's procedural matrix:

> At the film's center, the character Maya (Jessica Chastain) registers the experience of violence as a direct, intimate witnessing, a witnessing that sutures her to the larger social and historical world the film portrays. In her single-minded focus on the pursuit of Osama Bin Laden, a picture of a world emerges, a world defined by hidden networks of potential threats that may or may not be real, underlined by scenes of visceral injury, death and violent confrontation, conveyed in the aesthetic language of the procedural, a form that proliferates its own forms of anxiety.[23]

As the centre of perception and agency, Maya moves through a both real and virtual network of fragmented speculations, incorporating traces of physical

---

23 Robert Burgoyne, "The Violated Body: Affective Experience and Somatic Intensity in Zero Dark Thirty," in *The Philosophy of War Films*, ed. David LaRocca, Lexington 2014, 247–260, here: 247.

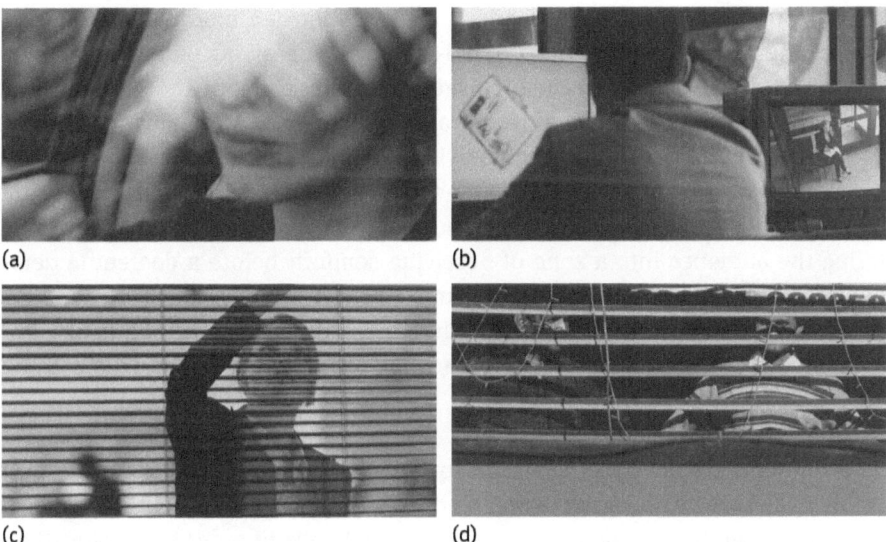

Figure 19: Behind the surface.

evidence, trying to turn them into a coherent image, while at the same time rejecting their impact on her own senses and emotions.[24] As Cilento also argues, Maya eventually succeeds in her job because she is "able to navigate the liveness and instantaneousness of the new multimedia environment in which she is immersed, surrounded as she is by statistics, metadata, visualizations of remote weaponry, satellite photographs, and an all-pervasive surveillance."[25] On the other hand, it is this obsessive navigation and investigation that the film frequently distances itself from. By occasionally depriving Maya from her agency and instead emplacing her (as well as the spectator) in unidentifiable environments ZERO DARK

---

[24] Here I do not want to further engage in debates about Maya's assumed motivations and behavioural traits, whether they could be interpreted as acts of revenge or as symptoms of "war autism." Cf. Agnieszka Piotrowska, "Zero Dark Thirty – 'War Autism' or a Lacanian Ethical Act?," *New Review of Film and Television Studies*, 12 (2), 2014, 143–155.

Although a psychoanalytical approach to ZERO DARK THIRTY is insofar helpful as it problematizes the way violence and torture are presented, (de)naturalized and, eventually, processed on the part of the audience, the focus nevertheless lies on the character (Maya) itself, whereas I am interested in the sensuous and spatial configurations that create a phenomenological rather than a psychological experience – more relying on the immediate interaction between body and space than on complex thought processes.

[25] Cilento, "The Aesthetics of the Procedural in Post-9/11 Cinema," 132.

THIRTY puts both its characters and it audience into an intermediary state of ever-changing perspectives, transitional spaces and deceiving perceptions.[26]

Another paradigmatic scene in this regard centres on Maya and her colleague Jessica having dinner at a hotel restaurant in Islamabad. After Maya has had to go through another security check outside the hotel building, the tension does not subside when she takes a seat at the table; only when Jessica tells her to stop looking at her phone does she (reluctantly) relax a little – a dramaturgical move luring the audience into a zone of deceiving comfort, before a deafening detonation shatters the room. Here, the filmic space is literally blown into pieces, as we see the same explosion from no less than seven different points of view, splintered into short successive shots showing people, furniture and glass being knocked over by the blast.

An alarm goes off, women scream in the distance, and we see Maya and Jessica stumbling through the smoke towards what seems to be the restaurant kitchen. Smoke and flickering lights complicate the navigation through the chaos; the two women have to hold on to each other's hands in order to stay together. We follow them through the almost apocalyptic scene (partially shot with a handheld camera), passing the many wounded employees, and getting a sense of the thick smoke and fire that surrounds them. Just this palpable claustrophobia, the somatic experience of a three-dimensional maze, is then immediately turned into the flat image of a TV news broadcast about the attack. Having been witnesses affectively engaged in a scene of pure confusion, that is, in a mediated experience of terror, we now become consumers of another layer of mediated images – one exposing the dynamics of TV journalism and image production.

As a mapping process, realized through a calculated mixture of screen aesthetics and nervous orientation in space, ZERO DARK THIRTY therefore proposes a thoroughly *paranoid corpography*. Sight and sound alternate in creating a tense atmosphere oscillating between anxiety and obsession that we most of all share with Maya, but that is just as often dissociated from any of the film's characters and complicates cinematic processes of emplacement and embodiment; we simultaneously navigate the film's cinematic space through various bodies, or

---

26 Conversely, Charles-Antoine Courcoux links what I would attribute to the film's overall expressive quality to Maya's intermediary position as an unconventional heroine: "[F]rom the very first scene, the movie shows that Maya is constantly in search of a fair distance between reflection and action, inside and outside, the East and the West, masculinity and femininity. In this respect, one can even argue that she is the person most on the outside in a business of insiders." Charles-Antoine Courcoux, "There's Something about Maya: On Being/Becoming a Heroine and the 'War on Terror,'" in *Heroism and Gender in War Films*, ed. Karen A. Ritzenhoff, Jakub Kazecki, New York 2014, 233.

media images, without being able to take or keep a fixed point of view. In this dissociation of perspectives on war as a mediated experience, corporeality thus seems to be a concept that is either literally "embodied" or technically abstracted.

6.3 Tracking Shots

The constant disjunction of sensory perception becomes especially tangible – however in a quite exceptional way – in one of the film's last segments, which is entitled "Tradecraft." Here, sounds and voices are of paramount importance. The way the sequence is initiated is in fact very similar to the film's prologue: a black screen, agitated voices. This time, however, the spoken language is Arabic, and given the information provided in the previous scene, it soon becomes clear that we are listening in on a phone conversation between a main Al-Quaeda intermediary, Saheed, and his mother. Instead of connecting their voices to visible bodies, the film offers a complementary diagrammatic image in the form of graphic sound waves on a computer screen. In the following shot, the vocals drown in a tangle of other phone calls as the camera tracks along a deserted server room, following the voices through a sea of cables. Again, a computer screen is to be seen, this time showing the sound graph under a geographical map of the Middle East. The programme zooms in on the city of Rawalpindi, Pakistan, where, instead of the source of the call (Saheed himself) the voice of his mother is singled out once more.

The aesthetic composition of this sequence deviates remarkably from ZERO DARK THIRTY's main staging patterns. While the film's corpography oftentimes comprises the display of a vulnerable "other" body, or the effects of an invisible Other on the sensuous configuration of the filmic body, the film itself seems establish virtual spaces that develop a life of their own. The buzzing voices inhabiting the empty space of the server room not only point to the invisibility and ubiquity of corresponding bodies, but they also highlight their inaudibility. That is, the portrayal of sounds travelling through cables is in fact an audiovisualization of actually unhearable electronic processes. The sequence thus becomes a metaphor for a communication network that is too complex to grasp by means of human perception, but one that is governed by an unmistakable – and unforgiving – technological construct (see Figure 20).

But instead of conforming to what Garrett Stewart conceives of as the "digital fatigue"[27] of contemporary war thrillers, this scene in ZERO DARK THIRTY once

---

27 Cf. Garrett Stewart, "Digital Fatigue: Imaging War in Recent American Film," *Film Quarterly* 62 (4), 2009, 45–55.

164 — 6 Zero Dark Thirty: Corpographies of the War on Terror

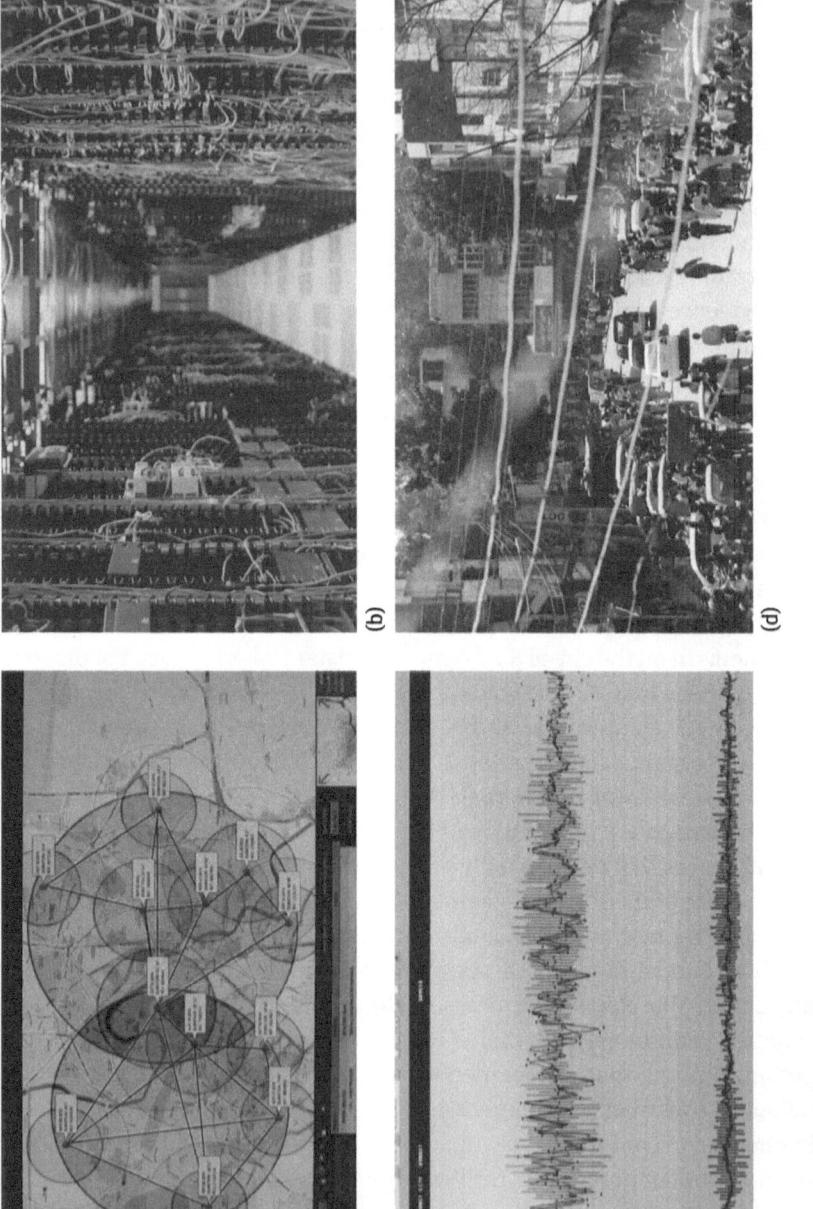

Figure 20: Technological conjunction and disjunction.

again visualizes both a technological recalibration of our sensuous system to time, space, and the body, as well as the films' impetus to uncover a "truth" behind the surface of clandestine or terrorist operations – and failing to do so by only disclosing the complexity of respective networks itself. This dramaturgy has already been constitutive for conspiracy films of the 1970s, where said desire to move beyond superficial structures is essentially spatialized. With special regard to Sydney Pollack's THE THREE DAYS OF THE CONDOR (1975), Fredric Jameson writes:

> [T]he representational confirmation that telephone cables and lines and their interchanges follow us everywhere, doubling the streets and buildings of the visible social world with a secondary secret underground world, is a vivid, if paranoid, cognitive map, redeemed for once only by the possibility of turning the tables, when the hero is able to tap into the circuits and bug the buggers, abolishing space with his own kind of simultaneity by scrambling all the symptoms and producing his messages from all corners of the map at the same time.[28]

Further developing Jameson's argument, this conception of cinematic space and time is also to be conceived of as *affective experience* communicated to the spectator by the same filmic techniques of cognitive mapping. Through image composition, cinematography, editing, and the interplay of disjunctive images and sounds, this experience unfolds over time, based on sensorial perceptions that challenge and eventually contradict a film's cognitive map.

Within the scene's unsettling amorphous set-up, the voice of Saheed's mother, in turn, provides an acoustic framing, if not a "sonorous envelope," as Kaja Silverman would call it.[29] The conversation between mother and son seems to weave through the presented data network like an umbilical cord, which, as it is traceable, is turned into a communicative flaw and a sign of vulnerability. The space, or better, the "non-space" of the scene thereby destabilizes the supposed hierarchy between hunters and hunted, between violator and victim, thus turning them into interchangeable factors in the equation of terror. ZERO DARK THIRTY, then, is not only ambiguous in its portrayal of torture, but shifts between various bodies of violence, ranging from detainees to CIA agents to the body of the film itself. The resulting paranoia arises from the fact that none of these bodies allows for an unquestionable identification with the spectator, but affects them on an intuitive somatic level instead – a level that provokes a physical prior to a cognitive reflection.

---

28 Fredric Jameson, *The Geopolitical Aesthetic*, Bloomington, IN 1992, 15.
29 For further discussion of the voice, and especially the female voice in film, cf. Kaja Silverman, *Acoustic Mirror: The Female Voice in Psychoanalysis and Cinema*, Bloomington, IN 1988.

Several times, this shift is indeed realized as a rhythmical pattern that constantly oscillates between visual and sonic elements of the filmic image. Formally rooted in the aforementioned tracking sequence, a later sequence in the film takes the notion of paranoia to an urban environment, subverting the ordinary atmosphere of an everyday space into a distressing experience.

In this scene, the Ground Branch team led by Larry (Édgar Ramírez) tries to track Saheed's phone signal from inside a van. While they drive through the crowded city centre of Rawalpindi, one of the technicians communicates the changes in signal strength, as visualized on his laptop. Saheed seems to constantly move in and out of the tracking range, but the dense traffic makes it impossible to locate him visually. After Larry concludes that Saheed must be driving in circles, the team decides to do the same, and then to wait for his car to pass by. Close-ups of the three men inside the van are juxtaposed with shots of numerous civilians talking on the phone, looking through window blinds, or walking and driving past the vehicle. On the one hand, space and architecture of the city are too dense to get a clear overview; on the other hand, the dominating uncertainty about the physical source of Saheed's signal renders every visible figure a possible suspect. Thus, the montage of the sequence evokes the uncomfortable feeling of being seen, but not being able to see. Additionally, the noisy atmosphere of the city fills the already overcrowded images, turning a scene of surveillance into one of paranoid claustrophobia. The way the signal continually changes directions not only underpins the impression of restless and crowded chaos but implies an almost choreographed movement of its transmitter through a non-transparent space. Ultimately, the source of the signal is located by means of rhythmical calculation. Larry and his colleagues correlate the signal's virtual movement to the physical movement of their van, attuning one to another. That is, the actual tracking process works neither entirely on a visual nor on a sonic level. Rather, the tracking data displayed on the team's computer is translated into a bodily perception, or measuring, of their environment; it is an intuitive kinetic interpretation of the signal's strength, whereby the metric quality of its frequency designates an estimated distance from one body (or vehicle) to another. The war film genre hereby homes in on phenomenological, or even psychological conceptions of urban space, as they have already been articulated in early twentieth century sociology.

In his book, *Acoustic Territories*, artist Brandon LaBelle refers to Georg Simmel's 1903 essay on "The Metropolis and Mental Life"[30] when he writes:

---

[30] Georg Simmel, "The Metropolis and Mental Life," in *The Sociology of Georg Simmel*, ed. and trans. K.H. Wolff, New York 1950, 409–424; originally published as "Die Großstädte und das

> The city and the body thus intertwine to operate as an emanating, medial network through which the here and now is immediately augmented with the potential of elsewhere. Being in the city is to not only experience the physical and direct environment, but to sense the extensiveness of functioning dynamics surrounding and invading the body. The geographic contours of urban life are thus networks between material environments and the intensities of perception, imagination, and fantasy, creating a feverish topography.[31]

What is most striking about this description is that LaBelle, by using the term "feverish topography," both hints at the paranoid potential of urban space and relates the individual body to a larger, interrelational system of experiences, where it takes part in interactions of material and immaterial forces. Interestingly, although one could get the impression that LaBelle mainly focuses on horizontal urban structures, the chapter in which this paragraph can be found is in fact titled "Sky: Radio, Spatial Urbanism, and Cultures of Transmission." Radio towers, he writes at one point, generate aerial figures – "manifestations of terrestrial projections that in turn come back down to haunt or invade life on earth."[32] Implicitly, without actually showing (or assuming the presence of) any radio towers yet all the more emphasizing the effects of radio transmission, ZERO DARK THIRTY's signal tracking sequence portrays the city as an acoustic territory that is heavily influenced by a form of *vertical mediation* which subsumes horizontal spaces under the controlling (over)view of technology (in this case the actual tracking device's screen that is shown frequently in this scene).

Lisa Parks most prominently attributes the remote modulation of terrestrial life to drones, stating that they would be as much a technology of inscription as they would be a technology of sensing or representation.[33] However, LaBelle's account of sound as having the potential to "disrupt or cohere given orders"[34] is surprisingly close to what Parks calls *vertical mediation*, "the technical process of transforming material phenomena into framed images" enhanced by "a multitude of imprints, traces, or residues left in the air, on the ground, or in the water by acts of war."[35] In this sense, acoustic signals would inscribe someone's or something's

---

Geistesleben", in *Die Großstadt. Vorträge und Aufsätze zur Städteausstellung. Jahrbuch der Gehe-Stiftung Dresden*, Band IX, ed. Theodor Petermann, Dresden 1903, 185–206.
31 Brandon LaBelle, *Acoustic Territories: Sound Culture and Everyday Life*, London 2010, 215.
32 LaBelle, *Acoustic Territories*, 207.
33 Cf. Lisa Parks, "Drones, Vertical Mediation, and the Targeted Class," *Feminist Studies* 42 (1), 2016, 227–235, here: 232.
34 LaBelle, *Acoustic Territories*, 207.
35 Lisa Parks, "Vertical Mediation: Geospatial Imagery and the US Wars in Afghanistan and Iraq," in *Mediated Geographies and Geographies of Media*, ed. Susan P. Mains, Julie Cupples, Chris Lukinbeal, Heidelberg / New York / London 2015, 159–175, here: 161.

physical presence into the urban network, and they would define the measures by which this presence is located. As foregrounded in ZERO DARK THIRTY, the scene's space is navigated through (traces of) communication devices, guided by the aim to attaching a signal to an identifiable body. The film thus draws a poignant picture of what Goodman calls the "urban audiosocial," and describes as "a system of speeds and channels, dense pressure pockets, vortices of attraction, basins of acoustic immersion and abrasion, vibratory and turbulent: a whole cartography of sonic force."[36] Ultimately, the sonic maps out the space of the film more intricately than any visual coordinates ZERO DARK THIRTY provides us with, which challenges, if not undermines the configurations of vision and visibility so often attributed to modern warfare.

6.4 Night Visions / Night Calls: The Canaries

The immersion of simultaneous sights and sounds, as demonstrated in the film's tracking sequences, results in a loss of both visual and auditory focus and thus amplifies the impression of an omnipresent (but undetectable) threat. Another aspect of paranoia, however, would stem from the exact opposite condition: the disjunction of sight and sound would be equally unsettling in forcing the perceiving subject to focus on one sense at a time, while being deprived of other senses. Here, too, ZERO DARK THIRTY offers a telling example: the most extreme disjunction of sight and sound occurs in the film's concluding segment, "The Canaries." In a final strike, a team of skilled Navy SEALs raids Bin Laden's compound at night, while Maya monitors and listens in on their actions from a safe distance. As the compound is shrouded in darkness, the soldiers have to use night vision goggles to proceed. Interestingly, this condition causes the subsequent filmic images to be divided into two perspectives: the green-hued night vision shots representing the SEAL's point of view on the one hand, and almost completely dark shots of the same action that vaguely frame the soldiers from an external position on the other. The two visual styles alternate through rapid editing, and although the film thus frequently detaches us from the soldiers' visual point of view, the dark images of compromised vision let us focus even more on the intimate sensuous perception that is foregrounded in this sequence. That is, in drawing our attention from faint animal sounds in the background to

---

[36] Steve Goodman, *Sonic Warfare: Sound, Affect, and the Ecology of Fear*, Cambridge, MA 2010, 9.

the breathing and whispering of the soldiers, the sonic coordinates given enable the creation of a rough aural topography that comprises more distant locations as well as the physical closeness to the SEALs. In terms of film form, this space is created through a distinct composition of *materializing sound indices* (M.S.I.) and *elements of auditory setting* (E.A.S.), both of which being terms coined by Michel Chion. While M.S.I.s help to express the texture and material condition of a sound's source as well as the circumstances of its production (an impact, periodic movement, etc.),[37] E.A.S.s are "sounds with a more or less punctual source, which "define a film's space by means of specific, distinct touches."[38] The animal sounds in this sequence, i.e. the barking of a dog and the mooing of cows, are to be conceived as E.A.S.s to enhance the spatial feel and rhythm of the scene, whereas M.S.I.s such as the rustling of the soldiers' armoured suits, the clicking sounds of their rifles, or the creaking floor in Bin Laden's house add a tactile quality to the depicted actions and movements. What is established here is a somatic point of view split into an internal perspective marked by images of night vision, and an external perspective deploying a rudimentary topography of sound. This is not to say that sound and image could be clearly differentiated from one another. Chion, in an admittedly oversimplifying manner, speaks of cinema using auditory and visual channels to communicate with the spectator, whereby "everything spatial in a film, in terms of image as well as sound, is ultimately encoded into a so-called visual impression, and everything which is temporal, including elements reaching us via the eye, registers as an auditory impression."[39] Whether we perceive a film in spatial or in temporal terms, it is always both image and sound contributing to this feeling. With regard to ZERO DARK THIRTY, this thought can be concretized to the following: visual and sonic cues, in both their combination and disjunction, elaborate the spatiotemporal construct of an intensified corpography.

This is in fact a modulated form of what Kevin McSorley calls "embodied soldiering," the idea of a somatic perception of war recorded and expressed by helmetcams:

> The embodied presence of the soldier is constantly felt in helmetcam footage, via the restless point-of-view, the sounds of breathing and vocalizations, the reverberations of corporeal movement, the presence of shadows cast by the body, the sight of the soldier's rifle pointing the way ahead, the sense of hands shielding the sun. Helmetcam footage also emphasizes the choreography of martial embodiment, as in patrol, where the shared rhythms of bodily

---

37 Chion, *Audio-Vision*, 114.
38 Chion, *Audio-Vision*, 55.
39 Chion, *Audio-Vision*, 136.

movement and the collective grammars of bodily spacing and formation are foregrounded as the means through which territory [...] is apprehended and occupied.[40]

According to McSorley, such footage "highlights the sensory modalities through which threat becomes palpable."[41] Hence, in the case of ZERO DARK THIRTY, the physical rendering of space compensating a lack of vision, which is epitomized with the final raid sequence, adds to the sensation of threat – to a bodily perception of paranoia. For although the use of night vision oculars speaks for a significant technological advance on the part of the American soldiers, the green hue illuminating their visual field even alters the possible presence of hidden antagonists. Even more so, the SEALs literally produce their enemies by calling or pulling them into the frame at any one time. As no one is progressively attacking the soldiers, we hear them hissing the names Khalid and Osama, upon which vague figures come into view and are shot immediately. The women and children, in turn, are (with one exception) not harmed, but, once detected, physically fixated within the given image space.

This, again, is not only a strategic action within the scene's compositional structure. Although it might not be a comparable instance, the SEALs' act of pulling their targets into the frame nevertheless recalls the infamous military practice of taking "trophy" photos as an act of self-suggested control. As McClintock points out in her article on the "Specters from Guantánamo and Abu Ghraib," this might have been

> a means of fixing as spectacle, in the photographs' fraudulent promise of permanence, their own unsteady oscillations of paranoia. The photographs promised to memorialize, in the fixity of the image, what was ephemeral in the realm of power. In a context of great fear and vulnerability, the photographs promised to capture and fix, in the stopped-time of the image, the soldiers' fleeting moments of grand omnipotence [...] But because this omnipotence was borrowed and phantasmagoric, it could not be sustained and was therefore destined to recur for ritualistic repetition.[42]

Strikingly, the "fleeting moments of omnipotence" that McClintock describes designate once more the illusion of overview as an integral narrative and affective configuration of the war film genre. Here, however, it is not – or not primarily – a specific terrain that is supposedly controlled by means of cartographic opera-

---

40 Kevin McSorley, "Helmetcams, Militarized Sensation and 'Somatic War,'" *Journal of War and Culture Studies* 5 (1), 2012, 47–58, here: 53. McSorley technically refers to the practice of embodied soldiering in the Afghanistan war, but his observations also account for other contemporary battle zones.
41 McSorley, "Helmetcams, Militarized Sensation and 'Somatic War,'" 53.
42 McClintock, "Paranoid Empire," 60.

tions before it is lost through disorientation in battle; in this case, it is the attempt to take control over certain "other" bodies, which takes the form of creating a visual field and creating an enemy to behold. With regard to ZERO DARK THIRTY's raid sequence, then, the soldiers' navigation through the uncanny space of Bin Laden's compound depends both on any given sonic coordinates and the visible elimination of several opponents that, in an almost topographical manner, mark the decreasing distance to Bin Laden himself as the ultimate nemesis. Yet although there are eventually taken photos of his corpse at the end of the scene, the pictures themselves are out of focus, leaving doubts about his identity. Here the film reflects on the actual politics concerning Bin Laden's body, which, according to Jessica Auchter, still lingers on as a "specter" of terrorism: the fact that his corpse was not shown in the media seems to justify the on-going war on terror, as Bin Laden is thus not undoubtedly fixed within a photographic frame.[43]

This, in turn, leads back to what Baudrillard once called "leitmotif of precision": although we see or assume that Bin Laden is killed point-blank, the film leaves us with the thought that this efficacy nevertheless results in uncertainty, or, as Baudrillard would put it, that it is "impossible to discern whether or not he is dead."[44] Conforming to this interpretation, ZERO DARK THIRTY's entire raid sequence bears strong resemblance to scenes from a generic horror film or a first-person shooter game, as it features a compellingly restricted sense of vision in the form of short panning shots and images of technologically advanced, subjective points of view. But this is not only due to the fact that video game aesthetics are an important dimension of many films about the wars in Afghanistan and Iraq, or, to quote Patricia Pisters, that "[v]ideo games look like war and war looks like a video game."[45]

Moreover, style and composition of the scene expose, in a contemporary media-aesthetical mode, what Auchter calls a "politics of haunting,"[46] as it oscil-

---

[43] Auchter points out that, in contrast, images of Libyan dictator Muammar Gaddafi's corpse were instrumentalized to symbolise the triumph of democracy over dictatorship. I am referring here to a talk given by Auchter at the University of Reading in 2015. Her paper, entitled "Visible dead bodies and the technologies of erasure in the war on terror," was part of a research workshop ("'Disappearing War,' Cinema and the Politics of Erasure in the War on Terror") organized by the Department of Film, Theatre & Television and the Department of Politics and International Relations, and held on April 13, 2015.
[44] Jean Baudrillard, *The Gulf War Did Not Take Place*, trans. Paul Patton, Bloomington, IN 1995, 43.
[45] Pisters, "Logistics of Perception 2.0," 243.
[46] In her book, *The Politics of Haunting and Memory in International Relations*, Auchter explores "the role of practices and performances of statecraft in constructing the line between life

lates between the poles of human emotion and efficient proceduralism. Through its meticulous disjunction of sight and sound, ZERO DARK THIRTY deploys a cinematic experience of uncertainty, which is grounded in the instability of sensuous perception. In Bigelow's film, ghostly voices, violent sounds, and disembodied gazes populate fragile and transitory spaces, constantly haunting the cinematic image and blurring the line between life and death.

In effect, ZERO DARK THIRTY is a "spectral configuration" at its most cinematic, comparable to a recent multimedia installation of the same title, which Lisa Parks has created with a group of Lebanese and Slovenian artists: the installation's centrepiece is a drone-like human body floating in mid-air, with military video footage projected onto its almost translucent surface.[47] In the case of ZERO DARK THIRTY, it is the filmic body (and the body of the spectator) that is equally enveloped "within the luminous footprint of world history and militarization, cycling through a series of spectral suspects, framed targets, and aerial strikes,"[48] unsettled by the techno-logical effects of fragmented audiovisual perception. It is this condition as both aesthetic concept and viewing experience, which marks another evolutionary stage in war cinema and its corpographic modes of staging. Channelled through the numerous audiovisual renditions of past wars, the terror of contemporary political conflict is already implemented in today's media culture – a context within which war is not only being re-mediated but also, disconcertingly, anticipated.

---

and death," (4) from a hauntological perspective, defining statecraft as "processes of ordering, bordering, and limitation that construct subjectivity/ies through an iterative and performative process" (5). Statecraft can therefore be regarded as part of constructing "architectures of enmity," which then contributes to the emergence of paranoia. With regard to her research, Auchter indeed takes into account that haunting has "material, bodily, affective, and ethical implications." (3) For further discussion see Jessica Auchter, *The Politics of Haunting and Memory in International Relations*, London 2014.

47 The installation was part of the "Vertical Collisions" exhibition at the Beirut Station Art Gallery (May 2015). Cf. Parks, "Drones, Vertical Mediation, and the Targeted Class."

48 Parks, "Drones, Vertical Mediation, and the Targeted Class," 233.

7 Conclusion

Having looked at various audiovisual representations of war throughout media history, from the post-WWI period to today, it becomes evident how important renditions of bodily sensations in relation to space have been (and continue to be) for our cultural understanding of military conflict. At the same time, this importance has been surprisingly underrated in film and media studies.

The role of the body in and for the mediation of war is indeed central to approaches to cultural identity and gender representation, and, from a dialectical point of view, even to all those discussing the problematic *absence* of the body in modern warfare – ranging from conceptions of so-called "bodiless wars" to the anaesthetizing effects of digital images. However, what all these perspectives focus on is the involvement of the body in combat as a situation based on visual parameters and cultural imaginations, a condition arising from the so-called "military dispositif" within which bodies and perceptions of war are organized from a distance, and organizing distances themselves.[1] But while these easily allow for a reflection on images as stereotypes, and conventions of conflict representation in audiovisual media, they also prohibit any closer look at how these images are shaping, and shaped by, complex aesthetic experiences in the first place.

Before further engaging with this issue, quite a few rather reductionist approaches to filmic renditions of war refer to Virilio's analogy of cinematic and military technology in which he criticizes the "fusion-confusion of eye and camera lens, the passage from vision to visualization,"[2] postulating:

> But what does one see when one's eyes, depending on sighting instruments, are reduced to a state of rigid and practically invariable structural immobility? One can only see instantaneous sections seized by the Cyclops eye of the lens. *Vision, once substantial, becomes accidental.*[3]

Here, Virilio indeed calls up the shortcomings of cinematic / photographic technology in relation to a "panperceptual" experience of war; yet this argument would only seem valid if we were to measure all audiovisual accounts of war against an absolute reality of combat, in which case they would obviously fail

---

[1] Cf. Paul Virilio, "A Topographical Amnesia," in *The Visual Culture Reader*, ed. Nicolas Mirzoeff, London / New York 1998, 108–122, here: 112.
[2] Paul Virilio, *The Vision Machine*, Bloomington, IN 1994, 13.
[3] Virilio, *The Vision Machine*, 13.

to convey the physical experience of battle they tried to recreate.[4] War films, however, and films as artistic media in general, are never authentic reproductions of actual events; rather, as I have pointed out, they are analytical reflections of and on sensuous perception, relating the spectator to a specific expression, an affective dimension of war. And is this process of putting us in a sensory relation to filmic images that is grounded in bodily experience before it can be concretized in the form of mental images or simulations. As Deleuze and Guattari have already noted in *What is Philosophy?*, art provides us not with the resemblance but the "pure sensation" of an object, when "the material [is] passing completely into the sensation, into the percept or affect."[5]

Thus, where a limited discussion of technology and accidental vision prevents theories of cinematic embodiment from coming into being, corpography offers an analytical model to further explore the possibilities of mediating the experience of combat as a multisensory, and spatial, phenomenon. Most importantly, it diverges from cognitivist notions of media and virtual realities to critically re-engage with genuinely phenomenological concepts concerning the interrelations of art, space and the body.

When we, for instance, consider Merleau-Ponty's idea of the body as "an intertwining of vision and movement"[6] and Edward Casey's take on landscapes (and artistic renditions of landscape) as appealing to the "full bodily sensorium,"[7] we have identified two theoretical premises that not only inform *corpography* as a way to navigate and physically apprehend space, but which also form basic points of reference for an affective theory of film viewing. In this line of argument, the orientation within cinematic spaces of concrete sensory experiences makes up the foundation for all processes of meaning making in film – as an interaction between audiovisual movement-images and the body of the spectator.

Consequently, the Hollywood war film would have to be understood as a genre not based on representations of factual events and glorifications of heroic deeds but, above all, on the staging of a relationship between the individual body, the larger military corps, and figurations of militarized nature. It is on the basis of this correlation that a central historical dimension of the war film can be described and investigated: similar to how Gregory conceptualizes the theoretical

---

4 As Kappelhoff also notes, in this (improbable) case the audiovisual document itself would have to be understood as an undistorted reference point for the mediation of a transparent reality of war. Cf. Kappelhoff, *Front Lines of Community*, 78.
5 Gilles Deleuze and Félix Guattari, *What Is Philosophy?* trans. Graham Burchell and Hugh Tomlinson, London 2003, 67.
6 Merleau-Ponty, "Eye and Mind," 124.
7 Edward Casey, *Representing Place: Landscape Painting and Maps*, Minneapolis 2002, 6.

fundamentals of Human Geography, *cinematic corpography* can propose a sensuous connection to the world by means of which "time and space are no longer absolutes but defined in relation to people, events and objects, and these are not located 'in' time and space but enter into the co-production of time-space."[8]

With regard to film, corpography is a mode of generating and communicating a subjective perspective of physical space which can be contextualized within a distinct cultural and historical framework. This, in turn, implies an understanding of genre as "a system of shaping, addressing and differentiating emotional experience" that situates the spectators "within a shared world of sentiment, a sense of belonging to a common world of aesthetic, emotional, and moral judgment"[9] – a conception which differs profoundly from narrative and iconographic "anatomies" of genre cinema. For if we look at the aesthetic function of combat movies as historical films, they do not just present us with images *of* the past, but with the past turned *into* audiovisual images with which we engage somatically and emotionally (an almost material dimension of time which becomes most evident in Kubrick's PATHS OF GLORY). That is, what Burgoyne calls a "feeling for the past" in this context therefore entails a different, and more complex, type of spectatorial involvement than cognitive processes of image recognition and identification. It does, for example, make a difference whether we qualify the notion of haunting in films about the Great War as an arrangement of symbolic images or as an affective dimension unfolding as a series of expressive movements. Opting for the latter, the fact that we actually see depictions of ghost soldiers at the end of ALL QUIET ON THE WESTERN FRONT only epitomizes the overall sense and sensation of haunting developed over the course of the film; and it is not only called up by means of uncanny portrayals of night and fog but through the ways we navigate and perceive these cinematic scenes as harrowing spaces of physical threat – how we are compelled to relate to the soldiers' tension, and their apprehension of No Man's Land as a "haptic geography."

It is thus no arbitrary tautological shortcut to compare Hollywood war films about WWI to First World War poetry and literature, as I have done in Chapter Two. Obviously, written accounts of war cannot simply be equated with the aesthetic principles of moving images; however, the way we approach them in terms of their affective engagement with the reader / viewer offers insights about the

---

[8] Gregory and Castree, "Editors' Introduction: Human Geography," xlix.
[9] Hermann Kappelhoff, Matthias Grotkopp, and David Gaertner, "The Poetics of Mobilization: Gung Ho!" *mediaesthetics – Journal of Poetics of Audiovisual Images*, no. 1, June 2016, http://www.mediaesthetics.org/index.php/mae/article/view/41/91 (accessed November 24, 2016).

effectiveness of poetic concepts – an effectiveness that goes beyond the realm of mimetic representation.

The metaphoric renditions of landscape and physicality both Santanu Das and Derek Gregory found in poems and novels about the Great War testify to what Sten Pultz Moslund has termed the "topopoetics" of literature: "the production – or the *poiesis* or *presencing* – of place in literature through the enduring interconnections between place, language, and bodily sensation."[10] Moreover, he not only describes the characteristics of somatic representation in literary texts but also sheds light on how these are embodied through a "topopoetic" mode of reading. Here, drawing on Josephine Machon, Pultz Moslund further elaborates on how the "preconceptual or corporal dimension of language"[11] refers human perception back to its "primordial impulse"[12] and moves from "the detached contemplation of place as scenery" in order to "enter into the complex cultural and sensuous experiences of place as a lived-in world."[13]

This theoretical perspective is fairly close to Kappelhoff's approach to genre cinema via the Hollywood war film, where he investigates how films can be described as poetic acts of film viewing,[14] embodied by the spectators as processes of feeling and thinking – which, for the purposes of this study, implies that cinematic spaces are not to be understood as preconditioned representations of place but as affective zones realized both through filmic movement and the spectators' capability of *being moved*.

When war films therefore make frequent use of maps (as representations and organizations of place), they do not just set cartographic texts against the disorienting physical experience of battle; rather, these texts become part of this experience, starting points for a specific *movement*, a corpography of combat that we perceive as a successive deconstruction of overview in favour of an intensified physicality. Seen in this way, the war film's cartographic, or Icarian, views not only signify certain visual perspectives of control but they translate them into affective categories, or, more precisely, into what Teresa Castro would call "cartographic sensation." It is this trajectory from overview to chaos that lies at the heart of the war film's genre poetics, and forms the basis for the melodramatic

---

10 Sten Pultz Moslund, "The Presencing of Place in Literature: Toward an Embodied Topopoetic Mode of Reading," in *Geocritical Explorations: Space, Place and Mapping in Literary and Cultural Studies*, ed. Robert T. Tally Jr., New York 2011, 9–43, here: 30.
11 Cf. Josephine Machon, *(Syn)aesthetics: Redefining Visceral Performance*, New York 2009, 6.
12 Machon, *(Syn)aesthetics*, 34.
13 Machon, *(Syn)aesthetics*, 34.
14 Cf. Kappelhoff, *Front Lines of Community*, 108.

journey of the individual soldier which the spectators are able to adopt as their own, cinematic, subjectivity.

What the analysis of Raoul Walsh's OBJECTIVE, BURMA! has shown in this regard is that the political discourses arising from the production and consumption of war films always need to be traced back to the ways this subjectivity is created as a shared communal feeling, a feeling that not only refers to an individual somatic experience of combat but also to the actual historical experience of war in the form of collective memories and media images. The conflict between OBJECTIVE, BURMA! and the documentaries BURMA VICTORY and THE STILWELL ROAD, for instance, is mainly grounded in their opposing staging patterns, their different treatments of sensory perception and their ambivalent educational rhetoric while all are based on the same documentary footage of the Burma campaign. Interestingly, the question as to whether either of these works could be qualified as propaganda has been tied to their degree of somatic representation. Whereas THE STILWELL ROAD (an American production) focuses on aerial views, depictions of a functioning military corps, and a rather authoritative rendering of events, the British BURMA VICTORY in fact highlights the physical ordeal of soldiers fighting in the campaign. Oscillating between these two perspectives, OBJECTIVE, BURMA! incorporates said documentary material into an opening newsreel sequence preceding the film's fictional narrative in order to set up a media-historical ground from where the somatic effects of jungle warfare can unfold as an impactful spectatorial experience.

However, the war film's cinematic corpography comprises more than a soldier's conflict between overview and chaos, or discrepancies between cartographic abstractions of nature and the actual navigation through the battle zone; it is also about a profound transformation of the soldier's body itself, the process of attuning to the overall physical charge of war. Like many other combat movies about tank warfare, David Ayer's recent film FURY highlights the intricate relationship of human bodies to military technology and describes the tragic process of an individual's physical unification with, and the eventual separation from, the machinery of battle. On the one hand, both the tank and the figure of the tank operator move within a corpographic complex which Derek Gregory has defined as the "cyborg nature" of war – specific forms of militarized landscapes shaping the military operations that take place through them, and composed of both vibrant and deadly matter: "burned-out vehicles and bombed-out buildings, barbed wire and exploded munitions, discarded weapons and abandoned supplies, toxic residues and body parts."[15] On the other hand, the fact

---

[15] Gregory, "The Natures of War," 4–5.

that the tank operator navigates the war zone by means of his vehicle's technical instruments, and becoming one with the machine, makes him a "cyborg soldier" himself. Bearing in mind that Ayer's film was released in 2014, a time of advanced military technology and drone warfare, the implicit look at WWII through the lens of contemporary conflicts problematizes the historical (and contemporary) role of the soldier as both vector and object of war. As Cristina Masters reminds us with special regard to the American military apparatus, the "making of soldiers into machines is scarcely a new phenomenon, continuing to signify the constitution of the body as a primary site of technological inscription,"[16] a condition that creates a so-called "post-human" subjectivity:

> This post-human subjectivity is represented through the cyborg in the very processes of transferring human reasoning and thinking from human subjects onto technology, wherein technology is infused with the ability to reason and think without being interrupted by emotions such as guilt or bodily limitations such as fatigue, and in that the human body is no longer the subject that can produce and project desired representations of the American self.[17]

While this is certainly one of the war film's main concerns, the bodily limitations Masters talks about in fact always counterbalance, and mostly outweigh, representations of the machinic military corps. From cinematic portrayals of the Korean War to Vietnam and the Gulf Wars, it is not a purely post-human subjectivity that is established, but a profoundly visceral experience of war which may be influenced but never replaced by technological perception or cyborg phantasies.

Still, tactile and acoustic sensations are pivotal elements of the films' affective dramaturgy – contrasting the abstract and oftentimes de-individualized perspectives of generals, military group formations, and mediated images of war. Whenever spatial figurations of touch and intimacy are foregrounded in Hollywood war films, they both emphasize the need for the single soldier's corpographic orientation that exceeds vision (and the potential of military technology) and the nature of war as a system of interacting spatial, physical and mental confinements. A paradigmatic example in this regard is Anthony Mann's MEN IN WAR, which, through its frequent condensations of cinematic space, articulates the spatial limitations of its characters and also testifies to a shift in the audiovisual representation of war in the 1950s. As for the Korean War's problematic status in-between genres and ideological messages, Mann's focus on the soldier's corporeal interaction with a surrounding enemy nature also refers to the ambiguous

---

16 Masters, "Bodies of Technology," 113.
17 Masters, "Bodies of Technology," 114.

nature of Hollywood's genre system in the 1950s. While the Korean War as the "Forgotten War" was partially filtered through the family melodrama or the POW film, the conflict itself was mainly depicted in the mode of classical WWII combat movies. Thus, the struggle to accommodate it to established generic codes or to find alternative forms of representations becomes manifest in the film's circular structure and its expression of a problematic physical relationship between body and space, between an individual and its relation to the world.

If the Korean War, and also the subsequent Cold War, posed substantial challenges to the combat film genre, which, in its creation of a specific feeling for the past, had to account for the constantly changing nature of war and audiovisual media, the Vietnam War has to be conceived of as an even more consequential crisis for the representation of military conflict. New cinema technology, the self-reflexive aesthetics of New Hollywood Cinema, and the image politics of television and photo journalism between government-friendly coverage on the one hand and unfiltered or critical reporting on the other provoked certain changes within the war film genre. Despite the fact that there had been almost no Vietnam combat films until the release of THE BOYS IN COMPANY C, GO TELL THE SPARTANS, and THE DEER HUNTER, the portrayals of nearly undefined war zones in this first wave of Hollywood films about Vietnam dealt with altered, or even inverted, hierarchies of sensory perception: disorienting sounds and visions, vague acoustic geographies, and mythical imagery dissolving into opulent visions of destruction. While Coppola's APOCALYPSE NOW continues to be discussed as the most influential production in this regard, all Vietnam War films share a common trait in their resolute rejection of cartographic perspectives and what I have called a "shattering of the senses" concerning their corpography. What already becomes manifest in the form of conflicting sounds and images in THE BOYS IN COMPANY C eventually develops into an intensified sensuous apprehension of nature and a physical experience of captivity in RESCUE DAWN – a reduction of vision, movement and verbal communication, which, in turn, calls for the sense of touch as an instrument of both communication and orientation. Almost thirty years after THE DEER HUNTER, and twenty years after Oliver Stone's PLATOON, Werner Herzog takes up on both the classical war film's depiction of an unforgiving enemy nature and the earlier Vietnam film's critique of American national myths and phantasies of power by centring on the fallen pilot as a metaphor for military hubris.

As the fighter pilot is usually not physically involved in the destruction he is causing from above, his situation epitomizes the idea of "war at a distance," that is, as part of the war film's cartographic imagery, the detached Icarian perspectives and technologies of aerial warfare initiate a problematic feeling of omnipotence and inviolability in relation to an in fact uncontrollable terrain, embodied in the figure of the pilot.

This issue is now pivotal for current debates on drone warfare and other remote-controlled battle technology, the difference being that the pilots' position at a military base is even more detached from the actual combat zone they are operating in. While, in media studies, related points have largely been discussed with regard to drone surveillance, the compression of time and space through advanced technology, and what Garrett Stewart has termed "digital fatigue," I chose not to focus on Virilian argumentations on "war at the speed of light" (which is the subtitle for his essay collection, *Desert Screen*), as they still tend to centre on the pre-eminence of the image and the paradigm of the informational. For my take on post-9/11 war cinema, as exemplified by ZERO DARK THIRTY, I am relying on the paranoid mode of perception these militarized technologies and images facilitate – an affective experience of instability on all levels of cinematic form. Ultimately, this experience is corpographic insofar as it builds on disjunctions of sight and sound for the navigation of both geographical and data spaces.

In my view, the fact that war has become intensely mechanized and digitized does not imply that it is purely virtual or "bodiless" now. That is, even if Chris Hables Gray has argued that, "[i]n the war of mechanical speed against human reactions, bodies are the real losers,"[18] this does not mean combat, and the audiovisual representation thereof, would be less corporeal, or less affective. What it does point to, however, is that there have been profound shifts in the mediation of war, and in the ways it is rendered as an essentially somatic experience. This becomes especially evident when focusing on a defined production context like the Hollywood war film, as there are, of course, cultural differences in global (war) cinema that lie beyond the scope of this study.

To be able to describe these changes in detail, corpography has proved to be a fruitful concept, as it accounts for the intimate and precarious relationship between space and the body in war, and also makes for an illuminating approach to genre cinema in that it can be used to explore both cinematic form and the spectator's involvement in a specific aesthetic experience. Thus, cinematic corpography extends and concretizes Williams' idea of "body genres" to a phenomenological reading of filmic space and affect – an analytical method that, to my mind, enriches theories of cartographic cinema and can also be applied to other genres and production contexts insofar as the comparison of different national cinemas on the level of corpographic staging could not only facilitate, but concretize a transnational approach to genre poetics. Especially with regard to the horror film, corpography promises to be a useful instrument to analyse its spatial

---

18 Chris Hables Gray, *Postmodern War: The New Politics of Conflict*, New York 1997, 40.

figurations, acoustics, visibilities and invisibilities in relation to sensuous navigation. This corpographic dimension of an encounter with the unknown and the uncanny could, in turn, be extended to works of science fiction, and specifically to films that deal with the exploration of outer space. Furthermore, the concept could be traced in the adventure film and the historical film to further enquire the affective relation to spaces of the past that these genres establish. After all, a feeling for the past is a feeling of the present.

Bibliography

Adey, Peter, Mark Whitehead, and Alison J. Williams, eds. *From Above: War, Violence and Verticality*. London: Hurst & Company, 2014.
Aldgate, Tony. "Mr Capra Goes to War: Frank Capra, the British Army Film Unit, and Anglo-American travails in the production of 'Tunisian Victory,'" *Historical Journal of Film, Radio and Television* 11 (1) (1991), 21–39.
Ames, Eric. "Herzog, Landscape, and Documentary," *Cinema Journal* 48 (2) (2009), 49–69.
Anderegg, Michael, ed. *Inventing Vietnam: The War in Film and Television*. Philadelphia: Temple University Press, 1991.
Andreescu, Florentina C. "War, Trauma and the Militarized Body," *Subjectivity* 9 (2) (2016), 205–223.
Auchter, Jessica. *The Politics of Haunting and Memory in International Relations*. London: Routledge, 2014.
Bachelard, Gaston. *The Poetics of Space: The Classic Look at How We Experience Intimate Places*. Translated by Maria Jolas. Boston: Beacon Press, 1994.
Bakhtin, Mikhail. *Problems of Dostoevsky's Poetics*. Translated by Caryl Emerson. Minneapolis: University of Minnesota Press, 1984.
Balázs, Béla. *Early Film Theory*. Edited by Erica Carter and translated by Rodney Livingstone. New York / Oxford: Berghahn Books, 2011.
Balla, Giacomo et. al. "Manifesto of Aeropainting (1929)." In *Futurism: An Anthology*, eds. Lawrence Rainey, Christine Poggi, and Laura Wittman. New Haven / London: Yale University Press, 2009, 283–285.
Barbusse, Henri. *Light*. Translated by Fitzwater Wray. London / Toronto: J.M. Dent & Sons, 1919.
Barbusse, Henri. *Under Fire*. Translated by Fitzwater Wray 1928. Everyman's Library ed., 2nd ed. New York: E.P. Dutton & Co, 1937.
Barker, Jennifer. *The Tactile Eye: Touch and the Cinematic Experience*. Berkeley: University of California Press, 2009.
Barker, Martin. *A 'Toxic Genre': The Iraq War Films*. Chicago: University of Chicago Press, 2011.
Basinger, Jeanine. *The World War II Combat Film: Anatomy of a Genre*. New York: Columbia University Press, 2003.
Basinger, Jeanine. *Anthony Mann*. Middletown, CT: Wesleyan University Press, 2007.
Baudrillard, Jean. *The Gulf War Did Not Take Place*. Translated by Paul Patton. Bloomington: Indiana University Press, 1995.
Baudrillard, Jean. *The Spirit of Terrorism and Requiem for the Twin Towers*. Translated by Chris Turner. London / New York: Verso, 2003.
Bazin, André. "Beauty of a Western [1956]." In *Cahiers du Cinéma, Vol. 1, The 1950s: Neo-Realism, Hollywood, New Wave*, ed. Jim Hillier. London: Routledge, 2005, 165–168.
Beidler, Philip D. *American Literature and the Experience of Vietnam*. Athens: University of Georgia Press, 1982.
Benjamin, Walter. *Illuminations*. Translated by Harry Zohn. New York: Schocken Books, 1969.
Boxwell, David. "Anthony Mann," *Senses of Cinema* 24 (2003), http://sensesofcinema.com/2003/great-directors/mann_anthony/ (March 25, 2016).
Bronfen, Elisabeth. *Specters of War: Hollywood's Engagement with Military Conflict*. New Brunswick, NJ: Rutgers University Press, 2012.

Brooke, Jocelyn. "Landscape near Tobruk." In *Poems in Pamphlet V (1952)*, ed. Jon Manchip White. Kent: The Hand and Flower Press, 1952, 360.

Bruno, Giuliana. *Atlas of Emotion: Journeys in Art, Architecture, and Film*. New York: Verso, 2002.

Buci-Glucksmann, Christine. "From the Cartographic View to the Virtual," *Media Art Net. Themes. Mapping and Text*, medienkunstnetz.de, http://www.medienkunstnetz.de/themes/mapping_and_text/carthographic-view/1/ (August 29, 2016).

Bühler, Karl. *Theory of Language: The Representational Function of Language*. Translated by D. Fraser Goodwin. Amsterdam / Philadelphia: Benjamins, 1990.

Burgoyne, Robert. *The Historical Film*. Malden, MA: Wiley Blackwell, 2008.

Burgoyne, Robert. "Embodiment in the War Film: Paradise Now and The Hurt Locker," *Journal of War & Culture Studies* 5 (1) (2012), 7–19.

Burgoyne, Robert. "Haunting in the War Film: Flags of Our Fathers." In *Eastwood's Iwo Jima: Critical Engagement With Flags of Our Fathers and Letters From Iwo Jima*, eds. Rikke Schubart and Anne Gjelsvik. New York: Wallflower Press, 2013, 157–172.

Burgoyne, Robert. "Generational Memory and Affect in Letters from Iwo Jima." In *A Companion to the Historical Film*, eds. Robert A. Rosenstone and Constantin Parvulescu. Malden, MA: Wiley Blackwell, 2013, 349–364.

Burgoyne, Robert. "The Violated Body: Affective Experience and Somatic Intensity in Zero Dark Thirty." In *The Philosophy of War Films*, ed. David LaRocca. Lexington: The University Press of Kentucky, 2014, 247–260.

Burgoyne, Robert and Eileen Rositzka. "Goya on his Shoulder: Tim Hetherington, Genre Memory, and the Body at Risk," *Frames Cinema Journal* 7 (2015), http://framescinemajournal.com/article/goya-on-his-shoulder-tim-hetherington-genre-memory-and-the-body-at-risk/.

Caputo, Philip. *A Rumor of War*. New York: Henry Holt, 1977.

Carruthers, Susan L. *The Media at War: Communication and Conflict in the Twentieth Century*. Second Edition. New York: Palgrave, 2011.

Casey, Edward. *Representing Place: Landscape Painting and Maps*. Minneapolis: University of Minnesota Press, 2002.

Castro, Teresa. "Cinema's Mapping Impulse: Questioning Visual Culture," *The Cartographic-Journal* 46 (2009), 9–15.

Cavell, Stanley. *The World Viewed: Reflections on the Ontology of Film*. Cambridge, MA: Harvard University Press, 1979.

Chambers II, John Whiteclay. "'All Quiet on the Western Front' (1930): The Anti-War Film and the Image of the First World War," *Historical Journal of Film, Radio and Television* 14 (4) (1994), 377–411.

Chapman, James and Nicholas J. Cull, eds. *Projecting Empire: Imperialism and Popular Cinema*. London / New York: I. B. Tauris, 2009.

Chapman, James. *War and Film*. London: Reaktion Books, 2008.

Chion, Michel. *Audio-Vision: Sound on Screen*. Edited and translated by Claudia Gorbman. New York: Columbia University Press, 1994.

Chion, Michel. *The Voice in Cinema*. Edited and translated by Claudia Gorbman. New York: Columbia University Press, 1999.

Cilento, Fabrizio. "The Aesthetics of the Procedural in Post-9/11 Cinema," *Cinema Journal* 56 (1) (2016), 131–136.

Clark, Michael P. "The Work of War after the Age of Mechanical Reproduction." In *The Vietnam War and Postmodernity*, ed. Michael Bibby. Amherst: University of Massachusetts Press, 2000, 17–47.
Cobb, Humphrey. *Paths of Glory* [1935]. New York: Penguin, 2010.
Cole, Sarah. *At the Violet Hour: Modernism and Violence in England and Ireland*. Oxford / New York: Oxford University Press, 2012.
Coll, Steve. "'Disturbing' and 'Misleading,'" *New York Review of Books* (2013), http://www.nybooks.com/articles/archives/2013/feb/07/disturbing-misleading-zero-dark-thirty/?pagination=false (December 3, 2016).
Conley, Tom. *Film Hieroglyphs: Ruptures in Classical Cinema* (new introduction). Minneapolis: University of Minnesota Press, 1991; 2006.
Conley, Tom. *Cartographic Cinema*. Minneapolis: University of Minnesota Press, 2007.
Conley, Tom. "The Fall of the Roman Empire: On Space and Allegory." In *The Epic Film in World Culture*, ed. Robert Burgoyne. New York / London: Routledge, 2010, 144–160.
Cook, David A. *A History of Narrative Film*, 3rd ed. New York: W.W. Norton & Co, 1996.
Corrigan, Timothy. *A Cinema Without Walls: Movies and Culture After Vietnam*. New Brunswick, NJ: Rutgers University Press, 1991.
Corrigan, Timothy, ed. *The Films of Werner Herzog*. New York / London: Methuen, 1986.
Cosgrove, Denis. *Geography and Vision*. London: I.B. Tauris, 2008.
Courcoux, Charles-Antoine. "There's Something about Maya: On Being/Becoming a Heroine and the 'War on Terror.'" In *Heroism and Gender in War Films*, eds. Karen A. Ritzenhoff and Jakub Kazecki. New York: Palgrave, 2014, 225–243.
Crean, Jeffrey. "Something to Compete with 'Gunsmoke': 'The Big Picture' Television series and selling a 'modern, progressive and forward thinking' Army to Cold War America," *War & Society* 35 (3) (2006), 204–218.
Crowther, Bosley. "The Screen in Review; 'Bridges at Toko-ri' Is Fine Film of War," *The New York Times*, January 21 (1995).
Cubitt, Sean. *The Cinema Effect*. Cambridge, MA: MIT Press, 2004.
Curtis, Robin. "Deixis and the Origo of Time-based Media: Blurring the "Here and Now" from the Dickson Experimental Sound Film of 1894 to Janet Cardiff's Installation Ghost Machine." In *Möglichkeitsräume: Zur Performativität von sensorischer Wahrnehmung*, eds. Christina Lechtermann, Kirsten Wagner, and Horst Wenzel. Berlin: Erich Schmidt Verlag, 2007, 255–266.
Curtis, Robin. "Immersion und Einfühlung: Zwischen Repräsentationalität und Materialität bewegter Bilder," *montage/av* 17 (2) (2008), 89–107.
Dargis, Manohla. "By Any Means Necessary," *The New York Times* (2012), http://www.nytimes.com/2012/12/18/movies/jessica-chastain-in-zero-dark-thirty.html (December 3, 2016).
Das, Santanu. *Touch and Intimacy in First World War Literature*. Cambridge: Cambridge University Press, 2005.
Daughtry, J. Martin. "Thanatosonics: Ontologies of Acoustic Violence," *Social Text* 32 (2:119) (2014), 25–51.
De Certeau, Michel. *The Practice of Everyday Life*. Translated by Steven Rendall. Berkeley: University of California Press, 1988.
Deleuze, Gilles and Félix Guattari. *What Is Philosophy?* Translated by Graham Burchell and Hugh Tomlinson. London: Verso 2003.
Delezen, John Edmund. *Eye of the Tiger*. Jefferson, NC: McFarland, 2003.

Der Derian, James. *Virtuous War: Mapping the Military–Industrial–Media–Entertainment Network*, 2nd edition. London: Routledge, 2009.
Dittmar, Linda and Gene Michaud, eds. *From Hanoi to Hollywood: The Vietnam War in American Film*. New Brunswick / London: Rutgers University Press, 1990.
Doherty, Thomas. "Full Metal Genre: Stanley Kubrick's Vietnam Combat Movie," *Film Quarterly* 42 (2) (1988–1989), 24–30.
Dombrowski, Lisa. *The Films of Samuel Fuller: If you die, I'll kill you!*, Middletown, CT: Wesleyan University Press, 2008.
Downs, Frederick. *The Killing Zone: My Life in the Vietnam War*. New York: Norton, 1978.
Duncan, Paul. *Stanley Kubrick: Visual Poet 1928–1999*. Cologne: Taschen, 2003.
Eagle, Jonna K. "A Rough Ride: Strenuous Spectatorship and the Early Cinema of Assaults," *Screen* 53 (1) (2012), 18–35.
Easthope, Anthony. *What a Man's Gotta Do: The Masculine Myth in Popular Culture*. New York / London: Routledge, 1990.
Eberwein, Robert. *The Hollywood War Film*. Chichester / Malden, MA: Wiley-Blackwell, 2010.
Ebert, Roger. "The Boys in Company C." In *rogerebert.com* (1978), http://www.rogerebert.com/reviews/the-boys-in-company-c-1978 (December 10, 2016).
Eisenstein, Sergei M. "Montage and Architecture," with an introduction by Yves-Alain Bois. *Assemblage* 10 (1989), 111–131.
Elsaesser, Thomas and Michael Wedel. "Apocalypse Now: The Hollow Heart of Hollywood." In *Joseph Conrad on Film*, ed. Gene Moore. Cambridge: Cambridge University Press, 1997, 151–175.
Empirische Medienästhetik. Database "Mobilization of Emotions in War Films." Categories. "A sense of community as the shared filmic remembrance of shared suffering." In *Freie Universität Berlin, Languages of Emotion* (2011), http://www.empirische-medienaesthetik.fu-berlin.de/en/emaex-system/affektdatenmatrix/kategorien/gemeinschaftsgefuehl/index.html (January 6, 2015).
Empirische Medienästhetik. Database "Mobilization of Emotions in War Films." Categories. "Battle and nature." In *Freie Universität Berlin, Languages of Emotion* (2011), system/affektdatenmatrix/kategorien/kampfnatur/index.html (March 25, 2015).
Empirische Medienästhetik. Database "Mobilization of Emotions in War Films." Categories. "Battle and technology." In *Freie Universität Berlin, Languages of Emotion* (2011), http://www.empirische-medienaesthetik.fu-berlin.de/en/emaex-system/affektdatenmatrix/kategorien/kampftechnologie/index.html (March 25, 2015).
Empirische Medienästhetik. Database "Mobilization of Emotions in War Films." Categories. "Homeland, woman, home." In *Freie Universität Berlin, Languages of Emotion* (2011), http://www.empirische-medienaesthetik.fu-berlin.de/en/emaex-system/affektdatenmatrix/kategorien/heimatfrau/index.html (March 25, 2015).
Empirische Medienästhetik. Database "Mobilization of Emotions in War Films." Categories. "Injustice and humiliation / moral self-assertion." In *Freie Universität Berlin, Languages of Emotion* (2011), http://www.empirische-medienaesthetik.fu-berlin.de/en/emaexsystem/affektdatenmatrix/kategorien/unrechtdemuetigung/index.html (March 25, 2015).
Empirische Medienästhetik. Database "Mobilization of Emotions in War Films." Categories. "Suffering / victim / sacrifice." In *Freie Universität Berlin, Languages of Emotion* (2011), http://www.empirische-medienaesthetik.fu-berlin.de/en/emaex-system/affektdatenmatrix/kategorien/leidenopfer/index.html (March 25, 2015).

Empirische Medienästhetik. Database "Mobilization of Emotions in War Films." Categories. "Transition between two social systems." In *Freie Universität Berlin, Languages of Emotion* (2011), http://www.empirische-medienaesthetik.fu-berlin.de/en/emaex-system/affektdatenmatrix/kategorien/uebergang/index.html (March 25, 2015).

Epstein, Jean. "Magnification." In *French Film Theory and Criticism: A History / Anthology, 1907–1939. Vol. 1: 1907–1929*, ed. Richard Abel. Princeton: Princeton University Press, 1988, 235–241.

Erdheim, Mario. *Psychoanalyse und Unbewußtheit in der Kultur*. Frankfurt a. M.: Suhrkamp, 1988.

Falsetto, Mario. *Stanley Kubrick: A Narrative and Stylistic Analysis*. New and expanded second edition. Westport, CT: Praeger, 2001.

Fischer, Ralf Michael. "'… a pleasant atmosphere in which to work': Wechselwirkungen zwischen Schein und Sein im filmischen Raum von Stanley Kubricks 'Paths of Glory' (USA 1957)," *Marburger Jahrbuch für Kunstwissenschaft* 32 (2005), 271–312.

Fisher, Jaimey. "Demythologization and Convergence: Herzog's Late Genre Pictures and the Rogue Cop Film in *Bad Lieutenant: Port of Call–New Orleans*." In *A Companion to Werner Herzog*, ed. Brad Prager. Malden, MA: Wiley-Blackwell, 2012, 208–229.

Fore, Steven James. *The Perils of Patriotism: The Hollywood Film as Generic and Cultural Discourse*. Doctoral Dissertation. Austin: University of Texas at Austin, 1986.

Fox, Jo. *Film Propaganda in Britain and Nazi-Germany: World War II Cinema*. New York: Berg, 2007.

Fulbright, J. William. *The Pentagon Propaganda Machine*. New York: Random House, 1970.

Gareis, Torsten. "Put your helmet on! Der Helm im amerikanischen Kriegsfilm." In *Mobilisierung der Sinne: Der Hollywood-Kriegsfilm zwischen Genrekino und Historie*, eds. Hermann Kappelhoff, Cilli Pogodda, and David Gaertner. Berlin: Vorwerk 8, 2013, 345–382.

Geiger, Jeffrey and Karin Littau. "Introduction: Cinematicity and Comparative Media." In *Cinematicity in Media History*, eds. Jeffrey Geiger and Karin Littau. Edinburgh: Edinburgh University Press, 2013, 1–20.

Geiger, Jeffrey. "Making America Global: Cinematicity and the Aerial View." In *Cinematicity in Media History*, eds. Jeffrey Geiger and Karin Littau. Edinburgh: Edinburgh University Press, 2013, 133–156.

Gledhill, Christine. "Rethinking Genre." In *Reinventing Film Studies*, eds. Christine Gledhill and Linda Williams. London: Bloomsbury, 2000, 221–243.

Godard, Jean-Luc. "SuperMann: Man of the West." In *Godard on Godard*. Edited and translated by Tom Milne. New York / London: Da Capo, 1972, 116–120.

Gollbach, Michael. *Die Wiederkehr des Weltkrieges in der Literatur. Zu den Frontromanen der späten Zwanziger Jahre*. Kronberg (Ts.): Scriptor Verlag, 1978.

Goodman, Steve. *Sonic Warfare: Sound, Affect, and the Ecology of Fear*. Cambridge, MA: The MIT Press, 2010.

Gregory, Derek. "The Natures of War." Geographical Imaginations. Downloads. November 2014. 1–87, https://geographicalimaginations.files.wordpress.com/2012/07/gregory-the-natures-of-war-final-may-2015.pdf (accessed March 2, 2018).

Gregory, Derek. "Moving Targets and Violent Geographies." In *Spaces of Danger: Culture and Power in the Everyday*, eds. Heather Merrill and Lisa M. Hoffman. Athens, GA: University of Georgia Press, 2015, 256–296.

Gregory, Derek. "The Natures of War," *Antipode* 48 (1) (2016), 3–56.

Gregory, Derek, and Noel Castree. "Editors' Introduction: Human Geography." In *Human Geography*, Vol. 2, eds. Derek Gregory and Noel Castree. London: Sage, 2012, xxv–lxxix.

Gunning, Tom. "The Attraction of Motion: Modern Representation and the Image of Movement." In *Film 1900: Technology, Perception, Culture*, eds. Annemone Ligensa and Klaus Kreimeier. Eastleigh / Bloomington: Libbey and Indiana University Press, 2009, 165–174.

Gwin, Larry. *Baptism: A Vietnam Memoir*. New York: Random House, 1999.

Hables Gray, Chris. *Postmodern War: The New Politics of Conflict*. New York: The Guilford Press, 1997.

Hallin, Daniel C. *The Uncensored War: The Media and Vietnam*. Berkeley, CA: University of California Press, 1986.

Haraway, Donna. "A Cyborg Manifesto: Science, Technology and Socialist-Feminism in the Late Twentieth Century." In *The Cybercultures Reader*, eds. David Bell and Barbara M. Kennedy. London / New York: Routledge, 2000, 291–324.

Harley, J. B. "The Map and the Development of the History of Cartography." In *The History of Cartography Vol. I: Cartography in Prehistoric, Ancient and Medieval Europe and the Mediterranean*, eds. J.B. Harley and David Woodward. Chicago, IL: Chicago University Press, 1987, 1–42.

Heisler, Hermann. *Krieg oder Frieden. Randbemerkung zu Remarques Buch „Im Westen nichts Neues"*. Stuttgart: Verlag der Christengemeinschaft, 1929.

Herr, Michael. *Dispatches*. New York: Avon, 1977.

H. H. T. "Wartime Romance Flourishes in Korea." In *The New York Times*, May 28 (1953), http://www.nytimes.com/movie/review?res=9800E4DB163DE23BBC4051DFB3668388649EDE (March 21, 2016).

Hoskins, Andrew and Ben O'Loughlin. *War and Media: The Emergence of Diffused War*. Cambridge, UK: Polity Press, 2010.

Huhtamo, Erkki. "Unterwegs in der Kapsel. Simulatoren und das Bedürfnis nach totaler Immersion," *montage/av* 17 (2) (2008), 41–68.

Jacobs, Andrew. "Peace Signs Amid Calls for War" In *The New York Times*, September 20 (2001), http://www.nytimes.com/2001/09/20/nyregion/peace-signs-amid-calls-for-war.html (December 5, 2016).

Jameson, Fredric. *The Geopolitical Aesthetic*. Bloomington: Indiana University Press, 1992.

Jameson, Fredric. *Signatures of the Visible* [1992]. New York: Routledge Classics, 2007.

Jarvie, Ian. "The Burma Campaign on Film: 'Objective Burma' (1945), 'The Stilwell Road' (1945) and 'Burma Victory' (1945)," *Historical Journal of Film, Radio and Television* 8 (1) (1988), 55–73.

Johnson, Laurie Ruth. *Forgotten Dreams: Revisiting Romanticism in the Cinema of Werner Herzog*. Rochester, NY: Camden House, 2016.

Johnson, Mark. *The Body in the Mind: The Bodily Basis of Meaning, Imagination, and Reason*. Chicago: University of Chicago Press, 1987.

Kane, Kathryn R. *Visions of War: Hollywood Combat Films of World War II*. Ann Arbor: UMI Research Press (Studies in Cinema), 1982.

Kappelhoff, Hermann. *Matrix der Gefühle. Das Kino, das Melodrama und das Theater der Empfindsamkeit*. Berlin: Vorwerk 8, 2004.

Kappelhoff, Hermann. "Kriegerische Mobilisierung: Die mediale Organisation des Gemeinsinns. Frank Capras Prelude to War und Leni Riefenstahls Tag der Freiheit," *Navigationen. Zeitschrift für Medien- und Kulturwissenschaften* 9 (1) (2009), 151–165.

Kappelhoff, Hermann. *Front Lines of Community: Hollywood Between War and Democracy.* Berlin: De Gruyter, 2018.
Kappelhoff, Hermann. "For Love of Country: World War II in Hollywood Cinema at the Turn of the Century." Unpublished manuscript, referenced with permission of the author.
Kappelhoff, Hermann and Jan-Hendrik Bakels. "Das Zuschauergefühl. Möglichkeiten qualitativer Medienanalyse," *Zeitschrift für Medienwissenschaft* 5 (2) (2011), 78–95.
Kappelhoff, Hermann and Cornelia Müller. "Embodied Meaning Construction: Multimodal Metaphor and Expressive Movement in Speech, Gesture, and Feature Film," *Metaphor and the Social World* 1 (2) (2011), 121–153.
Kappelhoff, Hermann, Matthias Grotkopp, and David Gaertner. "The Poetics of Mobilization: Gung Ho!" In *mediaesthetics – Journal of Poetics of Audiovisual Images* (2016), http://www.mediaesthetics.org/index.php/mae/article/view/41/91 (November 24, 2016).
Kelly, Andrew. "The Brutality of Military Incompetence: 'Paths of Glory' (1957)," *Historical Journal of Film, Radio & Television* 13 (2) (1993), 215–227.
Kester, Bernadette. *Film Front Weimar: Representations of the First World War in German Films of the Weimar Period (1919–1933).* Amsterdam: Amsterdam University Press, 2003.
Ketwig, John. *… And a Hard Rain fell: A GI's True Story of the War in Vietnam.* Napierville, IL: Sourcebooks, 2002.
Kitchin, Rob, Chris Perkins, and Martin Dodge, eds. *Rethinking Maps: New Frontiers in Cartographic Theory.* London: Routledge, 2009.
Kitchin, Rob and Martin Dodge. "Rethinking Maps," *Progress in Human Geography* 31 (3) (2007), 331–344.
Kolker, Robert. *A Cinema of Loneliness: Penn, Stone, Kubrick, Scorsese, Spielberg, Altman.* Oxford / New York: Oxford University Press, 2000.
Kolker, R.P. and J. Douglas Ousley. "A Phenomenology of Cinematic Time and Space," *British Journal of Aesthetics* 13 (4) (1973), 388–396.
Krämer, Sibylle. "Karten erzeugen doch Welten, oder?" *Soziale Systeme* 178 (1 & 2) (2012), 153–167.
LaBelle, Brandon. *Acoustic Territories: Sound Culture and Everyday Life.* London: Continuum Books, 2010.
Langewiesche, William. *American Ground: Unbuilding the World Trade Center.* New York: North Point Press, 2002.
Lastra, James. "Film and the Wagnerian Aspiration: Thoughts on Sound Design and History of the Senses." In *Lowering the Boom: Critical Studies in Film Sound*, eds. Jay Beck and Tony Grajeda. Chicago: University of Illinois Press, 2008, 123–138.
Lebow, Alisa. "The Unwar Film." In *A Companion to Contemporary Documentary Film*, eds. Alexandra Juhasz and Alisa Lebow. Hoboken, NJ: John Wiley & Sons, 2015, 454–474.
Lefebvre, Martin, ed. *Landscape and Film.* London / New York: Routledge, 2006.
Lehmann, Hauke. *Affektpoetiken des New Hollywood.* Berlin: De Gruyter, 2016.
Lenoir, Tim and Henry Lowood. "Theaters of War: The Military-Entertainment Complex." (2002), http://www.stanford.edu/class/sts145/Library/Lenoir-Lowood_TheatersOfWar.pdf (December 10, 2016).
Lentz, Robert J. *Korean War Filmography: 91 English Language Features through 2000.* Jefferson, NC: McFarland, 2003.
Lodder, Christina. "Transfiguring Reality: Suprematism and the Aerial View." In *Seeing from Above: The Aerial View in Visual Culture*, eds. Mark Dorrian and Frédéric Pousin. London / New York: I.B. Tauris, 2013, 95–117.

Lukinbeal, Chris. "The Map that Precedes the Territory: An Introduction to Essays in Cinematic Geography," *Geo-Journal* 59 (4) (2004), 247–251.
MacDonald, Fraser. "Visuality." In *Human Geography*, Vol. 2., eds. Derek Gregory and Noel Castree. London: Sage, 2012, 345–355.
Machon, Josephine. *(Syn)aesthetics: Redefining Visceral Performance*. New York: Palgrave Macmillan, 2009.
Manning, Frederic. *The Middle Parts of Fortune*. London: Vintage Classics, 2014 [1929].
Marinetti, F.T. "Multiplied Man and the Reign of the Machine (1911)" In *Futurism: An Anthology*, eds. Lawrence Rainey, Christine Poggi, and Laura Wittman. New Haven / London: Yale University Press, 2009, 89–92.
Marks, Laura U. *The Skin of the Film: Intercultural Cinema, Embodiment, and the Senses*. Durham, NC: Duke University Press, 2000.
Masters, Cristina. "Bodies of Technology: Cyborg Soldiers and Militarised Masculinities," *International Feminist Journal of Politics* 7 (1) (2005), 112–132.
Mather, Philippe. *Stanley Kubrick at Look Magazine: Authorship and Genre in Photojournalism and Film*. Bristol / Chicago: Intellect, 2013.
McClintock, Anne. "Paranoid Empire: Specters from Guantánamo and Abu Ghraib," *Small Axe* 13 (1) (2009), 50–74.
McSorley, Kevin. "Helmetcams, Militarized Sensation and 'Somatic War'," *Journal of War and Culture Studies* 5 (1) (2012), 47–58.
Meredith, James H. "Introduction." In *Paths of Glory* [1935], by Humphrey Cobb. New York: Penguin, 2010, xxiii–xxiv.
Merleau-Ponty, Maurice. *Phénoménologie de la Perception*. Paris: Gallimard, 1945.
Merleau-Ponty, Maurice. *The Visible and the Invisible*. Edited by Claude Lefort and translated by Alphonso Lingus. Evanston, IL: Northwestern University Press, 1968.
Merleau-Ponty, Maurice. "Eye and Mind." In *The Merleau-Ponty Aesthetics Reader: Philosophy and Painting*, ed. Galen A. Johnson. Evanston, IL: Northwestern University Press, 1993, 121–149.
Merleau-Ponty, Maurice. *Phenomenology of Perception*. Translated by Colin Smith. London: Routledge & Kegan Paul, 2002 [1962].
Missiaen, Jean-Claude. "A Lesson in Cinema," *Cahiers du Cinéma in English*, 12 (December 1967), 44–51.
Metz, Christian. *L'Enonciation impersonnelle, ou le site du film*. Paris: Meridiens / Klincksieck, 1991.
Midkiff DeBauche, Leslie. "The United States' Film Industry and World War One." In *The First World War and Popular Cinema: 1914 to the Present*, ed. Michael Paris. Edinburgh: Edinburgh University Press, 1999, 138–161.
Morsch, Thomas. *Medienästhetik des Films: Verkörperte Wahrnehmung und ästhetische Erfahrung im Kino*. Munich: Fink, 2011.
Müller Scheld, Wilhelm. *„Im Westen nichts Neues": Eine Täuschung*. Idstein: Georg Grandpierre, 1929.
Neale, Steve. "Aspects of Ideology and Narrative Form in the American War Film," *Screen* 32 (1) (1991), 35–57.
Nelson, Thomas Allen. *Kubrick: Inside a Film Artist's Maze*. Bloomington: Indiana University Press, 1982.
N.N. "Cinema: The New Pictures, Dec. 9, 1957," *Time* LXX (24) (1957).
N.N. "Confers on New War Film," *New York Times*, August 11 (1929), 8.

Nohr, Rolf F. *Karten im Fernsehen. Die Produktion von Positionierung*. Münster: LIT, 2002.
O'Brien, Tim. *If I Die in a Combat Zone*. New York: Broadway Books, 1975.
Owen, A. Susan. "Memory, War and American Identity: Saving Private Ryan as Cinematic Jeremiad," *Critical Studies in Media Communication* 19 (3) (2002), 249–282.
Panofsky, Erwin. "Style and Medium in the Motion Pictures," *Critique* Jan / Feb (1947), 5–28.
Parks, Lisa. "Vertical Mediation: Geospatial Imagery and the US Wars in Afghanistan and Iraq." In *Mediated Geographies and Geographies of Media*, eds. Susan P. Mains, Julie Cupples, and Chris Lukinbeal. Heidelberg / New York / London: Springer, 2015, 159–175.
Parks, Lisa. "Drones, Vertical Mediation, and the Targeted Class," *Feminist Studies* 42 (1) (2016), 227–235.
Pauli, Hansjörg. "Umgang mit Tönen." In *Stanley Kubrick*, eds. Peter W. Jansen and Wolfram Schütte. Munich / Vienna: Hanser, 1984, 247–284.
Piotrowska, Agnieszka. "Zero Dark Thirty – 'War Autism' or a Lacanian ethical act?" *New Review of Film and Television Studies* 12 (2) (2014), 143–155.
Pisters, Patricia. "Logistics of Perception 2.0: Multiple Screen Aesthetics in Iraq War Films," *Film-Philosophy* 14 (1) (2010), 233–252, http://www.film-philosophy.com/index.php/f-p/article/view/221/179 (accessed March 2, 2018).
Polan, Dana. "Stylistic Regularities (and Peculiarities) of the Hollywood World War II Propaganda Film." In *Warner's War: Politics, Pop Culture and Propaganda in Wartime Hollywood*, eds. Martin Kaplan and Johanna Blakley. Los Angeles: USC Norman Lear Center, 2004, 38–47.
Polan, Dana. "Auteurism and War-teurism: Terrence Malick's War Movie." In *The War Film*, ed. Robert Eberwein. New Brunswick: Rutgers University Press, 2005, 53–61.
Prager, Brad. *The Cinema of Werner Herzog: Aesthetic Ecstasy and Truth*. London: Wallflower Press, 2007.
Prince, Stephen. *Savage Cinema: Sam Peckinpah and the Rise of Ultraviolent Movies*. Austin, TX: University of Texas Press, 1998.
Pultz Moslund, Sten. "The Presencing of Place in Literature: Toward an Embodied Topopoetic Mode of Reading." In *Geocritical Explorations: Space, Place and Mapping in Literary and Cultural Studies*, ed. Robert T. Tally Jr. New York: Palgrave Macmillan, 2011, 9–43.
Purse, Lisa. "Working through the Body: Textual-Corporeal Strategies in United 93 (2006)." In *Film Moments: Criticism, History, Theory*, eds. Tom Brown and James Walters. London: BFI Publishing, 2010, 157–161.
Rancière, Jacques. *Film Fables*. Translated by Emiliano Battista. London / Oxford: Bloomsbury, 2006.
Randell, Karen and Sean Redmond, eds. *The War Body on Screen*. London / New York: Continuum, 2012.
Remarque, Erich Maria. *All Quiet on the Western Front*. Translated by A.W. Wheen. London: Putnam, 1929.
Ritzenhoff, Karen and Jakub Kazecki, eds. *Heroism and Gender in War Films*. New York: Palgrave Macmillan, 2014.
Roberts, Les, ed. *Mapping Cultures: Place, Practice, Performance*. London / New York: Palgrave Macmillan, 2012.
Rodaway, Paul. *Sensuous Geographies: Body, Sense and Place*. London / New York: Routledge, 1994.
Ropars-Wuilleumier, Marie-Claire. *Ecrire l'espace*. Paris: Presses de l'Université de Paris-VIII, 2003.

Sassoon, Siegfried. *Counter-Attack and Other Poems*. New York: Dutton and Co., 1918.
Sassoon, Siegfried. *Memoirs of an Infantry Officer*. London: Faber & Faber, 1965.
Seydor, Paul. *Peckinpah – The Western Films: A Reconsideration*. Revised Edition. Urbana, IL: University of Illinois Press, 1997.
Shaviro, Steven. "A Brief Remark on Zero Dark Thirty," The Pinocchio Theory, January 18 (2013), http://www.shaviro.com/Blog/?m=201301 (June 5, 2016).
Shaviro, Steven. "Kathryn Bigelow," The Pinocchio Theory, March 10 (2010), http://www.shaviro.com/Blog/?p=862 (June 5, 2016).
Shaw, Tony. *Hollywood's Cold War*. Edinburgh: Edinburgh University Press, 2007.
Silverman, Kaja. *Acoustic Mirror: The Female Voice in Psychoanalysis and Cinema*. Bloomington, IN: Indiana University Press, 1988.
Simmel, Georg. *"The Metropolis and Mental Life."* In *The Sociology of Georg Simmel*. Edited and translated by K.H. Wolff. New York: Free Press, 1950, 409–424.
Slocum, J. David, ed. *Hollywood and War: The Film Reader*. New York / London: Routledge, 2006.
Sobchack, Vivian. *The Address of the Eye: A Phenomenology of Film Experience*. Princeton, NJ: Princeton University Press, 1992.
Sobchack, Vivian. *Carnal Thoughts: Embodiment and Moving Image Culture*. Berkeley: University of California Press, 2004.
Sokołowska-Paryż, Marzena. "The Naked Male Body in the War Film," *Journal of War and Culture Studies*, 5 (1) (2012), 21–32.
Sorlin, Pierre. "Cinema and the Memory of the Great War." In *The First World War and Popular Cinema: 1914 to the Present*, ed. Michael Paris. Edinburgh: Edinburgh University Press, 1999, 5–26.
Speier, Hans. "Magic Geography," *Social Research* 3 (1941), 310–330.
Stewart, Garrett. "Digital Fatigue: Imaging War in Recent American Film," *Film Quarterly* 62 (4) (2009), 45–55.
Takacs, Stacy. "The Changing Shape of Our Fears," *Cinema Journal* 56 (1) (2016), 124–131.
Theweleit, Klaus. *Male Fantasies, Vol. 2, Male Bodies: Psychoanalyzing the White Terror*. Translated by Erica Carter and Chris Turner. Minneapolis: University of Minnesota Press, 1989.
Tripp, Nathaniel. *Father, Soldier, Son: Memoir of a Platoon Leader in Vietnam*. South Royalton: Steerforth, 2010 [1996].
Ungaretti, Giuseppe. "Vigil [1915]." In *The Penguin Book of First World War Poetry*, ed. George Walter. London: Penguin, 2006, 264.
Vertov, Dziga. "Kinoks: A Revolution." In *Kino-Eye: The Writings of Dziga Vertov*, ed. Annette Michelson. Translated by Kevin O'Brien. Berkeley / Los Angeles: University of California Press, 1984, 11–20.
Virilio, Paul. *War and Cinema: The Logistics of Perception*. London: Verso, 1989.
Virilio, Paul. *The Vision Machine*. Bloomington, IN: Indiana University Press, 1994.
Virilio, Paul. "A Topographical Amnesia." In *The Visual Culture Reader*, ed. Nicolas Mirzoeff. London / New York: Routledge, 1998, 108–122.
Virilio, Paul. *Desert Screen: War at the Speed of Light*. Translated by Michael Degener. London: Continuum, 2002.
Von Moltke, Johannes. "Sympathy for the Devil: Cinema, History, and the politics of emotion," *New German Critique* 102 (3) (2007), 17–43.

Wedel, Michael. "Körper, Tod und Technik – Der postklassische Hollywood-Kriegsfilm als reflexives Body Genre." In *Körperästhetiken: Filmische Inszenierungen von Körperlichkeit*, ed. Dagmar Hoffmann. Bielefeld: Transcript, 2010, 77–99.

Weil, Simone. "The Iliad, or the Poem of Force," Translated by Mary Mc Carthy. *Chicago Review* 18 (2) (1965), 5–30.

Westwell, Guy. *War Cinema: Hollywood on the Front Line*. London / New York: Wallflower Press, 2006.

Westwell, Guy. *Parallel Lines*. New York: Columbia University Press, 2014.

Willemen, Paul. "Looking at the Male: Anthony Mann," *Framework: The Journal of Cinema & Media* 15–17 (1981), 16.

Williams, Linda. "Film Bodies. Gender, Genre, and Excess," *Film Quarterly* 44 (4) (1991), 2–13.

Williams, Raymond. *Marxism and Literature*. Oxford: Oxford University Press, 1977.

Williams, Tony. "Collision and Contradiction: The Steel Helmet." In *Senses of Cinema* 52 (2009), http://sensesofcinema.com/2009/cteq/collision-and-contradiction-the-steel-helmet/ (March 25, 2016).

Wilson, James C. *Vietnam in Prose and Film*. Jefferson, NC: McFarland, 1982.

Wood, Robin. "The American Nightmare: Horror in the 70s." In *Horror: The Film Reader*, ed. Mark Jancovich. London / New York: Routledge, 2002, 25–32.

Woodman, Brian J. "Represented in the Margins: Images of African American Soldiers in Vietnam Combat Films." In *The War Film*, ed. Robert Eberwein. New Brunswick, NJ: Rutgers University Press, 2004, 90–114.

Worland, Rick. "The Korean War Film as Family Melodrama: 'The Bridges at Toko-Ri' (1954)," *Historical Journal of Film, Radio and Television* 19 (3) (1999), 359–377.

Wylie, John. "A Single Day's Walking: Narrating Self and Landscape on the South West Coast Path," *Transactions of the Institute of British Geographers* 30 (2) (2005), 234–247.

Yeung, Heather. "Affective Mapping in Lyric Poetry." In *Geocritical Explorations: Space, Place and Mapping in Literary and Cultural Studies*, ed. Robert T. Tally Jr. New York: Palgrave Macmillan, 2011, 209–222.

Young, Charles S. "Missing Action: POW Films, Brainwashing and the Korean War, 1954–1968," *Historical Journal of Film, Radio and Television* 18 (1) (1998), 49–74.

Žižek, Slavoj. *Welcome to the Desert of the Real! Five Essays on 11 September and Related Dates*. London: Verso, 2002.

Zweig, Arnold. "Kriegsromane," *Die Weltbühne*, April 25, 1929.

Filmography

ALL QUIET ON THE WESTERN FRONT. Dir. Lewis Milestone. 1930.
AMERICAN SNIPER. Dir. Clint Eastwood. 2014.
APOCALYPSE NOW. Dir. Francis Ford Coppola. 1979.
ATTACK. Dir. Robert Aldrich. 1956.
BAMBOO PRISON. Dir. Lewis Seiler. 1954.
BATAAN. Dir. Tay Garnett. 1943.
BATTLE CIRCUS. Dir. Richard Brooks. 1953.
BURMA VICTORY. Dir. Roy Boulting. 1946.
CASABLANCA. Dir. Michael Curtiz. 1942.
CASUALTIES OF WAR. Dir. Brian De Palma. 1989.
CEASE FIRE! Dir. Owen Crump. 1953.
CHINA GIRL. Dir. Henry Hathaway. 1942.
DAWN. Dir. Herbert Wilcox. 1928.
DEVIL'S DOORWAY. Dir. Anthony Mann. 1950.
DRAGONFLY SQUADRON. Dir. Lesley Selander. 1954.
EL CID. Dir. Anthony Mann. 1961.
FAIR GAME. Dir. Doug Liman. 2010.
FEAR AND DESIRE. Dir. Stanley Kubrick. 1953.
FIXED BAYONETS! Dir. Samuel Fuller. 1951.
FLAGS OF OUR FATHERS. Dir. Clint Eastwood. 2006.
FULL METAL JACKET. Dir. Stanley Kubrick. 1987.
FURY. Dir. David Ayer. 2014.
GO TELL THE SPARTANS. Dir. Ted Post. 1978.
GUADALCANAL DIARY. Dir. Lewis Seiler. 1943.
HEARTS OF THE WORLD. Dir. D.W. Griffith. 1918.
HELL'S ANGELS. Dir. Howard Hughes. 1930.
HOMELAND. Produced by Showtime. Television. 2011–2015.
IN THE VALLEY OF ELAH. Dir. Paul Haggis. 2007.
J'ACCUSE. Dir. Abel Gance. 1919.
LEBANON. Dir. Samuel Maoz. 2009.
LES CROIX DE BOIS. Dir. Raymond Bernard. 1932.
LITTLE DIETER NEEDS TO FLY. Dir. Werner Herzog. 1997.
LOST PATROL. Dir. Walter Summers. 1929.
MAN OF THE WEST. Dir. Anthony Mann. 1958.
MEN IN WAR. Dir. Anthony Mann. 1957.
MERRILL'S MARAUDERS. Dir. Samuel Fuller. 1962.
OBJECTIVE, BURMA! Dir. Raoul Walsh. 1945.
PATHS OF GLORY. Dir. Stanley Kubrick. 1957.
PATTON. Dir. Franklin J. Schaffner. 1970.
PLATOON. Dir. Oliver Stone. 1986.
PORK CHOP HILL. Dir. Lewis Milestone. 1959.
PRISONER OF WAR. Dir. Andrew Marton. 1954.
QUO VADIS. Dir. Melvyn LeRoy. 1951.
RENDITION. Dir. Gavin Hood. 2007.

RESCUE DAWN. Dir. Werner Herzog. 2006.
SAHARA. Dir. Zoltan Korda. 1943.
SAVING PRIVATE RYAN. Dir. Steven Spielberg. 1998.
SERGEANT RYKER. Dir. Buzz Kulik. 1968.
SERGEANT YORK. Dir. Howard Hawks. 1941.
SHOULDER ARMS. Dir. Charlie Chaplin. 1918.
STANDARD OPERATING PROCEDURE. Dir. Errol Morris. 2008.
THE BIG PARADE. Dir. King Vidor. 1925.
THE BIG PICTURE. Produced by the United States Army Signal Corps Army Pictorial Service. Television. 1951–1971.
THE BOYS IN COMPANY C. Dir. Sidney Furie. 1978.
THE BRIDGE ON THE RIVER KWAI. Dir. David Lean. 1957.
THE BRIDGES AT TOKIO-RI. Dir. Mark Robson. 1954.
THE DAWN PATROL. Dir. Edmund Goulding. 1938.
THE DEER HUNTER. Dir. Michael Cimino. 1978.
THE FALL OF THE ROMAN EMPIRE. Dir. Anthony Mann. 1964.
THE FOUR HORSEMEN OF THE APOCALYPSE. Dir. Rex Ingram. 1921.
THE GREEN BERETS. Dir. Ray Kellogg and John Wayne. 1968.
THE HEART OF HUMANITY. Dir. Alan Holubar. 1918.
THE HURT LOCKER. Dir. Kathryn Bigelow. 2008.
THE JAZZ SINGER. Dir. Alan Crosland. 1927.
THE LONGEST DAY. Andrew Marton et al. 1962.
THE MANCHURIAN CANDIDATE. Dir. John Frankenheimer. 1962.
THE RACK. Dir. Arnold Laven. 1956.
THE STEEL HELMET. Dir. Samuel Fuller. 1951.
THE STILWELL ROAD. Written by Robert Presnell Sr. 1945.
THE THIN RED LINE. Dir. Andrew Marton. 1964.
THE THREE DAYS OF THE CONDOR. Dir. Sydney Pollack. 1975.
TIGERLAND. Dir. Joel Schumacher. 2000.
TIME LIMIT. Dir. Karl Malden. 1957.
T-MEN. Dir. Anthony Mann. 1947.
TOP GUN. Dir. Tony Scott. 1986.
UNITED 93. Dir. Paul Greengrass. 2006.
WESTFRONT 1918. Dir. Georg Wilhelm Pabst. 1930.
WE WERE SOLDIERS. Randall Wallace. 2002.
WHAT PRICE GLORY? Dir. Raoul Walsh. 1926.
WHITE TIGER (BELYY TIGR). Dir. Karen Shakhnazarov. 2012.
WILSON. Dir. Henry King. 1944.
WINCHESTER '73. Dir. Anthony Mann. 1950.
WINGS. Dir. William A. Wellman. 1927.
WTC – THE FIRST 24 HOURS. Dir. Étienne Sauret. 2002.
ZERO DARK THIRTY. Dir. Kathryn Bigelow. 2012.

Subject index

Acoustics 23, 137, 138, 139, 147, 181
Aerial view 23, 24, 25, 57, 58, 59, 63, 65, 67, 68, 73, 77, 79, 85, 94, 95, 96, 142, 157, 177
Affect 4, 13, 16, 18, 19, 21, 26, 43, 45, 61, 79, 80, 91, 129, 135, 142, 146, 149, 155, 159, 174
Agoraphobia 42
Apparatus theory 7

Battle action 1, 27, 44, 99, 138, 146
Battle zone 2, 22, 32, 43, 65, 66, 67, 77, 82, 97, 103, 107, 111, 122, 123, 170, 177
Being-in-the-world 15, 41
Bilocation 9, 11, 32, 33, 64
Body genre 17, 20, 21, 180
Burma campaign 59, 60, 61, 62, 63, 66, 67, 68, 69, 75, 177

Cartography 1, 2, 4, 5, 6, 10, 11, 12, 33, 63, 97, 168
Classical war film 23, 87, 89, 94, 119, 124, 130, 135, 140, 149, 179
Claustrophobia 23, 34, 41, 42, 87, 88, 106, 156, 162, 166
Cold War 23, 46, 100, 101, 106, 124, 179
Comedy 14, 29, 127
Control 12, 23, 25, 39, 49, 50, 58, 66, 67, 70, 74, 78, 79, 87, 91, 95, 97, 109, 119, 122, 134, 135, 138, 142, 144, 152, 155, 170, 171, 176
Combat film (combat movie) 17, 18, 22, 23, 45, 46, 57, 59, 60, 75, 80, 81, 82, 83, 85, 94, 97, 99, 100, 102, 104, 105, 118, 128, 135, 140, 144, 152, 175, 177, 179
Communication 8, 9, 61, 64, 68, 72, 93, 97, 133, 134, 138, 143, 158, 163, 168, 179
Community 17, 35, 70, 79, 80, 108, 118, 144
Conversion 80, 81, 85, 89, 90, 93, 95
Corpography 2, 3, 5, 6, 12, 15, 21, 22, 28, 32, 33, 49, 54, 59, 73, 79, 80, 85, 87, 88, 96, 98, 99, 106, 111, 116, 123, 152, 162, 163, 169, 174, 175, 176, 177, 179, 180
Corps 19, 20, 63, 71, 80, 81, 97, 105, 108, 135, 136, 171, 174, 177, 178

Crisis of vision 16, 25, 49, 59, 153
Cyborg nature 27, 42, 53, 86, 97, 177
Cyborg soldier 91, 97, 178

Disorientation 21, 23, 27, 31, 53, 97, 110, 127, 130, 138, 146, 149, 159, 171
Documentary 58, 60, 61, 65, 67, 68, 79, 143, 144, 157, 177

E.A.S. (elements of auditory setting) 169
Embodiment 5, 8, 44, 54, 64, 88, 89, 109, 146, 162, 169, 174
Emotion 11, 12, 15, 17, 19, 27, 28, 40, 41, 58, 59, 88, 90, 91, 94, 121, 139, 151, 157, 161, 172
Enunciation 9, 10
Experience
– Aesthetic experience 7, 8, 10, 12, 28, 60, 64, 87, 114, 131, 133, 173, 180
– Cinematic experience 4, 5, 49, 84, 147, 149, 172
– Sensory experience (sensuous experience) 7, 16, 22, 26, 55, 98, 124, 127, 132, 174, 176
– Somatic experience 1, 2, 5, 17, 20, 21, 28, 46, 56, 62, 97, 119, 162, 177, 180
Expressive movement 3, 18, 45, 119, 140, 175

Fatigue 62, 75, 104, 111, 163, 178, 180
Fear 14, 19, 21, 26, 27, 30, 34, 35, 36, 37, 42, 44, 45, 46, 52, 75, 79, 81, 82, 104, 117, 136, 139, 140, 142, 147, 148, 149, 156, 159, 170
Feeling 3, 19, 27, 29, 34, 40, 42, 45, 48, 53, 57, 68, 84, 89, 94, 97, 98, 107, 108, 109, 110, 119, 122, 123, 166, 169, 175, 176, 177, 179, 181
First World War (Great War, WWI) 3, 5, 21, 22, 25, 26, 27, 28, 29, 31, 32, 34, 38, 40, 42, 43, 44, 46, 47, 48, 49, 52, 54, 56, 57, 58, 76, 81, 97, 98, 99, 101, 103, 115, 173, 175
Fragmentation 23, 25, 38, 97, 160
Futurism 91

https://doi.org/10.1515/9783110580808-010

Generational memory 15
Genre poetics 4, 16, 46, 149, 159, 176
Gulf War 16, 25, 178

Haptic geographies 27, 33, 38, 98
History 1, 2, 3, 4, 9, 12, 15, 20, 21, 22, 23, 25, 48, 56, 59, 64, 67, 69, 77, 85, 100, 101, 104, 111, 121, 127, 153, 157, 172
Human Geography 2, 175
Horror 14, 19, 37, 53, 110, 112, 128, 142, 149, 155, 159, 171, 180

Icarian view 57, 94, 176
Iconography 17, 22, 32, 48, 50, 52, 54, 120
Illusion of overview 26, 27, 56, 59, 63, 94, 128, 130, 136, 170
Immersion 20, 84, 85, 88, 89, 159, 168
Intimacy 22, 23, 27, 34, 35, 36, 38, 39, 40, 51, 57, 75, 76, 77, 81, 83, 92, 94, 98, 99, 106, 134, 138, 178
Invisibility 76, 152, 163

Korean War 23, 99, 100, 102, 103, 104, 105, 106, 115, 116, 118, 124, 126, 178, 179

Landscape 1, 2, 7, 9, 12, 21, 22, 25, 26, 27, 28, 38, 39, 42, 45, 46, 51, 52, 65, 67, 76, 81, 82, 84, 86, 97, 98, 107, 108, 109, 110, 111, 112, 114, 118, 119, 120, 121, 123, 138, 139, 142, 145, 146, 174, 176

Map 1, 2, 6, 7, 8, 9, 10, 11, 21, 22, 25, 26, 27, 33, 49, 58, 59, 62, 63, 64, 66, 67, 68, 71, 74, 75, 77, 94, 119, 130, 145, 146, 152, 163, 165, 176
Mapping 2, 6, 7, 8, 9, 10, 11, 27, 63, 64, 65, 74, 97, 124, 157, 159, 162, 165
Masculinity 36, 97, 103, 136, 162
Meaning making 8, 10, 11, 12, 174
Metageneric film 48, 49, 56
Metaphor 1, 32, 33, 38, 42, 53, 64, 97, 98, 124, 143, 153, 163, 179
Melodrama 14, 23, 93, 100, 105, 127, 179
Mise-en-scène 30, 49, 86, 104, 114, 139, 147
Movement 18, 29, 32, 33, 36, 43, 45, 47, 49, 50, 51, 52, 53, 56, 57, 58, 70, 71, 74, 82, 83, 84, 85, 86, 87, 89, 94, 95, 102, 110, 112, 117, 119, 120, 121, 122, 123, 129, 133, 135, 140, 141, 143, 146, 147, 160, 166, 169, 170, 174, 176, 179
M.S.I. (materializing sound indices) 169

Nature 2, 3, 10, 19, 21, 22, 27, 34, 44, 53, 59, 70, 71, 73, 74, 75, 81, 97, 106, 107, 109, 115, 119, 123, 124, 129, 139, 142, 143, 145, 146, 147, 148, 150, 174, 177, 179
New Hollywood 17, 130, 158, 159, 179
News 13, 22, 103, 129, 156, 162
Newsreel 60, 69, 79, 177
No Man's Land 36, 42, 53, 57, 175

Omnipotence 20, 27, 43, 44, 57, 128, 170
Optics 2, 49, 50, 56
Orientation 1, 2, 6, 19, 21, 26, 34, 36, 45, 56, 75, 93, 111, 123, 143, 146, 156, 162, 174, 178, 179

Pacific War 75, 76, 81, 82, 140
Paranoia 104, 151, 156, 158, 165, 166, 168, 170, 172
Pathos 14, 17, 18, 20, 40, 41, 85, 121
– Pathos scene 18, 19, 20, 40, 41, 43, 119, 129, 136, 142
– Pathos formula 18, 95
Phenomenology 7, 8
Photograph 27, 37, 41, 49, 68, 69, 70, 77, 161, 170
Pilot 23, 57, 142, 143, 144, 145, 146, 149, 179, 180
Poetry 4, 12, 22, 28, 47, 50, 98, 175
Post-classical war film 17, 26, 127, 130, 131, 133, 142
POW 103, 143, 147, 179
Proceduralism 151, 172
Propaganda 12, 62, 63, 67, 79, 177

Reterritorialization 6, 21
Rhythm 10, 37, 52, 91, 118, 119, 154, 169

Second World War (WWII) 3, 5, 14, 21, 22, 23, 45, 57, 59, 60, 79, 81, 82, 83, 85, 90, 94,

Subject index — **197**

97, 99, 100, 101, 102, 103, 104, 105, 118, 126, 134, 142, 178, 179
Sensorium 16, 22, 40, 47, 49, 52, 53, 73, 130, 131, 153, 159, 174
Sound 18, 22, 23, 24, 26, 27, 29, 30, 32, 33, 34, 38, 40, 41, 49, 51, 52, 55, 56, 59, 61, 62, 65, 66, 69, 73, 74, 75, 76, 77, 87, 94, 117, 118, 127, 128, 130, 131, 132, 133, 134, 135, 136, 137, 139, 140, 141, 143, 147, 149, 151, 152, 153, 154, 156, 157, 162, 163, 165, 167, 168, 169, 172, 179, 180
Subjectivity 8, 9, 12, 25, 57, 91, 98, 99, 117, 135, 172, 177, 178
Surveillance 12, 152, 160, 161, 166, 180
Symmetry 47, 54

Tactility 28, 111
Tank 22, 81, 82, 83, 84, 85, 86, 87, 88, 89, 90, 93, 94, 95, 96, 97, 177
Technology 20, 22, 23, 25, 44, 49, 54, 59, 70, 71, 72, 81, 89, 91, 149, 150, 167, 174, 178, 179, 180
– Media technology 17, 25
– Military technology 16, 17, 127, 149, 173, 177, 178
Television 101, 126, 128, 129, 130
Temporalities 22, 108, 147
Terrorism 16, 171
Topography 7, 10, 167, 169
Touch 21, 22, 23, 26, 28, 30, 33, 35, 36, 38, 39, 40, 42, 50, 51, 52, 56, 59, 76, 77, 93, 94, 97, 98, 104, 106, 108, 115, 122, 128, 143, 147, 178, 179

Vietnam War 3, 5, 13, 21, 22, 23, 26, 73, 76, 96, 100, 105, 114, 122, 126, 127, 128, 129, 130, 131, 133, 135, 142, 143, 144, 150, 178, 179
Voyeurism 78
Vulnerability 20, 41, 44, 73, 77, 78, 81, 92, 114, 115, 135, 165, 170

War on Terror 5, 24, 151, 153, 156, 158, 159, 171
Western Front 21, 27, 73

Name index

Albert, Eddie 103
Alexander, Ben 115
Aldrich, Robert 83, 103
Ames, Eric 146
Auchter, Jessica 171, 172
Ayer, David 22, 81, 85, 87, 88, 92, 94, 95, 178
Ayres, Lew 32

Bachelard, Gaston 98, 99
Bakhtin, Mikhail 48
Balázs, Béla 114
Bale, Christian 145
Barber, Samuel 131
Barbusse, Henri 29, 42, 98
Barker, Jennifer M. 28, 39
Barthes, Roland 50
Basinger, Jeanine 14, 18, 100, 102, 104, 107, 110, 111, 112, 113, 115, 124
Baudrillard, Jean 25, 171
Bazin, André 10, 109, 119
Beidler, Philip 127
Benjamin, Walter 128, 131, 151
Bernard, Raymond 29
Bernthal, Jon 87
Bigelow, Kathryn 24, 121, 151, 152, 155, 157, 158, 172
Bin Laden, Osama 152, 153, 154, 160, 168, 169, 171
Bogart, Humphrey 83, 104
Bronfen, Elisabeth 13, 18
Brooke, Jocelyn 86
Brooks, Richard 104
Bruno, Giuliana 4, 11, 12, 39
Bühler, Karl 64
Burgoyne, Robert 3, 4, 15, 48, 77, 121

Canning, James 141
Capra, Frank 60, 61
Caputo, Philip 122
Carruthers, Susan L. 13
Casey, Edward 174
Castro, Teresa 10, 58, 59, 73, 176
Cavell, Stanley 133
Chaplin, Charlie 29

Chapman, James 13
Chastain, Jessica 160
Chion, Michel 134, 137, 140, 169
Cilento, Fabrizio 151, 155, 157, 161
Clark, Michael P. 127
Cobb, Humphrey 45
Cole, Sarah 50, 51
Conley, Tom 4, 9, 32, 61, 69, 110
Coppola, Francis Ford 130, 134, 143, 144, 179
Corrigan, Timothy 128, 137, 145
Crowther, Bosley 104
Crump, Owen 101
Cubitt, Sean 131
Curtis, Robin 64
Curtiz, Michael 80

Das, Santanu 22, 26, 27, 28, 29, 34, 36, 37, 38, 42, 43, 44, 81, 98, 176
Deleuze, Gilles 28, 174
Delezen, John 84, 115, 149
Dengler, Dieter 143
Der Derian, James 13
Dodge, Martin 6
Douglas, Kirk 53

Eastwood, Clint 15, 76, 151
Eberwein, Robert 14
Edwards, James 112
Eisenstein, Sergei M. 54
Elsaesser, Thomas 17, 134
Erdheim, Mario 135, 136

Flynn, Errol 57, 61
Ford, John 60
Fore, Steven 116
Fuller, Samuel 67, 83, 106, 115
Furie, Sidney 23, 133, 134, 149

Gance, Abel 29
Garnett, Tay 75
Geiger, Jeffrey 68, 69, 73
Gledhill, Christine 14
Godard, Jean-Luc 119, 120
Goulding, Edmund 57

Name index

Gregory, Derek 2, 3, 4, 5, 6, 16, 18, 27, 28, 50, 73, 82, 97, 98, 111, 114, 115, 148, 174, 176, 177
Griffith, D.W. 29
Guattari, Félix 174
Gunning, Tom 84

Hables Gray, Chris 180
Haggis, Paul 151
Hallin, Daniel C. 129
Harley, John B. 63, 64
Hathaway, Henry 80
Hawks, Howard 80, 101
Herzog, Werner 23, 142, 143, 144, 145, 146, 147, 148, 149, 179
Holden, William 104
Holubar, Allen 29
Hood, Gavin 151
Hoskins, Andrew 13
Hughes, Howard 57
Hull, Henry 78
Huston, John 60

Ingram, Rex 29

Jameson, Fredric 48, 50, 165
Johnson, Mark 8
Joyce, James 51

Kane, Kathryn 61, 71, 82, 83
Kappelhoff, Hermann 3, 4, 12, 14, 15, 18, 19, 35, 40, 44, 118, 119, 136, 142, 159, 174, 176
Kelly, Grace 104
King, Henry 101
Kitchin, Rob 6
Kolker, Robert 7, 8
Korda, Zoltan 83
Krämer, Sibylle 7, 9
Kubrick, Stanley 22, 45, 46, 47, 48, 49, 50, 53, 54, 56, 103, 114, 129, 131, 136, 137, 144, 175

LaBelle, Brandon 166, 167
LaBeouf, Shia 87
Laemmle, Carl 31

Langewiesche, William 155, 156
Lastra, James 130, 132, 133, 135
Lean, David 103
Lehmann, Hauke 158
Lentz, Robert J. 100, 105
Lerman, Logan 81
LeRoy, Mervyn 110
Liman, Doug 158
Lucy, Arnold 34

Macdonald, David 62
Machon, Josephine 176
Macready, George 49
Mann, Anthony 23, 97, 100, 106, 107, 108, 109, 110, 111, 114, 115, 116, 117, 118, 119, 120, 123, 124, 178,
Manning, Frederic 111
Maoz, Samuel 96
Marinetti, F.T. 67, 91
Marks, Laura U. 28, 39
Marton, Andrew 75, 103, 126
Masters, Cristina 91, 178
McCarthy, Joseph 99, 102
McClintock, Anne 153, 170
McSorley, Kevin 23, 169, 170
Menjou, Adolphe 49
Meredith, James H. 47, 54
Merleau-Ponty, Maurice 8, 15, 28, 108, 174
Metz, Christian 10
Milestone, Lewis 22, 30
Mitchum, Robert 130
Morris, Errol 158
Mouly, Françoise 155

Neale, Steve 61, 70, 72

O'Loughlin, Ben 13
Ousley, J. Douglas 7, 8

Pabst, G.W. 29
Palance, Jack 103
Parks, Lisa 167, 172
Peckinpah, Sam 132
Peña, Michael 87
Persoff, Nehemiah 121
Phillippe, Ryan 77

Pisters, Patricia 23, 25, 158, 171
Pitt, Brad 87
Polan, Dana 79, 80
Pollack, Sydney 165
Pultz Moslund, Sten 176
Purse, Lisa 156

Ramírez, Édgar 166
Rancière, Jacques 108, 109, 120
Ray, Aldo 107
Reagan, Ronald 62
Remarque, Erich Maria 29, 30, 31, 38
Roberts, Les 6
Robson, Mark 104
Rodaway, Paul 33, 38
Ropars-Wuilleumier, Marie-Claire 10
Rosenberg, Isaac 37, 40
Ryan, Robert 107

Sassoon, Siegfried 26, 27
Sauret, Étienne 157
Schaffner, Franklin J. 85
Selander, Lesley 101
Shaviro, Steven 159, 160
Shaw, Stan 139
Shaw, Tony 99, 101
Seiler, Lewis 75, 103
Shakhnazarov, Karen 83
Silverman, Kaja 165
Simmel, Georg 166
Sobchack, Vivian 1, 8, 9, 84
Spiegelman, Art 155
Spielberg, Steven 20, 83, 95

Stevens, George 60
Stewart, Garrett 163, 180
Stilwell, Joseph 60, 65
Stone, Oliver 131, 179

Taylor, Don 104
Theweleit, Klaus 91
Tripp, Nathaniel 149

Ungaretti, Giuseppe 38

Vertov, Dziga 43
Vidor, King 29
Virilio, Paul 16, 20, 25, 38, 49, 131, 158, 173

Walsh, Raoul 22, 29, 60, 177
Wasson, Craig 137, 143
Waxman, Franz 62
Wayne, John 126, 130, 135
Wedel, Michael 17, 20, 127, 134
Wehner, Josef Magnus 31
Weil, Simone 47
Wellman, William A. 30, 57
Westwell, Guy 13, 157
Willemen, Paul 120, 121
Williams, Linda 17
Williams, Raymond 3
Williams, Tony 116, 120
Wolheim, Louis 33
Wray, John 34
Wyler, William 60
Wylie, John 28

Film index

ALL QUIET ON THE WESTERN FRONT 22, 30, 31, 32, 34, 37, 38, 39, 40, 41, 42, 43, 44, 45, 46, 52, 53, 54, 56, 57, 84, 103, 175
AMERICAN SNIPER 151
APOCALYPSE NOW 96, 126, 130, 131, 132, 133, 134, 135, 141, 142, 179
ATTACK 85, 103

BAMBOO PRISON 103
BATAAN 75
BATTLE CIRCUS 104
BURMA VICTORY 61, 62, 63, 67, 75, 76, 177

CASABLANCA 80
CEASE FIRE! 101
CHINA GIRL 80

DAWN 29
DEVIL'S DOORWAY 107
DRAGONFLY SQUADRON 101

EL CID 110
EN DIRIGEABLE SUR LES CHAMPS DE BATAILLE 58

FAIR GAME 158
FEAR AND DESIRE 103
FIXED BAYONETS! 83, 106
FLAGS OF OUR FATHERS 76, 77
FULL METAL JACKET 96, 114, 129, 131, 132, 133, 135, 136, 137, 142, 144
FURY 22, 80, 81, 85, 86, 87, 88, 89, 90, 92, 93, 94, 95, 96, 97, 177

GO TELL THE SPARTANS 126, 179
GUADALCANAL DIARY 75

HEARTS OF THE WORLD 29
HELL'S ANGELS 57
HOMELAND (TV) 158

IN THE VALLEY OF ELAH 151, 158

J'ACCUSE 29, 103

LEBANON 96
LES CROIX DE BOIS 29
LETTERS FROM IWO JIMA 15, 20
LITTLE DIETER NEEDS TO FLY 143, 144
LOST PATROL 29

MAN OF THE WEST 107
MEN IN WAR 23, 97, 100, 106, 107, 108, 109, 110, 111, 114, 115, 116, 118, 119, 120, 121, 122, 124
MERRILL'S MARAUDERS 67, 68

OBJECTIVE, BURMA! 22, 60, 61, 62, 63, 65, 67, 68, 69, 70, 71, 73, 75, 76, 77, 78, 79, 81, 82, 85, 94, 97, 177

PATTON 85
PATHS OF GLORY 22, 45, 46, 47, 48, 49, 51, 52, 53, 54, 55, 56, 57, 175
PLATOON 131, 135, 142, 179
PRISONER OF WAR 103

QUO VADIS 110

RENDITION 151, 158
RESCUE DAWN 23, 128, 142, 143, 144, 145, 146, 147, 149, 150, 179

SAHARA 83, 85
SAVING PRIVATE RYAN 20, 83, 85, 95, 96
SERGEANT YORK 80, 101
SHOULDER ARMS 29
STANDARD OPERATING PROCEDURE 158

T-MEN 107
THE BIG PARADE 29
THE BIG PICTURE (TV) 129, 130
THE BOYS IN COMPANY C 23, 126, 128, 133, 134, 135, 136, 137, 138, 139, 141, 142, 143, 149, 150, 179
THE BRIDGE ON THE RIVER KWAI 103
THE BRIDGES AT TOKIO-RI 104, 105
THE DEER HUNTER 96, 126, 131, 147, 179
THE DAWN PATROL 57

The Fall of the Roman Empire 110
The Four Horsemen of the Apocalypse 29
The Green Berets 126, 135
The Heart of Humanity 29
The Hurt Locker 121, 151
The Steel Helmet 106, 116, 120
The Stilwell Road 61, 62, 63, 65, 67, 177
The Thin Red Line 75
The Three Days of the Condor 165

Westfront 1918 29
What Price Glory? 29
White Tiger (Belyy Tigr) 83
Wilson 101
Winchester '73 107
Wings 30, 57
WTC – The First 24 Hours 157

Zero Dark Thirty 24, 151–172, 180

www.ingramcontent.com/pod-product-compliance
Lightning Source LLC
Chambersburg PA
CBHW031620210526
45464CB00004B/1677